Corrective Reading

Workbook

SRA Comprehension Skills

Comprehension B2

Siegfried Engelmann
Steve Osborn
Susan Hanner

McGraw Hill SRA

Columbus, OH

SRAonline.com

 SRA

Send all inquiries to this address:
SRA/McGraw-Hill
4400 Easton Commons
Columbus, OH 43219

ISBN: 978-0-07-611184-8
MHID: 0-07-611184-9

6 7 8 9 QPD 13 12 11 10

The *McGraw-Hill* Companies

A INFERENCE

Read the passage and answer the questions.
- Circle the **W** if the question is answered by words in the passage, and underline those words.
- Circle the **D** if the question is answered by a deduction.

> Your respiratory system brings oxygen, which is a gas in the air, into contact with your blood. When you breathe in, air goes down your trachea and into the bronchial tubes in each lung. The bronchial tubes branch off into smaller and smaller tubes. When the air reaches the ends of the bronchial tubes, capillaries in the lungs take in some of the oxygen. That oxygen is now in contact with your blood.

1. What is oxygen?

   _____ **W** **D**

2. Where does your respiratory system bring oxygen?

   _____

   _____ **W** **D**

3. What's the first tube the air goes into?

   _____

4. What happens to the bronchial tubes?

   _____

   _____

   _____

5. What happens to the air when it reaches the ends of the bronchial tubes?

   _____

   _____

   _____ **W** **D**

6. Which body system does the oxygen start out in?

   _____

7. Which body system does the oxygen end up in?

   _____ **W** **D**

B SENTENCE COMBINATIONS

Underline the common part. Circle each sentence that tells **why.** Combine the sentences with **because.**

1. This gold is worth a lot.
   Robbers want this gold.

   _____

   _____

   _____

2. Pamela's humerus is broken.
   Pamela's humerus will have to be examined.

   _____

   _____

   _____

3. Diana ate carrots.
Carrots were good for her.

_____

_____

_____

4. He is constructing a shack.
He has no residence.

_____

_____

_____

C CONTRADICTIONS

Tell which fact each statement relates to.
Make each contradiction true.

> **A.** The ulna is a lower arm bone.
> **B.** The man wrote a sentence.

1. It is moved by the quadriceps. _____

2. It only had a subject. _____

3. It is under the humerus. _____

4. It had an end mark. _____

D BODY SYSTEMS

Fill in each blank.

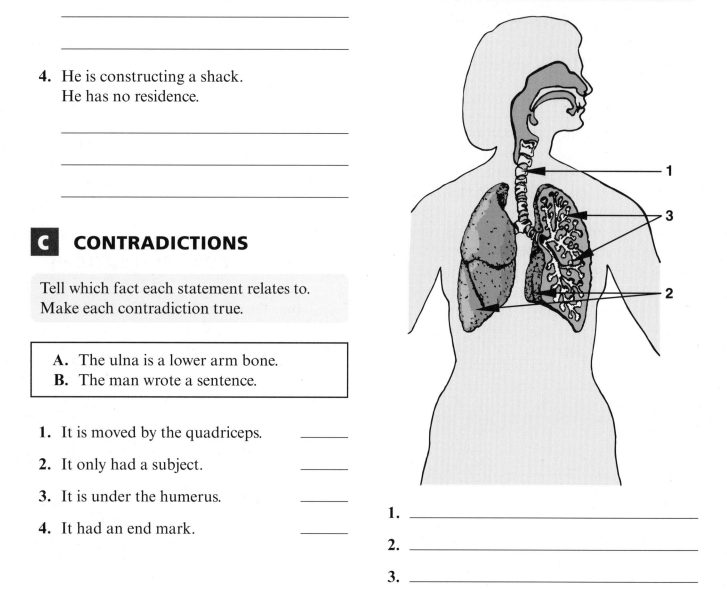

1. _____

2. _____

3. _____

E **SENTENCE COMBINATIONS**

Underline the common part. Circle the word that combines the sentences correctly. Combine the sentences with that word.

1. Vince runs every day.
   Barbara runs every day.

   and   who   which

   _____

   _____

2. A deer has hooves.
   An antelope has hooves.

   and   who   which

   _____

   _____

3. Sandra will run to the store.
   Neil will run to the store.

   and   who   which

   _____

   _____

4. Gene resides in that house.
   That house is painted white.

   and   who   which

   _____

   _____

   _____

5. A strong man lifted Tom.
   Tom had a broken leg.

   and   who   which

   _____

   _____

   _____

F **FOLLOWING DIRECTIONS**

Follow the directions about the sentence in the box.

> Tubes that carry blood away from the heart are called ___.
> > bronchial tubes
> > veins
> > arteries

1. Cross out the word that finishes the sentence correctly.
2. Circle the nouns in the sentence.
3. Above the first noun, write the name of the body system the sentence talks about.
4. Underline the word that means "a pump that moves blood."

G DEFINITIONS

Write a word that comes from **regulate** or **select** in each blank. Then write **verb, noun,** or **adjective** after each item.

1. I don't like traffic _____.

   _____

2. He is being very _____

   in filling that job. _____

3. I think her _____

   is ugly. _____

4. They tried to _____

   the cost of cars. _____

H SUBJECT/PREDICATE

Circle the subject and underline the predicate.

1. My pal Jean broke her femur.

2. Pigs, cows, and horses are all farm animals.

3. Some people have weak hearts.

4. Jumping up and down made the baby tired.

5. The trachea and the lungs are part of the respiratory system.

6. Riding a horse can be very tiring.

I WRITING STORIES

Write a story about this picture of a tornado approaching a farm. Your story should tell what happened **before** the picture, what happened **in** the picture, and what happened **after** the picture.

farmer	tornado	powerful	destroy	wind	storm clouds

_____

_____

_____

_____

_____

_____

_____

_____

_____

_____

_____

_____

_____

_____

_____

- **Does each sentence start with a capital letter?**
- **Does each sentence end with a period?**

Lesson 2

A SENTENCE COMBINATIONS

Underline the common part. Circle each sentence that tells why. Combine the sentences with **because**.

1. Don needs cash.
    Don is looking for a job.

    _____

    _____

    _____

2. Those bushes were too tall.
    Frank cut down those bushes.

    _____

    _____

    _____

3. That woman wants to catch fish.
    That woman got some bait.

    _____

    _____

    _____

B WRITING DIRECTIONS

Complete the instructions.

1. Draw a _____ line.

2. Draw a _____ line

    _____ from the

    _____ end of the

    _____ line.

3. Draw a _____ line from the

    _____ of the _____

    _____ to the _____

    _____ of the _____

    _____ .

C CONTRADICTIONS

Tell which fact each statement relates to. Make each contradiction true.

> **A.** The biceps bends the arm.
> **B.** The lower leg has many arteries.

1. This muscle covers the femur. _____

2. They carry blood away from the heart. _____

3. They are near the gastrocnemius. _____

4. It moves the humerus. _____

D INFERENCE

Read the passage and answer the questions.
- Circle the **W** if the question is answered by words in the passage, and underline those words.
- Circle the **D** if the question is answered by a deduction.

> The capillaries in your lungs take in oxygen from the air in your bronchial tubes. The capillaries also release carbon dioxide into this air. When you breathe out, the air with carbon dioxide leaves your bronchial tubes, goes up your trachea, and exits your body through your nose and mouth. Remember, you breathe in oxygen and you breathe out carbon dioxide.

1. What gas do the capillaries in your lungs take in? _____ **W D**

2. What gas do the capillaries in your lungs release? _____ **W D**

3. When you breathe out, where does the air begin? _____

_____

4. Through how many openings does the air exit your body? _____ **W D**

5. What gas do you breathe in?

_____ **W D**

6. What gas do you breathe out?

_____ **W D**

7. Which system takes oxygen from the lungs?

_____ **W D**

E DEFINITIONS

Write a word that comes from **reside** or **produce** in each blank. Then write **verb, noun,** or **adjective** after each item.

1. Those jobs need _____

workers. _____

2. There are many trees in that _____

part of town. _____

3. The boss wants the workers to

_____ more cars.

_____

4. Sam's _____ is too big

for him. _____

F DEDUCTIONS

Write the conclusion of each deduction.

1. Burning things need oxygen. Fires are

burning things. _____

_____

2. Burning things produce carbon dioxide.

Fires are burning things. _____

_____

3. Arteries carry blood away from the heart.

The aorta is an artery. _____

_____

_____

G SENTENCE COMBINATIONS

Underline the common part. Circle the
word that combines the sentences correctly.
Combine the sentences with that word.

1. Your body needs vitamin A.
   Vitamin A comes from carrots.
   and   who   which

   _____

   _____

   _____

2. The skeletal system is made up of bones.
   The skeletal system holds up your body.
   and   who   which

   _____

   _____

   _____

3. The player was arguing with the referee.
   Her coach was arguing with the referee.
   and   who   which

   _____

   _____

   _____

4. The lungs are part of the respiratory
   system.
   The respiratory system brings oxygen to
   the blood.
   and   who   which

   _____

   _____

   _____

   _____

5. New York is on the East Coast.
   Maine is on the East Coast.

   and   who   which

   _____

   _____

6. Bill criticized his sister.
   His sister had been mean.

   and   who   which

   _____

   _____

   _____

H SUBJECT/PREDICATE

Circle the subject and underline the predicate.

1. Drinking pop is not good for people.

2. The time is three o'clock.

3. To produce films takes a lot of cash.

4. A protective wall kept the fort from harm.

5. Horses and cows eat oats and grass.

6. Riding a bike is good for you.

I PARTS OF SPEECH

Underline the nouns. Draw **one** line **over** the adjectives. Draw **two** lines **over** the articles. Circle the verbs.

1. Burning things need oxygen.

2. That thermostat is regulating the heat in this room.

3. Some burning things produce heat and smoke.

4. The bronchial tubes are inside the lungs.

Lesson 3

A WRITING DIRECTIONS

Complete the instructions.

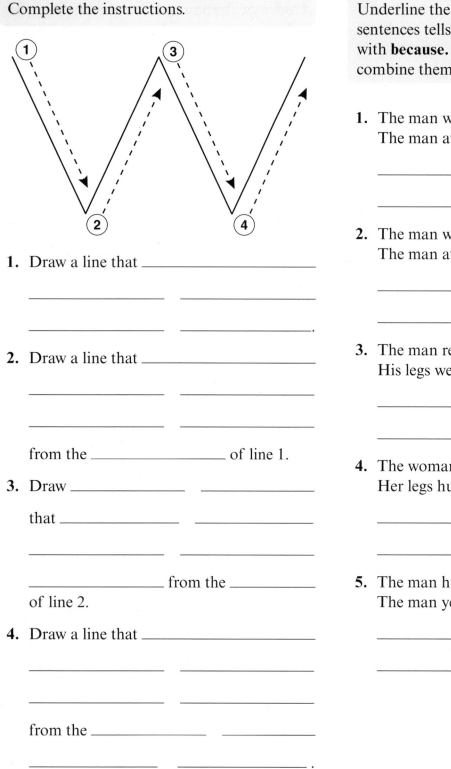

1. Draw a line that _____

   _____ _____

   _____ _____.

2. Draw a line that _____

   _____ _____

   _____ _____

   from the _____ of line 1.

3. Draw _____ _____

   that _____ _____

   _____ _____

   _____ from the _____
   of line 2.

4. Draw a line that _____

   _____ _____

   from the _____ _____

   _____ _____.

B SENTENCE COMBINATIONS

Underline the common part. If one of the
sentences tells why, combine the sentences
with **because.** If neither sentence tells why,
combine them with **who, which,** or **and.**

1. The man went home.
   The man ate dinner.

   _____

   _____

2. The man was hungry.
   The man ate dinner.

   _____

   _____

3. The man rested his legs.
   His legs were long.

   _____

   _____

4. The woman rested her legs.
   Her legs hurt.

   _____

   _____

5. The man hurt himself.
   The man yelled.

   _____

   _____

10   *Lesson 3*

C SIMILES

Tell how the things are the same.

1. The woman ran like a bullet.

   _____

   _____

2. The man had a fist like a brick.

   _____

   _____

3. The woman's hair was like coal.

   _____

   _____

D SUBJECT/PREDICATE

Circle the subject and underline the predicate.

1. The respiratory system brings oxygen to the blood.

2. Hammers and hoes are tools.

3. To write a book takes lots of time.

4. Jumping down the stairs is not safe.

5. Containers hold things.

6. The abdominal muscle goes from the ribs to the pelvis.

E DEDUCTIONS

Write the middle part of each deduction.

1. Burning things need oxygen.

   _____

   So, fires need oxygen.

2. Burning things produce carbon dioxide.

   _____

   So, fires produce carbon dioxide.

3. Some veins carry oxygen.

   _____

   So, maybe the vena cava carries oxygen.

F EVIDENCE

Write **R** for each fact that is **relevant** to what happened. Write **I** for each fact that is **irrelevant** to what happened.

The doctor looked at the man's lungs.

1. The doctor had a white coat.   _____

2. The man wheezed.   _____

3. The man didn't breathe very well.   _____

4. The man didn't like the doctor.   _____

G INFERENCE

Read the passage and answer the questions.
- Circle the **W** if the question is answered by words in the passage, and underline those words.
- Circle the **D** if the question is answered by a deduction.

> Your circulatory system keeps fresh blood moving to all parts of your body. Your blood brings oxygen to your muscles and other body parts, and it carries carbon dioxide away. Your muscles and other body parts are made up of tiny objects called **cells.** Your cells, which are like burning things, need oxygen and produce carbon dioxide. If your cells don't get oxygen, you die. If your cells don't get rid of carbon dioxide, you die.

1. What does the circulatory system do?

_____

_____

_____ **W   D**

2. What gas does blood bring to your muscles?

_____ **W   D**

3. What gas does blood carry away from your muscles?

_____ **W   D**

4. Are your cells like fire?

_____ **W   D**

5. Why?

_____

_____

_____

6. What gas do your cells make?

_____

7. If a fire goes out, what gas isn't it getting?

_____ **W   D**

H CONTRADICTIONS

Make each statement mean the same thing as the statement in the box.

> **The digestive system modifies food.**

1. The digestive system constructs food.

2. The respiratory system modifies food.

3. The digestive system is a system that changes food.

4. Food is not changed by the digestive system.

I BODY SYSTEMS

Fill in each blank.

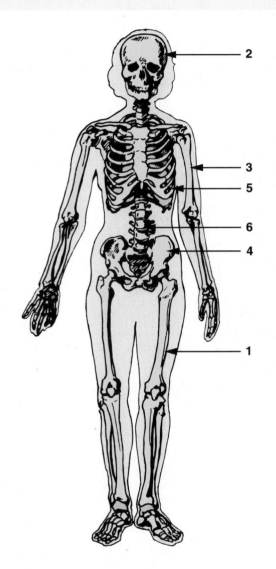

1. _____

2. _____

3. _____

4. _____

5. _____

6. _____

J   WRITING STORIES

Write a story about this picture of Tim and Rosie. Your story should tell what happened **before** the picture, what happened **in** the picture, and what happened **after** the picture.

| wallet | breakfast | cash register | bacon | hungry | discovered |

_____

_____

_____

_____

_____

_____

_____

_____

- **Does each sentence start with a capital letter?**
- **Does each sentence end with a period?**

Lesson 4

ERRORS	G	W	B	T

A SIMILES

Tell how the things are the same.

1. His dog eats like a pig.

   _____

   _____

2. His hair grows like weeds.

   _____

   _____

3. Her lips were like roses.

   _____

B DEFINITIONS

Write a word that comes from **modify** in each blank. Then write **verb, noun,** or **adjective** after each item.

1. The digestive system _____

   food. _____

2. This new car has many

   _____. _____

3. That hot rod is a _____

   truck. _____

4. The writer is _____

   his book. _____

5. That book has so many

   _____ that it is

   almost new. _____

C SENTENCE COMBINATIONS

Underline the common part. If one of the sentences tells why, combine the sentences with **because.** If neither sentence tells why, combine them with **who, which,** or **and.**

1. Linda was thirsty.
   Linda drank lots of water.

   _____

   _____

   _____

2. Roberta was thirsty.
   Roberta was hungry.

   _____

   _____

3. That silver is in a box.
   Antony protects that silver.

   _____

   _____

4. That silver is worth a lot.
   Ted protects that silver.

   _____

   _____

   _____

5. This cat was running down the street.
A man was running down the street.

_____

_____

_____

D INFERENCE

Read the passage and answer the questions.
- Circle the **W** if the question is answered by words in the passage, and underline those words.
- Circle the **D** if the question is answered by a deduction.

Your body is made of tiny cells that need oxygen and produce carbon dioxide. Your left biceps, for example, has billions of cells, and each one needs oxygen. Capillaries bring oxygen-filled blood to these cells and take away blood filled with carbon dioxide. Then the blood with carbon dioxide flows into veins and travels back to your heart. The blood in these veins is almost black.

When the blood with carbon dioxide gets to your heart, the heart pumps the blood to your lungs. Your heart doesn't change the blood; it just pumps the blood. The tube that carries blood from your heart to your lungs is called the **pulmonary artery.** It is one of the biggest arteries in your body.

---

1. How many cells are in your biceps?

_____ **W   D**

2. What gas does your blood carry from your biceps to your heart?

_____

3. Why is that blood almost black?

_____

_____

_____

_____ **W   D**

4. Where does your heart pump the blood with carbon dioxide?

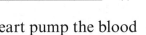 **W   D**

5. Does your heart change your blood?

_____

6. What color is blood in the pulmonary artery?

_____

7. Why is the pulmonary artery an artery?

_____

_____

_____ **W   D**

E EVIDENCE

Write **R** for each fact that is **relevant** to what happened. Write **I** for each fact that is **irrelevant** to what happened.

> The woman can't get food to her stomach.

1. She likes to eat ham.   _____

2. Her esophagus is blocked.   _____

3. She can't open her mouth.   _____

4. She liked her doctor.   _____

F SUBJECT/PREDICATE

Circle the subject and underline the predicate.

1. Vehicles take things places.

2. To sing well takes practice.

3. Every sentence is divided into two parts.

4. Boxes and paper bags are containers.

5. Making presents can be fun.

6. The skeletal system is made up of bones.

G BODY SYSTEMS

Fill in each blank.

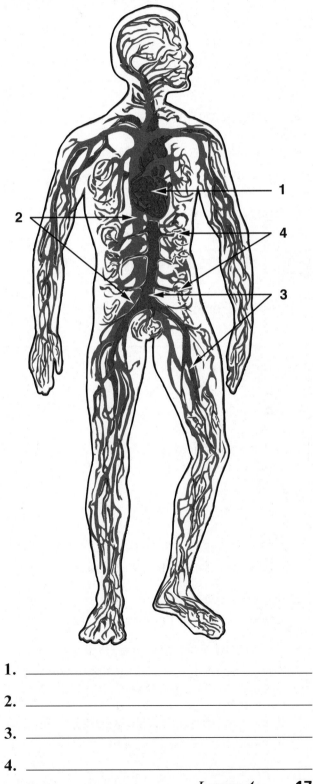

1. _____

2. _____

3. _____

4. _____

H CONTRADICTIONS

Tell which fact each statement relates to. Make each contradiction true.

> **A.** The stick was burning.
> **B.** The man had a cast on his chest.

1. It was below his pelvis. _____

2. It was producing oxygen. _____

3. He probably broke his ribs. _____

4. It needed carbon dioxide. _____

I FOLLOWING DIRECTIONS

Follow the directions.

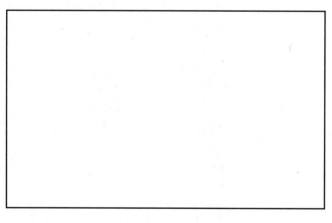

1. Draw a vertical line in the box.

2. Draw a line that slants down to the right from the bottom of the vertical line.

3. Draw a muscle that covers the right side of the vertical line and attaches to the right side of the slanted line.

4. Draw an arrow that shows which way the muscle will move the slanted line.

J ANALOGIES

Complete the analogies.

1. Tell what system each part is in.

   The heart is to the _____ system as the lungs are to the

   _____ system.

2. Tell how many of each part you have.

   The heart is to _____ as

   the lungs are to _____.

WORD LIST

abdominal muscle (n) the muscle that goes from the ribs to the pelvis

biceps (n) the muscle that covers the front of the humerus

criticize (v) to find fault with

gastrocnemius (n) the muscle that covers the back of the lower leg

produce (v) to make

quadriceps (n) the muscle that covers the front of the femur

regulate (v) to control

regulation (n) a rule

regulatory (a) that something regulates

residence (n) a place where someone resides

selection (n) something that is selected

trapezius (n) the muscle that covers the back of the neck

triceps (n) the muscle that covers the back of the humerus

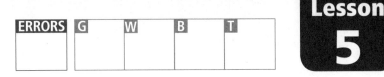
A SENTENCE COMBINATIONS

Underline the common part. If one of the sentences tells why, combine the sentences with **because.** If neither sentence tells why, combine them with **who, which,** or **and.**

1. Fred won the race.
   Fred was a fast runner.

   _____

   _____

   _____

2. Fred was a fast runner.
   Bob saw Fred.

   _____

   _____

3. The team lost the game.
   The team was sad.

   _____

   _____

   _____

4. The team lost the game.
   The game lasted ten innings.

   _____

   _____

   _____

5. The team criticized the coach.
   The coach was mean.

   _____

   _____

   _____

B INFERENCE

Read the passage and answer the questions.
- Circle the **W** if the question is answered by words in the passage, and underline those words.
- Circle the **D** if the question is answered by a deduction.

> Your pulmonary artery carries blood filled with carbon dioxide to your lungs. Capillaries in your lungs take away the carbon dioxide and replace it with oxygen. The blood, which is now filled with oxygen, then goes back to your heart through your pulmonary vein. When the blood gets to your heart, the heart pumps the blood into an artery called the **aorta.** Your aorta branches into smaller and smaller arteries, which carry the oxygen-filled blood to all parts of your body.

1. What color is blood in the pulmonary artery?

   _____ **W D**

2. What color is blood in the pulmonary vein?

   _____ **W D**

3. Why is blood that color in the pulmonary vein?

_____

_____

4. What color is blood in the aorta?

_____ **W   D**

5. Why is the aorta an artery?

_____

_____

_____ **W   D**

6. What gas does blood in the aorta carry?

_____

C   CONTRADICTIONS

In each passage, underline the contradiction and circle the statement it contradicts.

1. All dogs are called canines. Every dog has warm blood. Some dogs have spotted fur.* Some dogs are brown. Some dogs have cold blood. Most dogs have homes, but some roam the streets.

2. Pam had a race with her older brother. They ran ten blocks. They both wore sneakers.* Pam won the race. Her brother said, "You won because you are older than I am."

D   SIMILES

Tell how the things are the same.

1. That man's nose is like a banana.

_____

_____

2. Her hands were like sandpaper.

_____

_____

3. His eyes are like emeralds.

_____

_____

E BODY SYSTEMS

Fill in each blank.

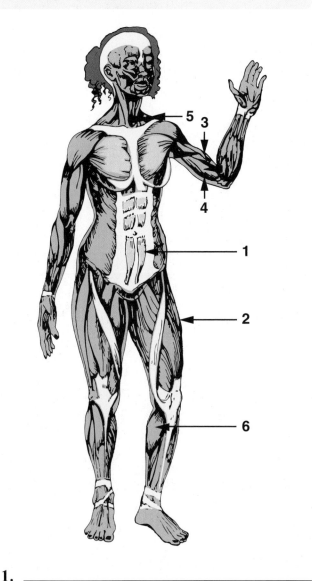

1. _____
2. _____
3. _____
4. _____
5. _____
6. _____

F PARTS OF SPEECH

Underline the nouns. Draw one line over the adjectives. Draw two lines over the articles. Circle the verbs.

1. Some arteries have red blood.
2. The man spent his time modifying his car.
3. His car has a modified carburetor.
4. The man modified his carburetor with a wrench.

G DEFINITIONS

Write a word that comes from **modify** in each blank. Then write **verb, noun,** or **adjective** after each item.

1. The woman will _____ the plane. _____
2. His dad made many _____ in their residence. _____
3. He said, "People like to _____ residences." _____
4. His wife said, "These _____ cost a lot of money." _____
5. So his dad stopped _____ the residence. _____

H SUBJECT/PREDICATE

Circle the subject and underline the predicate.

1. Keeping a secret can be hard.

2. School buses and yellow cabs are vehicles.

3. The digestive system changes food into fuel.

4. **Criticize, predict,** and **reside** are verbs.

5. To run in races is thrilling.

6. The esophagus and the trachea are both tubes.

▮ WRITING STORIES

Write a story about this picture of Rasheed. Your story should tell what happened **before** the picture, what happened **in** the picture, and what happened **after** the picture.

soccer	test	study	worried	cell phone	backpack

_____

_____

_____

_____

_____

_____

_____

_____

_____

_____

_____

_____

_____

_____

_____

- **Does each sentence start with a capital letter?**
- **Does each sentence end with a period?**

Fact Game

1

FACT GAME SCORECARD

1	2	3	4	5	6	7	8	9	10	11	12	13	14	15
16	17	18	19	20	21	22	23	24	25	26	27	28	29	30

FG	B	T

2. Combine the sentences in the box with **because.**

> Lynn's femur was broken. Lynn was wearing a cast.

3. Answer the questions about the sentence in the box.

> The glossy magazine has a large circulation.

    a. What are the nouns?
    b. What are the articles?
    c. What are the adjectives?
    d. What are the verbs?

4. Answer the questions about the sentence in the box.

> To breathe cold air can hurt.

    a. What's the subject?
    b. What's the predicate?

5. Combine the sentences in the box with **because.**

> He went running. He needed some exercise.

6. Name the part of speech for each underlined word.

    a. You can <u>digest</u> food more easily if you chew it well.
    b. Her <u>conclusive</u> comments changed my mind.
    c. His <u>digestion</u> was upset by the bad news.

7. Answer the questions about the sentence in the box.

> Swimming in that lake is a bad idea.

    a. What's the subject?
    b. What's the predicate?

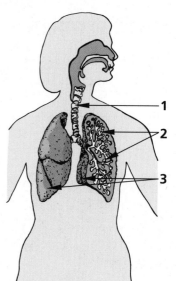

8. Answer the questions about the picture.

    a. What body system does the picture show?
    b. What's the name of part 1?
    c. What's the name of part 2?
    d. What's the name of part 3?

9. Answer the questions.

    a. What color is blood that carries oxygen?
    b. What color is blood that carries carbon dioxide?

10. Say each sentence using another word for the underlined part.

    a. He made many <u>changes</u> to his speech.
    b. She <u>changed</u> the plans for her new house.

11. Answer the questions about the picture.

    a. What gas do burning things need?
    b. What gas do burning things produce?

12. Say each sentence using another word for the underlined part.

    a. That office needs many <u>changes</u>.
    b. The racer <u>changed</u> her sports car.

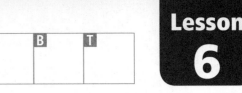

A REWRITING PARAGRAPHS

Rewrite the paragraph by combining the sentences that are joined with an underline. If one of the sentences tells **why**, combine the sentences with **because**.

> Birds make <u>nests. Birds</u> need a place to live. They make their nests from <u>twigs. They</u> make their nests from leaves. It is hard to see some <u>nests. Some</u> nests are hidden in trees.

_____

_____

_____

_____

_____

_____

B CONTRADICTIONS

Underline the contradiction in each passage. Circle the statement it contradicts.

1. Mr. Jones worked for a car maker. Mr. Jones spent all day at the factory putting on tires. When Mr. Jones came home in the evening, he was too tired to do anything. * He would watch TV all night and yell at the ads. "I would rather do anything than put tires on bikes," Mr. Jones told himself. "I think I'll quit this job and become a thinker."

2. People use their brains to think and feel. If you don't eat the right food when you are a baby, you can suffer damage to your brain. This damage cannot be corrected. Some people don't know this. * They don't feed their babies the right food. When the child grows up, he or she must have an operation to correct the damage. It is very important to eat the right kinds of foods.

C SIMILES

Tell how the things are the same.

1. Sam's arms are like sticks.

_____

_____

2. The room was like a cave.

_____

_____

3. Her smile was like the sun.

_____

_____

D INFERENCE

Read the passage and answer the questions.
• Circle the **W** if the question is answered by words in the passage. Then underline those words.
• Circle the **D** if the question is answered by a deduction.

> Your circulatory system is pretty easy to understand if you remember that your blood does four things. First, your blood carries carbon dioxide from your cells to your heart. Second, the blood goes through your heart and to your lungs, where the blood lets go of the carbon dioxide. Third, your blood gets oxygen from the lungs and travels back to your heart. Fourth, your heart pumps the blood filled with oxygen back to your cells.

1. What gas do your cells produce?

   _____

2. What color is blood that goes from your cells to your heart?

   _____ **W   D**

3. What gas is carried by blood that goes from the heart to the lungs?

   _____

4. What color is blood that goes from the lungs to the heart?

   _____ **W   D**

5. What gas is carried by blood that goes from the heart to the body cells?

   _____

6. What gas does the blood get after it is pumped to the lungs?

   _____

7. What kind of tubes carry blood away from the heart?

   _____

E BODY SYSTEMS

Fill in each blank.

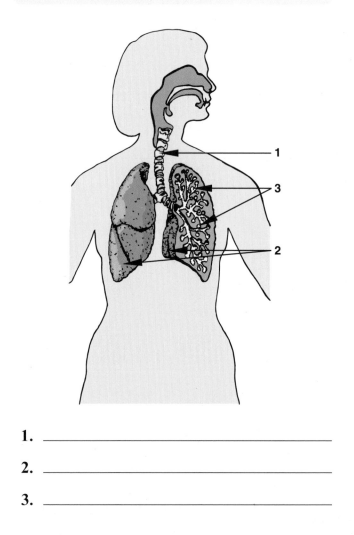

1. _____

2. _____

3. _____

F FOLLOWING DIRECTIONS

Follow the directions about the sentence in the box.

> The _____ is a tube that brings air to the lungs.

1. Finish the sentence.

2. Circle the articles.

3. Write the name of the body system the sentence describes.

_____

4. Cross out the verbs.

G BODY RULES

Circle each bone that will move. Then draw an arrow that shows which way it will move.

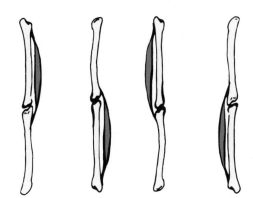

H PARTS OF SPEECH

Underline the nouns. Draw **one** line **over** the adjectives. Draw **two** lines **over** the articles. Circle the verbs.

1. A big float won the contest.

2. His boat will float when the leak is fixed.

3. Three thick logs floated down a slow stream.

4. Most students follow regulations.

I EVIDENCE

Write **R** for each fact that is **relevant** to what happened. Write **I** for each fact that is **irrelevant** to what happened.

> Pam wrote six adjectives in one sentence.

1. She wanted to tell about the nouns. _____

2. The sentence had two verbs. _____

3. She was writing at her desk. _____

4. She was writing with a pen. _____

A BODY RULES

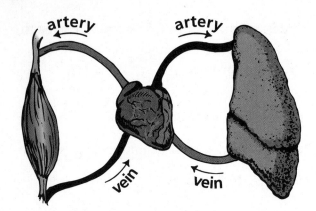

B BODY SYSTEMS

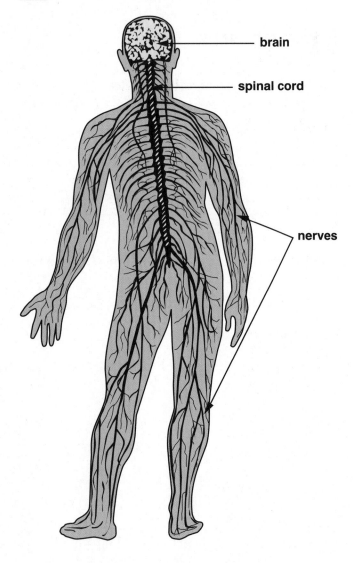

C REWRITING PARAGRAPHS

Rewrite the paragraph by combining the sentences that are joined with an underline. If one of the sentences tells **why,** combine the sentences with **because**.

James passed a big test. James was very happy. The test was in his French class. His French class met in the afternoon. James spoke French well. James studied hard.

_____

_____

_____

_____

_____

_____

D CONTRADICTIONS

Underline the contradiction in each passage. Circle the statement it contradicts.

1. Your body is often its own doctor. It can heal itself of many sicknesses. When you are sick, you are weak because your body is fighting with the sickness. If you are not healthy, your body is not in good shape for a fight.* Your body cannot heal many things, but it needs to be healthy to heal what it can. Some people heal faster than others. They watch what they eat, and they get lots of sleep.

2. You should learn about money. You will need money if you want a car, if you want to travel, or if you want some shoes. You have to be careful of stores that try to cheat you.* You have to stretch your dollar by looking for the best deals. No one will try to trick you, but you must learn to be smart. The smarter you are about money, the more you will have when you need it.

E SIMILES

Tell **two** ways that the things compared are **not** the same. Tell **one** way that the things compared **are** the same.

> The man ran like a bullet.

1. A man is not _____

_____

2. A bullet is not _____

3. _____

_____

F WRITING DIRECTIONS

Complete the instructions.

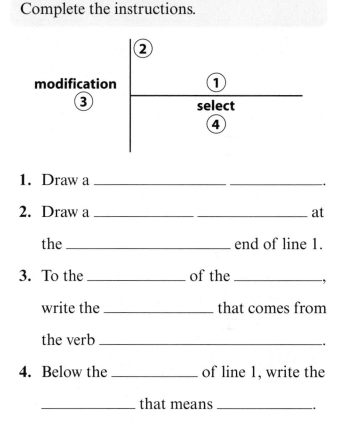

1. Draw a _____ _____.

2. Draw a _____ _____ at the _____ end of line 1.

3. To the _____ of the _____, write the _____ that comes from the verb _____.

4. Below the _____ of line 1, write the _____ that means _____.

G BODY RULES

Draw in the muscles.

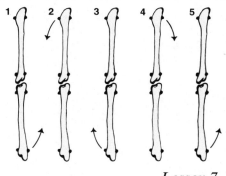

Lesson 7

H INFERENCE

> Ramone was in a place that was very dark when he cut his hand. He could feel it bleeding. He said to himself, "If a bandage stops my hand from bleeding, I know that a vein is bleeding. If a bandage does not stop my hand from bleeding, I know that an artery is bleeding.

1. What color is the blood in the arteries of your hand?

   _____

2. What color is the blood in the veins of your hand?

   _____

3. Why is the blood in your veins almost black?

   _____

   _____

4. Which would be harder to stop bleeding, a cut artery or a cut vein?

   _____ **W   D**

5. If the bandage stops the bleeding, what color is the blood that comes out of the cut?

   _____ **W   D**

6. If the bandage does not stop the bleeding, what color is the blood that comes out?

   _____ **W   D**

I DEFINITIONS

1. The man never watched _____

   games. _____

2. A carpenter will _____ this

   home. _____

3. The home needs many

   _____

   _____

4. The woman's _____

   about the game were wrong. _____

5. _____ a car can cost a

   lot of money. _____

J WRITING STORIES

Write a story about this picture of Alfonso and the dinosaur. Your story should tell what happened **before** the picture, what happened **in** the picture, and what happened **after** the picture.

scientist	dinosaur	jungle	bone	shovel

_____

_____

_____

_____

_____

_____

_____

_____

- **Does each sentence start with a capital letter?**
- **Does each sentence end with a period?**

ERRORS | G | W | B | T

A BODY RULES

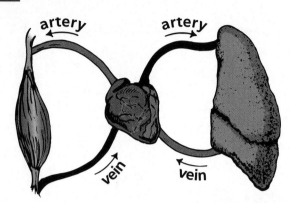

B INFERENCE

Read the passage and answer the questions.
- Circle the **W** if the question is answered by words in the passage. Then underline those words.
- Circle the **D** if the question is answered by a deduction.

John told Ramone that artery blood is red, and vein blood is black. Ramone said that he did not believe that. He told John about the time his father cut a vein when he was sawing down a tree. Ramone said, "His blood came from a vein but it was red."

John said, "It was red because there is oxygen in the air. When you cut yourself, the oxygen in the air comes into contact with the blood in the cut, and the blood rurns red. It doesn't matter if you cut an artery, a vein, or a capillary. The blood will always turn red."

Ramone thought about what John said and replied, "Maybe you're right."

1. What color is blood that carries carbon dioxide?

   _____

2. What color is blood that carries oxygen?

   _____

3. What is one gas in the air?

   _____ W D

4. What color will blood turn if you put it in the air?

   _____ W D

5. Why? _____

   _____

   _____

   _____ W D

6. If there is no oxygen in the air, will the blood be red when you cut yourself?

   _____ W D

C SIMILES

Tell **two** ways that the things compared are **not** the same. Tell **one** way that the things compared **are** the same.

> Their hair grows like weeds.

1. _____

   _____

2. _____

   _____

3. _____

   _____

D SENTENCE COMBINATIONS

Underline the common part. Then combine the sentences with **who** or **which**.

1. John lifts big boxes.
   John has strong biceps.

   _____

   _____

2. The stomach is under the heart.
   The stomach mixes food.

   _____

   _____

3. The biceps moves the lower arm.
   The biceps pulls like a rubber band.

   _____

   _____

   _____

4. The heart pumps blood.
   The heart is in the circulatory system.

   _____

   _____

   _____

E CONTRADICTIONS

Underline the contradiction. Circle the statement it contradicts.

Only some people like team sports. Other people like sports that they can do alone, like running. When you play on a team, you must depend on other people and work together.* When you run, you train yourself and depend on yourself. Although everyone likes team sports, single sports can be thrilling. Most track events are single sports, and the greatest of them all is the marathon.

F ANALOGIES

Write what each analogy tells.

- what burning things do with each gas
- what color each gas turns blood
- where you find each gas
- what your respiratory system does with each gas

1. Oxygen is to need as carbon dioxide is to produce.

_____

_____

_____

2. Oxygen is to breathing in as carbon dioxide is to breathing out.

_____

_____

_____

3. Oxygen is to red as carbon dioxide is to almost black.

_____

_____

G WRITING DIRECTIONS

Complete the instructions.

predictable (4)   (1) modify (3)   (2)

1. Draw a _____ line.

2. Draw a line that _____

up to the _____ from

the _____ of the

_____ line.

3. To the _____ of the

_____ line, write

the verb that means _____ .

4. Write the _____ that

comes from the verb _____

to the _____ of the

_____ line.

H SUBJECT/PREDICATE

Circle the subject and underline the predicate.

1. Blood that carries oxygen is red.

2. Gray whales and snakes are animals.

3. Blood that carries carbon dioxide is almost black.

4. To laugh at jokes is human.

5. Verbs tell the action that things do.

6. The muscular system is made up of muscles.

I DEDUCTIONS

Write the middle part of each deduction.

1. Blood that carries carbon dioxide is black.

_____

_____

So, blood in the arm veins is black.

2. Blood that carries oxygen is red.

_____

_____

So, blood in the aorta is red.

3. Arteries carry blood away from the heart.

_____

So, the aorta carries blood away from the heart.

J DEFINITIONS

In each blank, write the word that has the same meaning as the word or words under the blank.

1. Your skull _____
   (guards)
   your brain.

2. Those new cars have many

   _____.
   (changes)

3. She got glasses after her eyes were

   _____.
   (looked at)

4. My _____
   (choice)
   for lunch was a ham sandwich.

ERRORS	G	W	B	T

A CONTRADICTIONS

Underline the contradiction.
Circle the statement it contradicts.

Sam was running in a track meet. He hurt the muscle that covered the back of his lower left leg. Sam won the race, but he had to go to a doctor. *The doctor looked at Sam's leg and shook her head. "You hurt your quadriceps," she said. "You won't be able to run for a while." Then she taped up Sam's lower leg and gave him some crutches.

B SENTENCE COMBINATIONS

Underline the common part. Then combine the sentences with **who** or **which.**

1. The lungs bring fresh air to the blood.
   The lungs are large organs.

   _____

   _____

   _____

2. Pam makes boats.
   Pam is very productive.

   _____

   _____

   _____

3. This button regulates the heat.
   This button is yellow.

   _____

   _____

   _____

4. That doctor plays the trumpet.
   That doctor examined my femur.

   _____

   _____

   _____

C BODY RULES

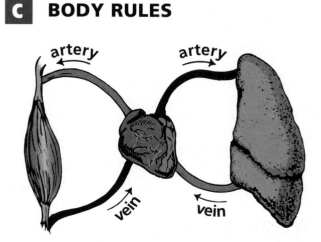

artery   artery

vein   vein

D DEFINITIONS

Write a word that comes from **digest** or **conclude** in each blank. Then write **verb, noun,** or **adjective** after each item.

1. She made a prediction about the

   _____ of the play.

   _____

2. The _____ system

   changes food into fuel. _____

3. Tom is _____ his

   comments now. _____

4. Her doctor made some _____

   remarks. _____

5. _____ is important to

   your body. _____

E BODY SYSTEMS

Write **brain, nerves,** or **spinal cord** in each blank.

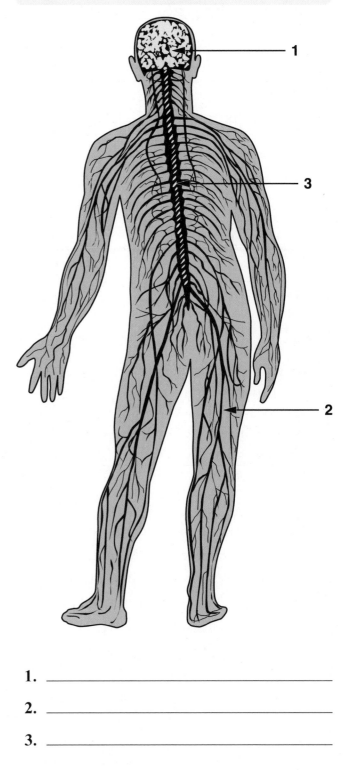

1. _____

2. _____

3. _____

F SIMILES

Tell **two** ways that the things compared are **not** the same. Tell **one** way that the things compared **are** the same.

> Their arms are like sticks.

1. _____

   _____

2. _____

   _____

3. _____

   _____

G INFERENCE

Read the passage and answer the questions.
- Circle the **W** if the question is answered by words in the passage. Then underline those words.
- Circle the **D** if the question is answered by a deduction.

> Your respiratory system brings oxygen, which is a gas in the air, into contact with your blood. When you breathe air in, the air goes down your trachea and into the bronchial tubes in each lung. The bronchial tubes branch off into smaller and smaller tubes. When the air reaches the ends of the bronchial tubes, capillaries in the lungs soak up the oxygen. That oxygen is now in contact with your blood.

1. What is oxygen?

   _____ **W** **D**

2. Where does your respiratory system bring oxygen?

   _____

   _____ **W** **D**

3. What's the first tube the air goes into?

   _____

4. What happens to the bronchial tubes?

   _____

   _____

   _____

5. What happens to the air when it reaches the ends of the bronchial tubes?

   _____

   _____

   _____ **W** **D**

6. Which body system does the oxygen start out in?

   _____

7. Which body system does the oxygen end up in?

   _____ **W** **D**

H DEDUCTIONS

Write the conclusion of each deduction.

1. Blood that carries oxygen is red.
   Blood in the aorta carries oxygen.

   _____

2. Blood that carries carbon dioxide is almost black.
   Blood in the arm veins carries carbon dioxide.

   _____

   _____

3. Veins carry blood back to the heart.
   The vena cava is a vein.

   _____

   _____

I FOLLOWING DIRECTIONS

Follow the directions.

[box]

1. Draw a horizontal line in the box.

2. Draw a line that slants down to the left from the left end of the horizontal line.

3. Draw a muscle that covers the bottom of the horizontal line and attaches to the right side of the slanted line.

4. Circle the line that will move.

J SUBJECT/PREDICATE

Circle the subject and underline the predicate.

1. **Cloud, cup,** and **book** are nouns.
2. Finding money is always fun.
3. The skull and the ribs are protective bones.
4. Constructive criticism is important to some people.
5. To run in school is not a good idea.
6. The circulatory system keeps fresh blood moving in your body.

WORD LIST
adjective (n) a word that comes before a noun and tells about the noun
carbon dioxide (n) a gas that burning things produce
construct (v) to build
constructive (a) that something is helpful
modification (n) a change
modified (a) that something is changed
modify (v) to change
noun (n) a word that names a person, place, or thing
obtain (v) to get
oxygen (n) a gas that burning things need
predict (v) to say that something will happen
predictable (a) that something is easy to predict
regulate (v) to control
regulatory (a) that something regulates
verb (n) a word that tells the action that things do

K   **Writing Stories**

Write a story about this picture of Tensing. Your story should tell what happened **before** the picture, what happened **in** the picture, and what happened **after** the picture.

wooden bridge	mountains	walking stick	supplies

- **Does each sentence start with a capital letter?**
- **Does each sentence end with a period?**

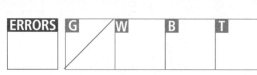

A SENTENCE COMBINATIONS

Underline the common part. Then combine the sentences with **who** or **which.**

1. The trachea brings air to the lungs.
The trachea is a tube.

_____

_____

_____

2. Tina does not like criticism.
Tina likes to play sports.

_____

_____

_____

3. The quadriceps covers the front of the femur.
The quadriceps is in the muscular system.

_____

_____

_____

_____

4. That old man resides on a farm.
That old man sells milk.

_____

_____

_____

B BODY RULES

Shade in each tube that carries dark blood.
Then write **vein** or **artery** in each blank.

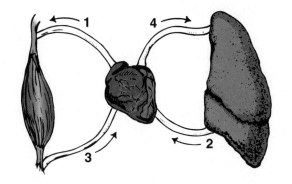

1. _____

2. _____

3. _____

4. _____

C REWRITING PARAGRAPHS

Rewrite the paragraph by combining the sentences that are joined with an underline. If one of the sentences tells **why**, combine the sentences with **because.**

Bill wanted to skate at the pond. Bill had red hair. He obtained a pair of skates from his pal. His pal was named Ted. But Bill did not get to skate at the pond. The pond was not frozen.

_____

_____

_____

_____

_____

_____

_____

_____

D WRITING DIRECTIONS

Complete the instructions.

③

②   ①

circulatory

④

1. Draw a _____

_____ .

2. Draw a _____

_____ down from the

_____ end of line 1.

3. Draw a _____

_____ up from the

_____ end of line 1.

4. Write the word _____

_____ the lower

_____ line.

E BODY SYSTEMS

Write **brain, nerves,** or **spinal cord** in each blank.

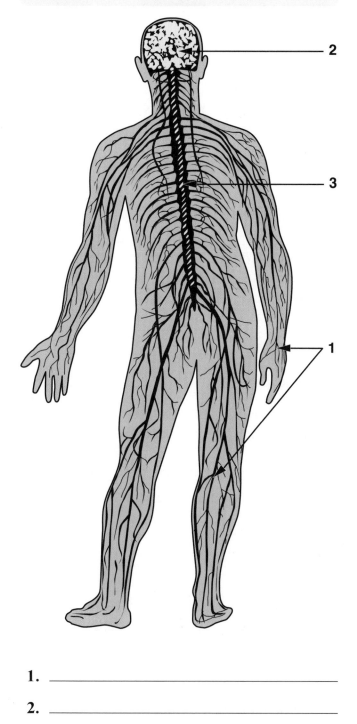

1. _____
2. _____
3. _____

F SIMILES

Tell **two** ways that the things compared are **not** the same. Tell **one** way that the things compared **are** the same.

Her hands were like velvet.

1. _____
_____

2. _____
_____

3. _____
_____

G CONTRADICTIONS

Underline the contradiction. Circle the statement it contradicts.

   Jim took a class on how to fix engines. He remembered everything that was irrelevant, and he forgot everything that was relevant. When he went to fix his car engine, Jim didn't know what to do.* He said, "Why can't I fix this engine? I remember everything that helps to explain engines." Finally, Jim took his car to a garage, where mechanics fixed his engine for him.

H INFERENCE

Read the passage and answer the questions.
- Circle the **W** if the question is answered by words in the passage. Then underline those words.
- Circle the **D** if the question is answered by a deduction.

> You know that the capillaries in your lungs soak up oxygen from the air in your bronchial tubes. After the air loses its oxygen, it soaks up carbon dioxide from the capillaries. When you breathe out, the air goes out your bronchial tubes. This air, which now has carbon dioxide in it, goes up your trachea, and out of your nose and mouth. Remember, you breathe in oxygen and you breathe out carbon dioxide.

1. What do the capillaries in your lungs do?

   _____

   _____

   _____ **W** **D**

2. What does the air do after it loses its oxygen?

   _____

   _____

   _____ **W** **D**

3. What do the capillaries give to the air?

   _____

4. What do the capillaries take to the air?

   _____

5. What gas do you breathe in?

   _____ **W** **D**

6. What gas do you breathe out?

   _____ **W** **D**

7. Which system takes oxygen from the lungs?

   _____ **W** **D**

I DEFINITIONS

Write a word that comes from **conclude** or **digest** in each blank. Then write **verb, noun,** or **adjective** after each item.

1. The body _____ food slowly. _____

2. Lin gave _____ proof that Tom ate the cake.

   _____

3. Rick did not make the right

   _____ in his

   deduction. _____

4. The mouth is part of the

   _____ system.

   _____

5. Your body _____ some foods faster than others.

   _____

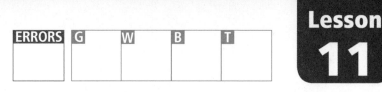

Lesson 11

ERRORS | G | W | B | T

A BODY SYSTEMS

Write **brain, nerves,** or **spinal cord** in each blank.

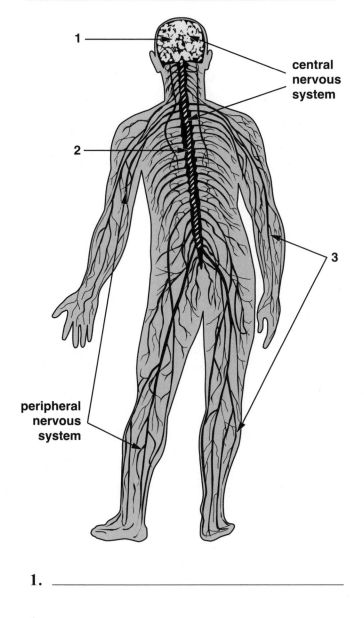

central
nervous
system

peripheral
nervous
system

1. _____

2. _____

3. _____

B REWRITING PARAGRAPHS

Rewrite the paragraph by combining the sentences that are joined with an underline. If one of the sentences tells why, combine the sentences with **because**.

The muscular system does many <u>jobs. The</u> muscular system is made up of muscles. The biceps moves the lower <u>arm. The</u> triceps moves the lower arm. The quadriceps moves the lower <u>leg. The</u> lower leg is very heavy. The fingers have many <u>bones. Tiny</u> muscles move the fingers.

_____

_____

_____

_____

_____

_____

_____

_____

_____

_____

Lesson 11

C SENTENCE COMBINATIONS

Underline the common part. Then combine the sentences with **who** or **which.**

1. Mr. Jones gave Jane some criticism.
   Mr. Jones is smart.

   _____

   _____

   _____

2. That story is too predictable.
   That story goes on forever.

   _____

   _____

   _____

3. The heart is connected to veins and arteries. The heart pumps blood.

   _____

   _____

   _____

4. A tall basketball player selected three CDs.
   A tall basketball player likes hot tunes.

   _____

   _____

   _____

D BODY RULES

Shade in each tube that carries dark blood. Write **vein** or **artery** in each blank.

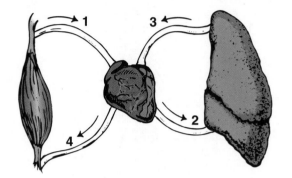

1. _____

2. _____

3. _____

4. _____

46 *Lesson 11*

E INFERENCE

Read the passage and answer the questions.
- Circle the **W** if the question is answered by words in the passage. Then underline those words.
- Circle the **D** if the question is answered by a deduction.

> Your brain has three parts: the **cerebrum,** the **cerebellum,** and the **brain stem.** Your cerebrum, which is by far the largest part of your brain, fills the top half of your skull. You use your cerebrum to think and feel. Your cerebellum is under the back part of your cerebrum. The cerebellum does a lot of things. One thing is to help you keep your balance. Your brain stem connects your cerebrum to your spinal cord. The brain stem controls your digestive, circulatory, and respiratory systems.

1. Name the three parts of your brain.

   _____

   _____

2. Which part is the largest?

   _____

3. Where is your cerebrum?

   _____

   _____

4. What is one thing your cerebellum does?

   _____

   _____ W   D

5. Where is your cerebellum?

   _____

   _____ W   D

6. Which brain part do you use when you make a deduction?

   _____

   _____ W   D

7. Which brain part regulates your heartbeat?

   _____

   _____ W   D

F CONTRADICTIONS

Tell which fact each statement relates to. Make each contradiction true.

> **A.** The cell needed oxygen.
> **B.** The cell was part of the biceps.

1. It was like a burning thing.   _____

2. It was in the lower leg.   _____

3. It was a muscle cell.   _____

G SIMILES

Tell **two** ways that the things compared are **not** the same. Tell **one** way that the things compared **are** the same.

His shirt was like Swiss cheese.

1. _____

_____

2. _____

_____

3. _____

_____

H DEDUCTIONS

Write the conclusion of each deduction.

1. Burning things produce carbon dioxide.
   Fires are burning things.

   _____

   _____

2. Blood that is red carries oxygen.
   Blood in the arm arteries is red.

   _____

   _____

3. Some bones protect body parts.
   The clavicle is a bone.

   _____

   _____

I WRITING DIRECTIONS

Complete the instructions.

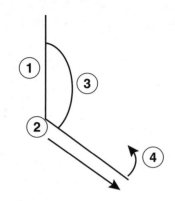

1. Draw a _____ _____.

2. Draw a line that _____

   _____ to the _____

   from the _____ of line 1.

3. Draw a _____ that covers the right side of line 1 and attaches to the

   _____ _____

   of line 2.

4. Draw an _____ that shows

   which way the _____ will

   _____ line 2.

J DEFINITIONS

Write a word that comes from **reside** or **produce** in each blank. Then write **verb, noun,** or **adjective** after each item.

1. Pam _____ in the woods last summer. _____

2. This factory is more _____ now. _____

3. Pete is afraid to _____ in that house. _____

4. The _____ part of town is on a hill. _____

5. New machines may increase the _____ of cars.

   _____

K BODY SYSTEMS

Fill in each blank.

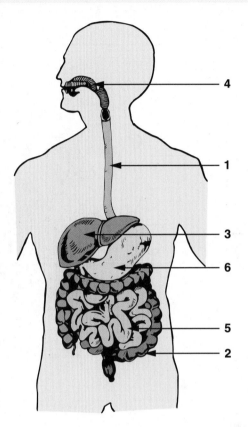

1. _____
2. _____
3. _____
4. _____
5. _____
6. _____

L WRITING STORIES

Write a story about this picture of Fernando. Your story should tell what happened **before** the picture, what happened **in** the picture, and what happened **after** the picture.

| questions | teacher | asleep | students | worried | almost |

_____

_____

_____

_____

_____

_____

_____

_____

_____

_____

- **Does each sentence start with a capital letter?**
- **Does each sentence end with a period?**

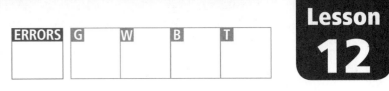
A **WRITING DIRECTIONS**

Write the instructions.

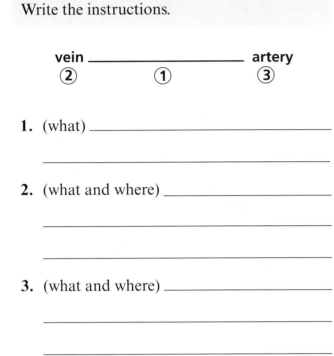

vein _____ artery
②   ①   ③

1. (what) _____

    _____

2. (what and where) _____

    _____

    _____

3. (what and where) _____

    _____

    _____

B **BODY SYSTEMS**

Write **brain, spinal cord, nerves, central,** or **peripheral** in each blank.

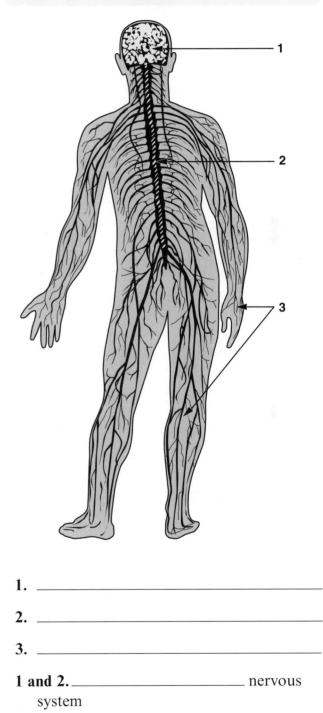

1. _____

2. _____

3. _____

1 and 2. _____ nervous system

3. _____ nervous system

C SENTENCE COMBINATIONS

Circle the common part that is at the beginning of two sentences. Then combine those sentences with **who** or **which.**

1. Tom has black hair.
   Tom is a football player.
   Black hair is good-looking.

   _____

   _____

2. The woman rode her spotted horse.
   Her spotted horse was eating oats.
   Her spotted horse is named Pinto.

   _____

   _____

   _____

3. A big cat digested its food.
   Its food was all meat.
   A big cat sat in the sun.

   _____

   _____

   _____

4. That construction is very old.
   That construction has many offices.
   Many offices are always hot.

   _____

   _____

   _____

D DEDUCTIONS

Write the middle part of each deduction.

1. Burning things need oxygen.

   _____

   So, fires need oxygen.

2. Blood that is almost black carries carbon dioxide.

   _____

   So, blood in the leg veins carries carbon dioxide.

3. Some arteries carry carbon dioxide.

   _____

   So, maybe the hepatics carry carbon dioxide.

E BODY RULES

Shade in each tube that carries dark blood.
Write **vein** or **artery** in each blank.

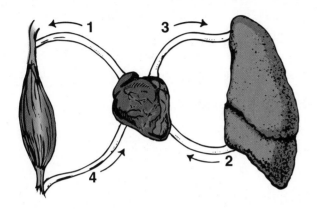

1. _____
2. _____
3. _____
4. _____

F CONTRADICTIONS

Tell which fact each statement relates to.
Make each contradiction true.

> **A.** The nerve went from the spinal cord
> to the quadriceps.
> **B.** The vein went from the quadriceps to
> the heart.

1. It was part of the central
   nervous system.   _____

2. It was carrying oxygen.   _____

3. It looked almost black.   _____

G SIMILES

Tell **two** ways that the things compared are
not the same. Tell **one** way that the things
compared **are** the same.

> His back is like a pole.

1. _____

   _____

2. _____

   _____

3. _____

   _____

H ANALOGIES

Complete the analogies.

1. **Tell which bone each nerve is near.**

   A biceps nerve is to the _____
   as a spinal cord nerve is to the

   _____.

2. **Tell which small system each nerve belongs to.**
   A biceps nerve is to the

   _____

   _____ as a spinal cord nerve

   is to the _____

   _____.

3. **Tell which big system each nerve belongs to.**
   A biceps nerve is to the

   _____

   as a spinal cord nerve is to the

   _____.

I DEFINITIONS

Write a word that comes from **protect** or **criticize** in each blank. Then write **verb, noun,** or **adjective** after each item.

1. Those people put up a _____

   fence. _____

2. Some chemicals _____ plants

   from bugs. _____

3. His _____ comments made

   me feel bad. _____

4. The man made many _____

   of the new play. _____

5. These locks will give you extra

   _____ . _____

J **INFERENCE**

Read the passage and answer the questions.
- Circle the **W** if the question is answered by words in the passage. Then underline those words.
- Circle the **D** if the question is answered by a deduction.

Your cerebrum, which is the top part of your brain, is divided into two halves. The right half is called the **right hemisphere** and the left half is called the **left hemisphere.** Your right hemisphere regulates the muscles on the **left** side of your body, and your left hemisphere regulates the muscles on the **right** side. For example, when you move your left biceps, that movement is controlled by your right hemisphere. And when you move your right quadriceps, that movement is controlled by your left hemisphere.

This same left-right switch happens with many other parts of your body. Sights you see with your left eye go to your right hemisphere, and sounds you hear with your right ear go to your left hemisphere. Both hemispheres work together to help you move, see, hear, think, and talk.

---

1. What are the two parts of the cerebrum?

_____

_____

_____

2. Which muscles does your right hemisphere regulate?

_____

_____

_____ **W   D**

3. Which hemisphere controls the muscles on your right side?

_____

_____ **W   D**

4. When somebody whispers into your right ear, to which hemisphere does the sound go?

_____

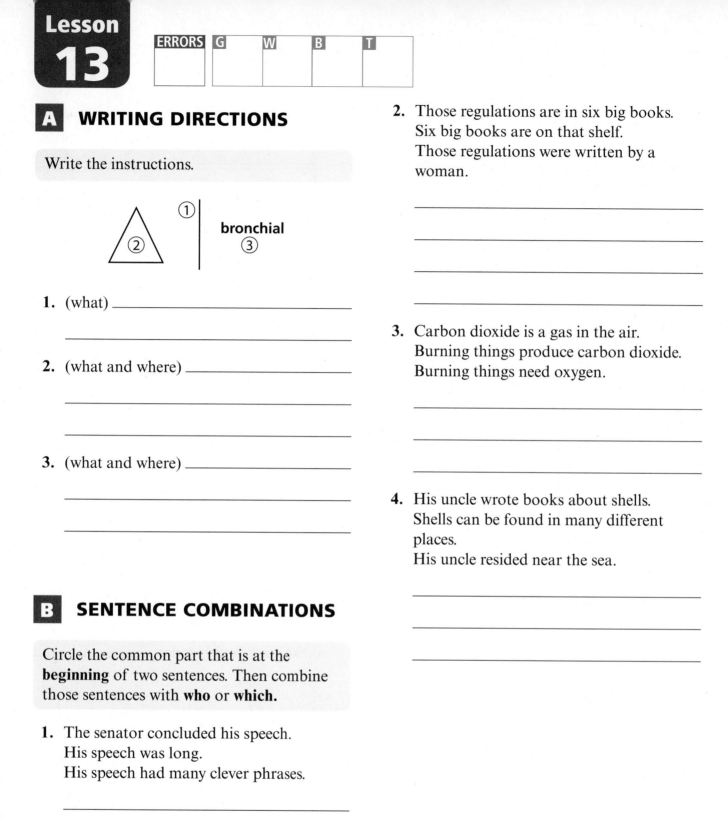

A WRITING DIRECTIONS

Write the instructions.

bronchial

1. (what) _____
   _____

2. (what and where) _____
   _____
   _____

3. (what and where) _____
   _____
   _____

B SENTENCE COMBINATIONS

Circle the common part that is at the **beginning** of two sentences. Then combine those sentences with **who** or **which.**

1. The senator concluded his speech.
   His speech was long.
   His speech had many clever phrases.
   _____
   _____
   _____

2. Those regulations are in six big books.
   Six big books are on that shelf.
   Those regulations were written by a woman.
   _____
   _____
   _____
   _____

3. Carbon dioxide is a gas in the air.
   Burning things produce carbon dioxide.
   Burning things need oxygen.
   _____
   _____
   _____

4. His uncle wrote books about shells.
   Shells can be found in many different places.
   His uncle resided near the sea.
   _____
   _____
   _____

C INFERENCE

Read the passage and answer the questions.
• Circle the **W** if the question is answered by words in the passage. Then underline those words.
• Circle the **D** if the question is answered by a deduction.

When you walk, your body is doing thousands of things every minute. Your heart is beating; your leg muscles are pulling; your blood is moving. If your cerebrum had to think about doing all those things, it wouldn't have much time for anything else. This is why you have the cerebellum and the brain stem. They regulate all the body parts you never think about. The cerebellum helps you keep your balance. The brain stem controls the digestive, circulatory, and respiratory systems.

1. When you walk, your heart is beating, your leg muscles are pulling, and your blood is moving. Name three other things that your body is doing.

   _____

   _____

   _____

   _____

   _____

2. Why doesn't your cerebrum think about all those things?

   _____

   _____

   _____

   _____ **W   D**

3. What does the cerebellum help you do?

   _____

   _____ **W   D**

4. Which systems does the brain stem regulate?

   _____

   _____ **W   D**

5. Tell which part of the brain you use for the following things:

   a. breathing _____

   b. reading _____

   c. thinking _____

   d. keeping your balance _____

   e. pumping blood _____

Lesson 13

D PARTS OF SPEECH

Underline the nouns. Draw **one** line over the adjectives. Draw **two** lines over the articles. Circle the verbs.

1. Cats were digesting their food on the porch.

2. The film had a strange conclusion.

3. His friends went to the park after dark.

4. The dark room is scaring the young baby.

E CONTRADICTIONS

Make each statement mean the same thing as the statement in the box.

> Your brain regulates everything your body does.

1. All the things you do are controlled by your brain.

2. Your brain is controlled by all the things your body does.

3. Your body is regulated by your brain.

4. Your body controls your brain.

F BODY SYSTEMS

Write **brain, nerves, spinal cord, central,** or **peripheral** in each blank.

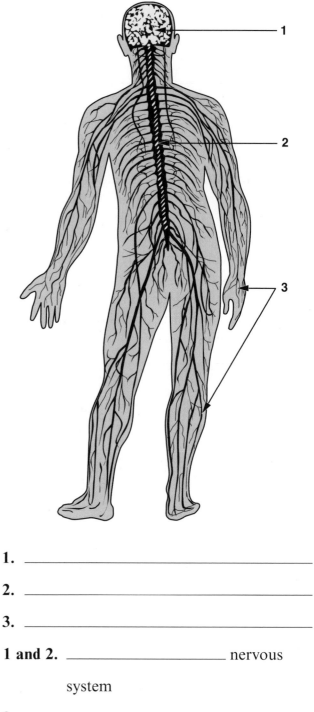

1. _____

2. _____

3. _____

1 and 2. _____ nervous system

3. _____ nervous system

G DEFINITIONS

Fill in each blank with the word that has the same meaning as the word or words under the blank.

1. Fish _____ oxygen from
   (get)
   water.

2. He was _____ after the
   (looked at)
   wreck.

3. The heart _____ the
   (controls)
   circulatory system.

4. You should _____ your
   (choose)
   food with care.

H BODY RULES

Shade in each tube that carries dark blood.
Write **vein** or **artery** in each blank.

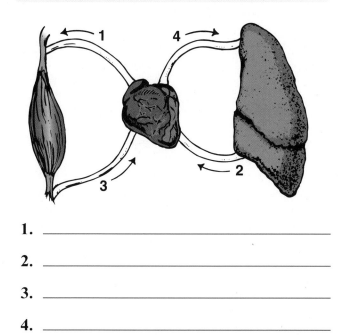

1. _____

2. _____

3. _____

4. _____

I SUBJECT/PREDICATE

Circle the subject and underline the predicate.

1. The brain and the spinal cord make up the central nervous system.

2. Running in the cold can be painful.

3. Stores sell many useful products.

4. Burning things produce carbon dioxide.

5. To make a recording is thrilling.

6. Some nerves let you feel.

J SIMILES

Tell **two** ways that the things compared are **not** the same. Tell **one** way that the things compared **are** the same.

Her eyes were like lights.

1. _____
   _____

2. _____

3. _____
   _____

Lesson 13

K WRITING STORIES

Write a story about this picture of Wanda. Your story should tell what happened **before** the picture, what happened **in** the picture, and what happened **after** the picture.

drumsticks	upset	pigtails	peace	tantrum

_____

_____

_____

_____

_____

_____

_____

_____

_____

_____

_____

_____

_____

_____

_____

_____

_____

_____

_____

- **Does each sentence start with a capital letter?**
- **Does each sentence end with a period?**

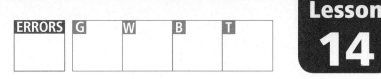

A INFERENCE

Read the passage and answer the questions.
- Circle the **W** if the question is answered by words in the passage. Then underline those words.
- Circle the **D** if the question is answered by a deduction.

> You use both your cerebrum and your cerebellum whenever you move. Let's say you want to walk across a room to open a door. First your **cerebrum** tells your leg muscles to start walking. Then your **cerebellum** makes sure that all your leg muscles are working together as you walk. If you trip over something, your cerebellum helps you find your balance again.
>
> When you get to the door, your cerebrum tells your arm muscles to turn the doorknob. Then your cerebellum helps guide your muscles as you reach for the knob and turn it.
>
> Remember, your cerebrum tells your muscles what to do, and your cerebellum helps your muscles work together.

1. What two parts of your brain do you use whenever you move?

   _____

   _____

2. Which part tells your muscles what to do?

   _____

   _____ **W D**

3. Which part helps your muscles work together?

   _____

   _____ **W D**

4. If someone has trouble keeping their balance, what part of their brain might have a problem?

   _____

   _____ **W D**

5. Pretend the different parts of your brain could talk. Which part might say, "Arm muscles, start bending"?

   _____

   _____

B SENTENCE COMBINATIONS

Circle the common part that is at the **beginning** of two sentences. Then combine those sentences with **who** or **which.**

1. The brain is part of the central nervous system.
   The central nervous system includes the spinal cord.
   The brain lets you think and feel.

   _____

   _____

   _____

   _____

2. The biceps does not move the humerus.
The humerus is part of the skeletal system.
The humerus is in the upper arm.

_____

_____

_____

_____

3. His older sister ran around the block.
His older sister has track shoes.
The block was very big.

_____

_____

_____

4. The man's dog was chasing a cat.
A cat had black fur.
The man's dog had brown feet.

_____

_____

_____

C   WRITING DIRECTIONS

Write the instructions.

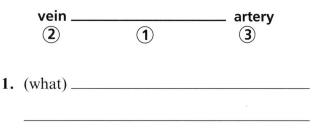

1. (what) _____

_____

2. (what and where) _____

_____

_____

3. (what and where) _____

_____

D   SENTENCE COMBINATIONS

Underline the common part. Circle the
word that combines the sentences correctly.
Combine the sentences with that word.

1. Sir Isaac Newton discovered many things.
Sir Isaac Newton was born in 1642.

because   **who**   **which**

_____

_____

_____

2. His dog has brown fur.
Her cat has brown fur.

and   **which**   **who**

_____

_____

3. An elephant digests food very slowly.
A whale digests food very slowly.

which   **and**   **because**

_____

_____

_____

4. The liver is part of the digestive system. The esophagus is part of the digestive system.

because   **who**   **and**

_____

_____

_____

5. A man was sitting in the yard. His wife was sitting in the yard.

and   **which**   **because**

_____

_____

_____

E SUBJECT/PREDICATE

Circle the subject and underline the predicate.

1. The nervous system is made up of the central and the peripheral nervous systems.

2. Plants breathe carbon dioxide.

3. Shoveling snow takes strong muscles.

4. To light the street costs money.

5. Blood that carries oxygen is red.

6. **Reside, produce,** and **modify** are verbs.

F CONTRADICTIONS

Underline the contradiction.
Circle the statement it contradicts.

Smoking hurts the circulatory system of people who smoke. Their blood can't get pure oxygen because their lungs are full of smoke. Their blood gets thick and heavy and moves slowly.* Because smokers' circulation is poor, their feet and hands get cold easily. Their blood is too thin to move quickly through their capillaries. Smokers could really help their circulatory system if they stopped smoking.

G BODY RULES

Draw in the arrows. Write **vein** or **artery** in each blank.

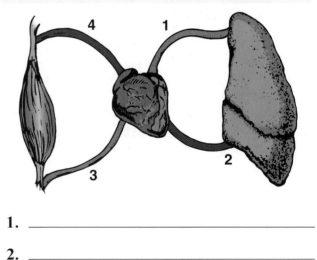

1. _____

2. _____

3. _____

4. _____

H BODY SYSTEMS

Write **brain, nerves, spinal cord, central,** or **peripheral** in each blank.

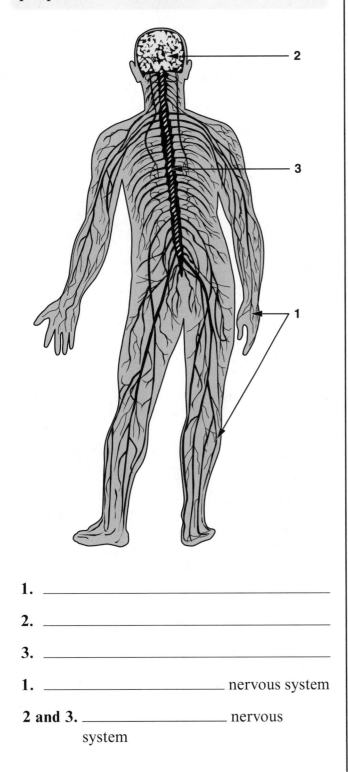

1. _____
2. _____
3. _____
1. _____ nervous system
2 and 3. _____ nervous system

I BODY SYSTEMS

Fill in each blank.

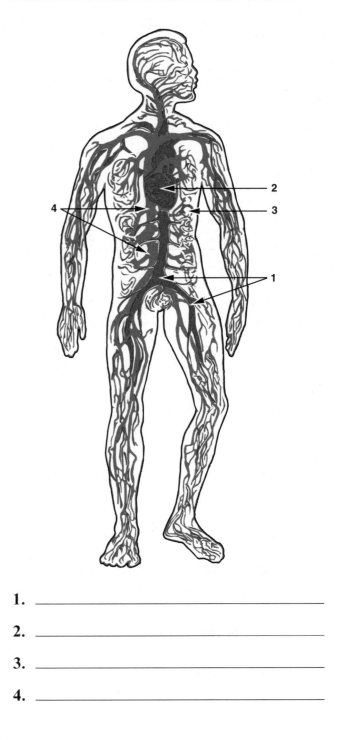

1. _____
2. _____
3. _____
4. _____

WORD LIST

brain (n) the organ that lets you think and feel

conclude (v) to end or figure out

conclusion (n) the end or something that is concluded

conclusive (a) that something is true without any doubt

criticism (n) a statement that criticizes

digest (v) to change food into fuel for the body

digestion (n) the act of digesting

digestive (a) that something involves digestion

modified (a) that something is changed

nerve (n) a wire in the body that carries messages

production (n) something that is produced

protective (a) that something protects

spinal cord (n) the body part that connects the brain to all parts of the body

Lesson 15

ERRORS	G	W	B	T

A WRITING DIRECTIONS

Write the instructions.

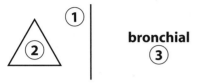

bronchial
③

1. (what) _____
   _____

2. (what and where) _____
   _____
   _____

3. (what and where) _____
   _____
   _____

B SENTENCE COMBINATIONS

Circle the common part that is at the **beginning** of two sentences. Then combine those sentences with **who** or **which.**

1. Carbon dioxide turns blood almost black.
   Carbon dioxide is a gas in the air.
   The air has many other gases.

   _____
   _____
   _____

2. The robber held up Bob's uncle.
   Bob's uncle got away from the robber.
   Bob's uncle was a police officer.

   _____
   _____
   _____
   _____

3. Her sentence was about trees.
   Trees are her favorite plant.
   Her sentence had a long subject.

   _____
   _____
   _____

C BODY RULES

Draw in the arrows. Write **vein** or **artery** in each blank.

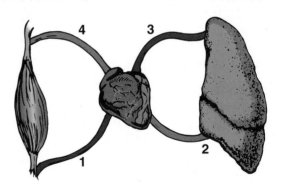

1. _____
2. _____
3. _____
4. _____

D INFERENCE

Read the passage and answer the questions.
- Circle the **W** if the question is answered by words in the passage. Then underline those words.
- Circle the **D** if the question is answered by a deduction.

When you stub your toe, the message "toe hurts" goes from your toe to your brain. Your nerves don't really carry the words "toe hurts." What they do carry is a little bit of electricity. The electricity comes in very short bursts called **impulses.** If the toe doesn't hurt too much, the message may have just a few impulses per second. If the toe hurts a lot, the message may have many impulses per second. The greater the pain, the more impulses per second.

1. Which system carries the message "toe hurts" to your brain?

_____ **W D**

2. How is a nerve like a lamp cord?

_____

_____ **W D**

3. What are impulses?

_____

_____

4. If a message has 10 impulses per second, how many impulses will it have in 5 seconds?

_____

5. Pain Message A has 50 impulses per second. Pain Message B has 120 impulses per second. Which message describes more pain?

_____ **W D**

6. Which gives more impulses per second: banging your knee against a door or touching your knee with a glove?

_____

_____

E SUBJECT/PREDICATE

Circle the subject and underline the predicate.

1. Buying new clothes is fun.
2. Burning things need oxygen.
3. Oxygen is needed by burning things.
4. The act of digesting is called digestion.
5. The predicate of a sentence tells more.
6. The nervous system is made up of nerves.

Lesson 15

F BODY SYSTEMS

Write **brain, nerves, spinal cord, central,** or **peripheral** in each blank.

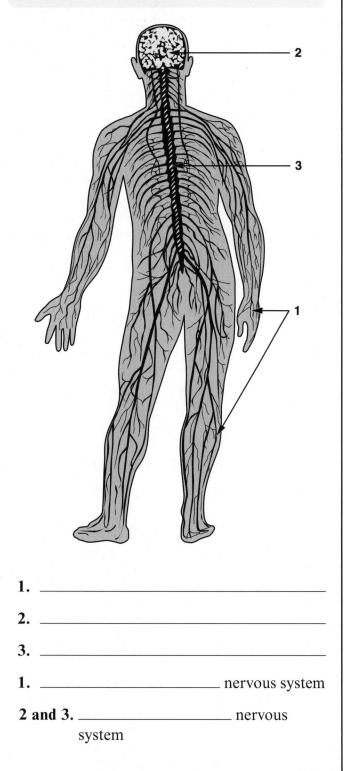

1. _____

2. _____

3. _____

1. _____ nervous system

2 and 3. _____ nervous system

G BODY SYSTEMS

Fill in each blank.

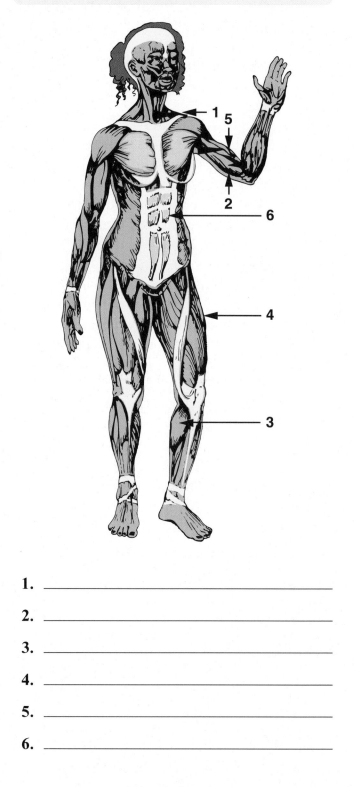

1. _____

2. _____

3. _____

4. _____

5. _____

6. _____

Lesson
15

H SENTENCE COMBINATIONS

Underline the common part. Circle the
word that combines the sentences correctly.
Combine the sentences with that word.

1. That student has sold many raffle tickets.
His teacher has sold many raffle tickets.

   who   **and**   **which**

   _____

   _____

2. Those women protect an army base.
A man protects an army base.

   and   **who**   **because**

   _____

   _____

   _____

3. The man was sick.
The man took pills.

   who   **which**   **because**

   _____

   _____

4. Sanford was riding in the truck.
His son was riding in the truck.

   and   **which**   **because**

   _____

   _____

   _____

5. Alabama is in the South.
Mississippi is in the South.

   because   **and**   **who**

   _____

   _____

I CONTRADICTIONS

Underline the contradiction.
Circle the statement it contradicts.

   Mary had a sore trachea. She ate lots of ice
cream to keep the pain down. She couldn't
breathe very well. She wanted to see a doctor.*
Her brother took her to the hospital.
A doctor there said, "The tubes inside your
lungs are hurting you. You will have to take
some pills." So Mary went home and took the
pills.

J WRITING STORIES

Write a story about this picture of a boat named Two Chimney Chuck. Your story should tell what happened **before** the picture, what happened **in** the picture, and what happened **after** the picture.

| attacked | ocean | monster | octopus | lifeboats | rescued |

_____

_____

_____

_____

_____

_____

_____

_____

_____

_____

- **Does each sentence start with a capital letter?**
- **Does each sentence end with a period**

Fact Game
2

FACT GAME SCORECARD

1	2	3	4	5	6	7	8	9	10	11	12	13	14	15
16	17	18	19	20	21	22	23	24	25	26	27	28	29	30

FG	B	T

2. Combine the sentences in the box with **who** or **which.**

> Pam is a baseball player. Pam lives in Fulton.

3. Name the part of speech for each underlined word.

   a. The stomach is part of the <u>digestive</u> system.
   b. Everyone liked the <u>conclusion</u> of the movie.

4. Answer the questions.

   a. What is the body system of nerves?
   b. What is the body system that brings oxygen to the blood?

5. Complete the sentences.

   a. The brain and the spinal cord make up the ▨▨▨▨▨ nervous system.
   b. The nerves that lead to and from the spinal cord and the brain make up the ▨▨▨▨▨ nervous system.

6. Combine the sentences in the box with **who** or **which.**

> Fulton is in New York State. Pam lives in Fulton.

7. Answer the questions about the picture.

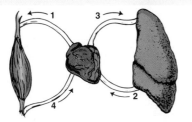

   a. Is tube 1 a vein or an artery?
   b. What gas does tube 2 carry?
   c. What gas does tube 3 carry?

8. Complete each sentence with a word that comes from **conclude.**

   a. The class ▨▨▨▨▨ when the bell rang.
   b. He completed the deduction by drawing a ▨▨▨▨▨

9. Name the part of speech for each underlined word.

   a. The evidence against the suspect was not <u>conclusive</u>.
   b. It was hard to <u>digest</u> the thick bread.

10. Answer the questions.

    a. What is the organ that lets you think and feel?
    b. What is the body part that connects the brain to all parts of the body?
    c. What are the wires in the body that carry messages?

11. Complete each sentence with a word that comes from **digest.**

    a. It takes a long time to ▨▨▨▨▨ your dinner.
    b. Too much candy can upset your ▨▨▨▨▨.

12. Answer the questions about the sentence in the box.

> His fingers were sausages.

    a. What is one way the things compared are **not** the same?
    b. What is one way the things compared **are** the same?

Copyright © SRA/McGraw-Hill. All rights reserved.

Fact Game 2   **71**

A SUBJECT/PREDICATE

Circle the subject and underline the predicate. Rewrite each sentence by moving part of the predicate.

> • The man was tired by noon.
> • By noon, the man was tired.

1. Kids were playing under the table.

_____

_____

2. She ate because she was hungry.

_____

_____

B WRITING DIRECTIONS

Write the instructions.

liver
③   ②

1. (what) _____

_____

2. (what and where) _____

_____

_____

3. (what and where) _____

_____

_____

C REWRITING PARAGRAPHS

Rewrite the paragraph by combining the sentences that are joined with an underline. If one of the sentences tells **why,** combine the sentences with **because.**

> Muscles need <u>oxygen. Muscles</u> are like burning things. Muscles can only <u>pull. Muscles</u> are made of things called fibers. An athlete has very strong <u>muscles. A</u> dancer has very strong muscles. Any person who exercises a lot will get strong <u>muscles. Strong</u> muscles are good to have.

_____

_____

_____

_____

_____

_____

_____

_____

_____

_____

_____

_____

_____

D BODY SYSTEMS

Fill in each blank.

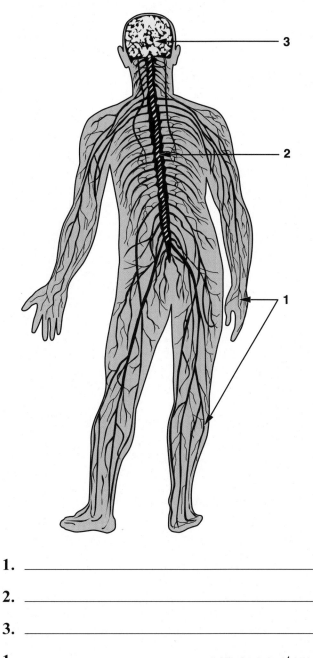

1. _____
2. _____
3. _____

1. _____ nervous system

2 and 3. _____ nervous system

E DEFINITIONS

Fill in each blank with the word that has the same meaning as the word or words under the blank.

1. Don't _____ him until he
   (find fault with)
   makes a mistake.

2. Some _____ don't make
   (rules)
   sense.

3. If you _____ that coat,
   (change)
   you can't return it.

4. He _____ his lunch.
   (changed into fuel for the body)

F PARTS OF SPEECH

Underline the nouns. Draw **one** line **over** the adjectives. Draw **two** lines **over** the articles. Circle the verbs.

1. Your arm nerves are in your peripheral nervous system.

2. His mother has many nervous habits.

3. Her conclusion was based on facts.

4. Their criticisms were printed in the newspaper.

G **INFERENCE**

Read the passage and answer the questions.
- Circle the **W** if the question is answered by words in the passage. Then underline those words.
- Circle the **D** if the question is answered by a deduction.

Your body is made of tiny cells that need oxygen and produce carbon dioxide. Your left biceps, for example, has billions of cells, and each one needs oxygen. Capillaries bring blood that is filled with oxygen to these cells. The blood takes away carbon dioxide. Then the blood with carbon dioxide flows into veins and travels back to your heart.

When the blood with carbon dioxide gets to your heart, the heart pumps the blood to your lungs. Your heart doesn't change your blood; it just pumps the blood. The tube that carries blood from your heart to your lungs is called the **pulmonary artery.** It is one of the biggest arteries in your body.

1. How many cells are in your biceps?

   _____ **W D**

2. What gas does your blood carry from your biceps to your heart?

   _____ **W D**

3. Why is that blood almost black?

   _____

   _____

   _____

   _____ **W D**

4. What happens to the blood when it gets to your heart?

   _____

   _____ **W D**

5. Does your heart change your blood?

   _____

6. What color is blood in the pulmonary artery?

   _____

7. Why is the pulmonary artery an artery?

   _____

   _____

   _____ **W D**

H EVIDENCE

Write **R** for each fact that is **relevant** to what happened. Write **I** for each fact that is **irrelevant** to what happened.

> The man had a pain in his central nervous system.

1. He had hurt his finger. _____

2. He had hurt his spinal cord. _____

3. His toe was over a fire. _____

4. He had hurt nerves inside his backbone. _____

I CONTRADICTIONS

Underline the contradiction.
Circle the statement it contradicts.

Bright red blood flowed through a maze of tubes in a scientist's laboratory. Some blood was being heated in flasks. Other blood was getting electrical jolts. The laboratory looked like a jungle. *The scientist said, "I think that blood can be used for many things. This blood has a lot of carbon dioxide. If I get that gas out of the blood, I will sell it to plant stores and make money."

J SENTENCE COMBINATIONS

Circle the common part that is at the **beginning** of two sentences. Then combine those sentences with **who** or **which.**

1. His older sister's cat had white feet.
   His older sister's cat was named Fats.
   White feet can get very dirty.

   _____

   _____

   _____

2. Dan was very fast.
   The race was long.
   Dan won the race.

   _____

   _____

   _____

3. Nerves carry messages.
   Messages are made up of electricity.
   Nerves are wires.

   _____

   _____

   _____

Lesson 17

ERRORS | G | W | B | T

A SENTENCE COMBINATIONS

You do 2 things for each item.
- **A.** Underline the common part that is at the **end** of one sentence and the **beginning** of another. Then combine those sentences with **who** or **which.**
- **B.** Circle the common part that is at the **beginning** of two sentences. Then combine those sentences with **who** or **which.**

1. Burning things produce carbon dioxide.
   Carbon dioxide is a gas in the air.
   Burning things need oxygen.

   A. _____

   _____

   _____

   B. _____

   _____

   _____

2. The biceps bends the arm.
   The biceps covers the front of the humerus.
   The humerus is the upper arm bone.

   A. _____

   _____

   _____

   B. _____

   _____

   _____

3. Bill had black hair.
   John was mad.
   Bill listened to John.

   A. _____

   _____

   B. _____

   _____

B WRITING DIRECTIONS

Write the instructions.

productive ②   ③ production ①

1. (what) _____

   _____

2. (what and where) _____

   _____

   _____

3. (what and where) _____

   _____

   _____

C SUBJECT/PREDICATE

Circle the subject and underline the predicate. Rewrite each sentence by moving part of the predicate.

- Ann and Jane played ball after school.
- After school, Ann and Jane played ball.

1. We can ski if it snows.

_____

2. Dinah went to sleep before ten o'clock.

_____

_____

D DEFINITIONS

Make each statement mean the same thing as the statement in the box.

The man modified his car because he wanted it to go faster.

1. The man changed his car so that it would go faster.
2. Because he wanted to make it go faster, the man digested his car.
3. To make it go more quickly, the man changed his car.
4. To make it go faster, the car changed the man.

E BODY SYSTEMS

Fill in each blank.

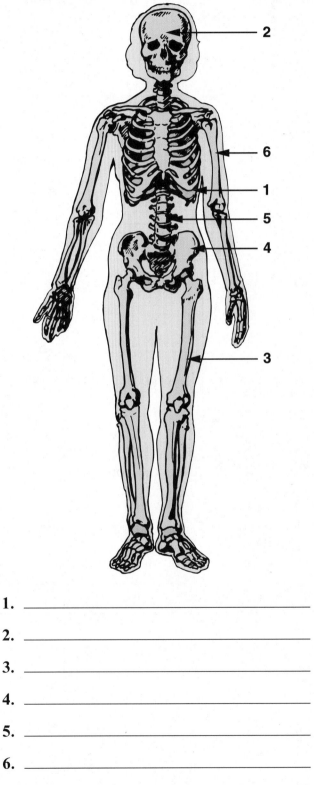

1. _____
2. _____
3. _____
4. _____
5. _____
6. _____

F DEFINITIONS

Write a word that comes from **reside** or **conclude** in each blank. Then write **verb, noun,** or **adjective** after each item.

1. The people clapped when Bob

   _____ his

   speech. _____

2. Many snakes _____

   in cool places. _____

3. The _____ of the

   story was sad. _____

4. Some _____ areas

   are for older people. _____

5. Jim _____ that the

   power was off because the lights went out.

   _____

G SIMILES

Tell **two** ways that the things compared are **not** the same. Tell **one** way that the things compared **are** the same.

| The basketball player moved like a rabbit. |

1. _____

   _____

   _____

2. _____

   _____

3. _____

   _____

H BODY RULES

Draw in the arrows. Shade in each tube that carries dark blood. Write **vein** or **artery** in each blank.

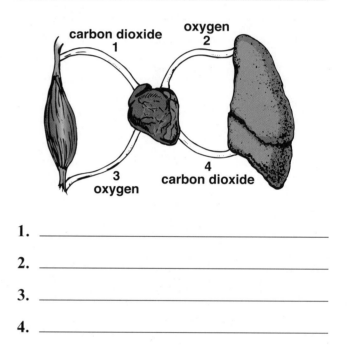

1. _____

2. _____

3. _____

4. _____

I INFERENCE

Read the passage and answer the questions.
- Circle the **W** if the question is answered by words in the passage, and underline those words.
- Circle the **D** if the question is answered by a deduction.

Your pulmonary artery carries blood filled with carbon dioxide to your lungs. Capillaries in your lungs take away the carbon dioxide and replace it with oxygen. The blood, which is now filled with oxygen, then goes back to your heart through your pulmonary vein. When the blood gets to your heart, the heart pumps the blood into an artery called the **aorta.** Your aorta branches into smaller and smaller arteries, which carry the oxygen-filled blood to all parts of your body.

---

1. What color is blood in the pulmonary artery?

   _____ **W   D**

2. What color is blood in the pulmonary vein?

   _____ **W   D**

3. Why is blood in the pulmonary vein that color ?

   _____

   _____

4. What color is blood in the aorta?

   _____ **W   D**

5. Why is the aorta an artery?

   _____

   _____

   _____ **W   D**

6. What gas does blood in the aorta carry?

   _____

J DEDUCTIONS

Use the rule to answer the questions.

The bigger the fire, the more oxygen it needs.

---

1. What needs more oxygen, a forest fire or a match?

   _____

2. Hector's fire needed a lot of oxygen. Hank's fire didn't need much oxygen. Whose fire was bigger?

   _____

3. How do you know?

   _____

   _____

4. Beverly lit a candle. Susan started a camp fire. Which person's fire needs less oxygen?

   _____

5. How do you know?

   _____

Lesson 17

K **BODY SYSTEMS**

Fill in each blank.

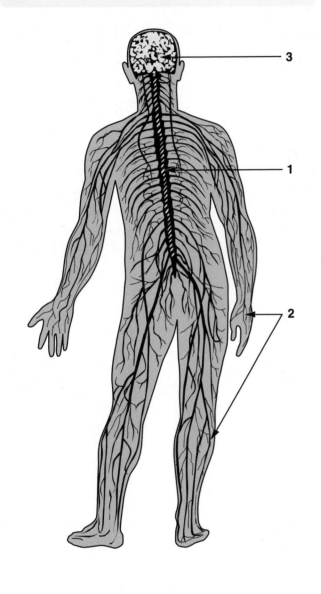

1. _____

2. _____

3. _____

1 and 3. _____ nervous system

2. _____ nervous system

L **WRITING STORIES**

Write a story about this picture of Javier. Your story should tell what happened **before** the picture, what happened **in** the picture, and what happened **after** the picture.

| birthday | pajamas | stuffed lion | wrapping | pillows |

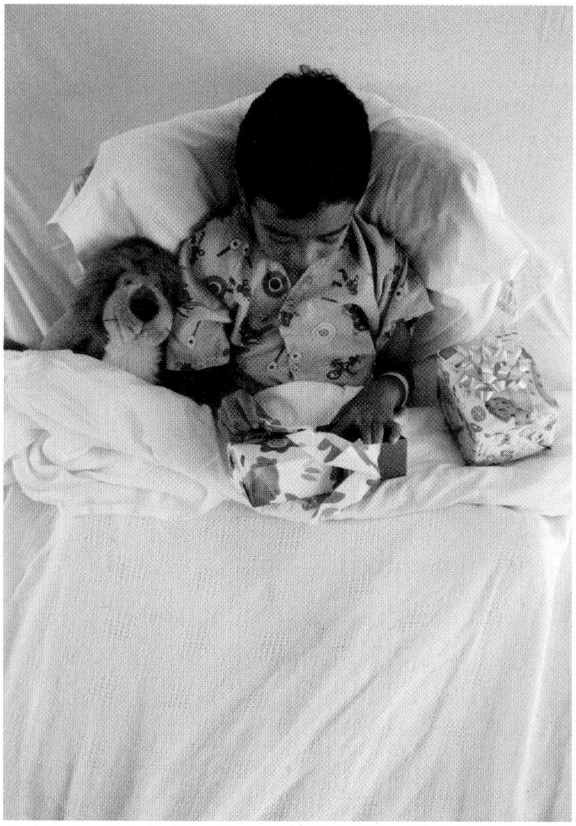

_____
_____
_____
_____
_____
_____
_____
_____
_____
_____
_____
_____
_____

_____
_____
_____
_____
_____
_____
_____

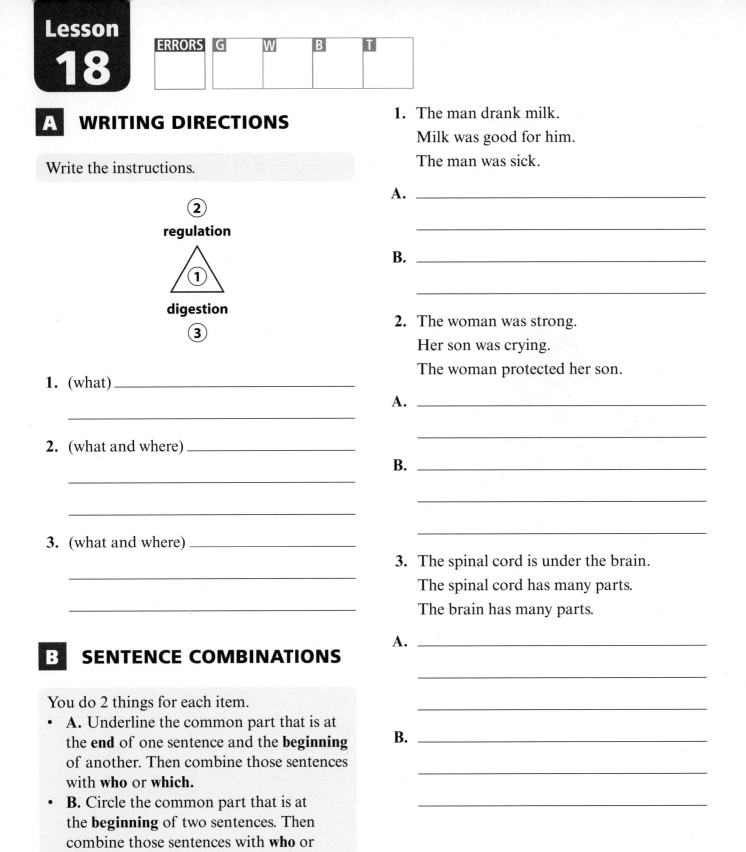

Lesson 18

ERRORS | G | W | B | T

A WRITING DIRECTIONS

Write the instructions.

② regulation

① (triangle)

digestion ③

1. (what) _____

_____

2. (what and where) _____

_____

_____

3. (what and where) _____

_____

_____

B SENTENCE COMBINATIONS

You do 2 things for each item.
- **A.** Underline the common part that is at the **end** of one sentence and the **beginning** of another. Then combine those sentences with **who** or **which.**
- **B.** Circle the common part that is at the **beginning** of two sentences. Then combine those sentences with **who** or **which.**

1. The man drank milk.
    Milk was good for him.
    The man was sick.

    A. _____

    _____

    B. _____

    _____

2. The woman was strong.
    Her son was crying.
    The woman protected her son.

    A. _____

    _____

    B. _____

    _____

3. The spinal cord is under the brain.
    The spinal cord has many parts.
    The brain has many parts.

    A. _____

    _____

    _____

    B. _____

    _____

    _____

C INFERENCE

Use the facts to fill out the form.

> **Facts:** Your name is James Renton. Your wife's name is Susan Renton. You are a police officer who is applying for a job as a fire fighter. You are now making $900 a week. Your address is 362 Pleasant Court, Flagstaff, Arizona.

A. Enter your name on line 4, last name first.
B. Write your wife's first name on line 5.
C. Write the state you live in on line 1.
D. Write the city you live in on line 2.
E. On line 3, write how much money you earn each week.
F. On line 6, write the sentence above that gives information you didn't use in filling out the form.

1. _____
2. _____
3. _____
4. _____
5. _____
6. _____
   _____
   _____

D SUBJECT/PREDICATE

Circle the subject and underline the predicate. Rewrite each sentence by moving part of the predicate.

1. Muscles pull like rubber bands when they work.

   _____
   _____
   _____

2. Your respiratory system works hard when you run.

   _____
   _____
   _____

3. The tree looks small next to that house.

   _____
   _____

4. The man went to the store yesterday.

   _____
   _____

E   BODY SYSTEMS

Fill in each blank.

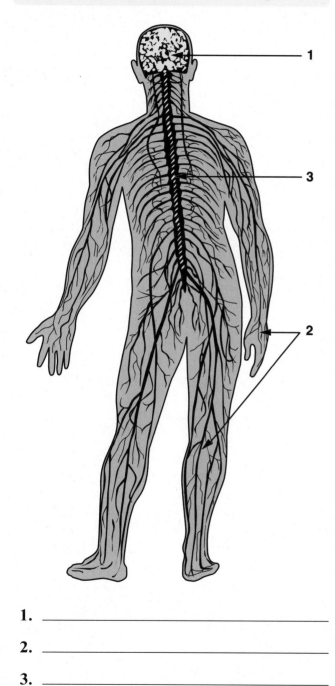

1. _____

2. _____

3. _____

1 and 3. _____ nervous system

2. _____ nervous system

F   DEDUCTIONS

Write the conclusion of each deduction.

1. Every heart has four chambers.
   Joe has a heart.

   _____

   _____

2. All nerves carry messages.
   The vagus is a nerve.

   _____

   _____

3. Some plants produce resin.
   Trees are plants.

   _____

   _____

G   SIMILES

Tell **two** ways that the things compared are **not** the same. Tell **one** way that the things compared **are** the same.

The town was like a beehive.

1. _____

   _____

2. _____

   _____

3. _____

   _____

H SENTENCE COMBINATIONS

Underline the common part. Circle the word that combines the sentences correctly. Combine the sentences with that word.

1. Maine is in the northeast.
   Vermont is in the northeast.
   and   **who**   **which**

   _____

   _____

2. Jim always obtains green apples.
   Marlene always obtains green apples.
   who   **and**   **which**

   _____

   _____

3. New York is one of the oldest states.
   New York has lots of people.
   who   **which**   **because**

   _____

   _____

   _____

4. Oxygen was in the lungs.
   Carbon dioxide was in the lungs.
   because   **who**   **and**

   _____

   _____

5. Montana is in the Great Plains.
   The Dakotas are in the Great Plains.
   which   **and**   **because**

   _____

   _____

   _____

I CONTRADICTIONS

Make each statement mean the same thing as the statement in the box.

> The film concluded with a shot of the sun setting.

1. A picture of the setting sun was the last shot in the film.

2. The film ended with a picture of the sunset.

3. A sunrise concluded the film.

4. The film started with a sunset.

Lesson 19

A DEFINITIONS

Write a word that comes from **consume** in each blank. Then write **verb, noun,** or **adjective** after each item.

1. That man has _____ too much coffee. _____

2. Regulatory agencies try to protect _____. _____

3. Crackers are a _____ product. _____

4. He can _____ great plates of meat. _____

5. Some _____ will buy anything that is on sale. _____

B WRITING DIRECTIONS

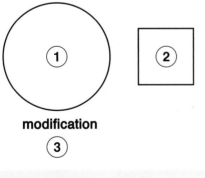

modification
③

Write the instructions.

1. (what) _____

2. (what and where) _____

_____

_____

3. (what and where) _____

_____

_____

C SUBJECT/PREDICATE

Circle the subject and underline the predicate. Rewrite each sentence by moving part of the predicate.

1. People eat lots of fish in Spain.

_____

_____

2. He had bacon and eggs for breakfast.

_____

_____

3. He modified the car before the race.

_____

_____

4. Your digestive system works hard after you eat.

_____

_____

_____

D INFERENCE

Use the facts to fill out the form.

Facts: Your name is Linda Carlson. You are 17 years old. You want to be a doctor when you grow up. You take photographs in your spare time. You earn $200 a week working part-time for the Royal Drug Store. You live at 5642 E. 63rd St., Chicago, Illinois.

A. State your age on line 4.
B. On line 6, tell what you want to be when you grow up.
C. On line 3, tell how much money you make in four weeks.
D. On line 2, write the name of the state you live in.
E. Write your first name on line 5.
F. On line 1, write the sentence above that gives information you didn't use in filling out the form.

1. _____

2. _____
3. _____
4. _____
5. _____
6. _____

E ANALOGIES

Write what each analogy tells.

- what shape each body part is
- what each body part carries
- what body system each body part is in
- what each body part lets you do

1. A **nerve** is to the **nervous system** as an **artery** is to the **circulatory system.**

_____

_____

2. A **nerve** is to **feeling** as an **artery** is to **getting blood.**

_____

_____

3. A **nerve** is to **messages** as an **artery** is to **blood.**

_____

_____

F CONTRADICTIONS

Underline the contradiction.
Circle the statement it contradicts.

Plants produce oxygen. Ellen lived in an apartment with lots of plants. The apartment had no windows, and it was very stuffy. *When Ted came to visit Ellen, he noticed all her plants. He said, "The air in your apartment has lots of oxygen." So Ellen opened the window to let new air in.

G SENTENCE COMBINATIONS

You do 2 things for each item.
- **A.** Underline the common part that is at the **end** of one sentence and the **beginning** of another. Then combine those sentences with **who** or **which.**
- **B.** Circle the common part that is at the **beginning** of two sentences. Then combine those sentences with **who** or **which.**

1. The dog consumed pork chops.
   The dog resided in a little house.
   Pork chops come from pigs.

   A. _____

   _____

   _____

   B. _____

   _____

   _____

2. Jill protects her gold.
   Jill examines silver.
   Her gold is worth a lot.

   A. _____

   _____

   B. _____

   _____

   _____

3. Oxygen is needed by the muscles.
   The aorta is the biggest artery in the body.
   The aorta carries oxygen.

   A. _____

   _____

   _____

   B. _____

   _____

   _____

H SENTENCE COMBINATIONS

Underline the common part. Circle the word that combines the sentences correctly. Combine the sentences with that word.

1. North Carolina was in the Confederacy.
   Virginia was in the Confederacy.
   which　　　**and**　　　**because**

   _____

   _____

   _____

2. The blood in your arm veins is dark.
   The blood in your arm veins has no oxygen.
   who　　　**because**　　　**which**

   _____

   _____

   _____

3. That swimmer has won many medals.
Her coach has won many medals.

and   **who**   **because**

_____

_____

_____

4. The woman put on her swimming suit.
The woman wanted to dive into the lake.

because   **and**   **which**

_____

_____

_____

_____

5. New Orleans is south of Chicago.
Memphis is south of Chicago.

and   **who**   **which**

_____

_____

_____

◼ BODY SYSTEMS

Fill in each blank.

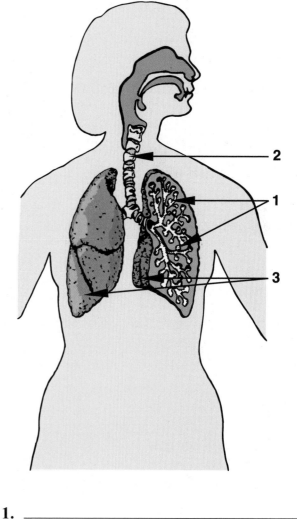

1. _____

2. _____

3. _____

J **DEDUCTIONS**

Write the middle part of each deduction.

1. All nerves carry messages.

   _____

   So, the vagus carries messages.

2. A cat has every kind of blood vessel.

   _____

   So, a cat has veins.

3. Some diseases affect the skin.

   _____

   So, maybe pellagra affects the skin.

WORD LIST

central nervous system (n) the body system made up of the brain and spinal cord

conclude (v) to end or figure out

conclusion (n) the end or something that is concluded

conclusive (a) that something is true without any doubt

digest (v) to change food into fuel for the body

examine (v) to look at

irrelevant (a) that something does not help to explain what happened

nervous system (n) the body system of nerves

peripheral nervous system (n) the body system made up of the nerves that lead to and from the spinal cord and the brain

regulation (n) a rule

relevant (a) that something helps to explain what happened

residential (a) that a place has many residences

selective (a) that something is careful about selecting things

---

K WRITING STORIES

Write a story about this picture of a volleyball game between the Panthers (in red shirts) and the Tigers (in blue shirts). Devon, the best player on the Panthers, has a broken leg. Your story should tell what happened **before** the picture, what happened **in** the picture, and what happened **after** the picture.

volleyball	bench	cast	broken	point	court

_____

_____

_____

_____

_____

_____

_____

_____

_____

_____

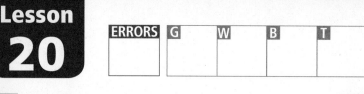

ERRORS | G | W | B | T

A INFERENCE

Use the facts to fill out the form.

Facts: Your name is Jim Morgan. You
want to open a checking account at the
bank. You make $400 a week. Your
address is 345 E. Locust St., Ames, Iowa.
You work as a janitor for John Jay High
School. You are 20 years old. You want a
checking account because you don't like
carrying cash in your wallet.

A. Write the name of your job on line 3.
B. State your age on line 4.
C. State your weekly income on line 1.
D. Give your street address only on line 2.
E. Tell what town you live in on line 6.
F. On line 5, give any reasons you have for
   opening a checking account.
G. On line 7, write the first sentence above
   that gives information you didn't use in
   filling out the form.

1. _____

2. _____

3. _____

4. _____

5. _____

   _____

   _____

6. _____

7. _____

   _____

B WRITING DIRECTIONS

Write the instructions.

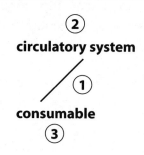

circulatory system

consumable

1. (what) _____

   _____

   _____

2. (what and where) _____

   _____

   _____

   _____

3. (what and where) _____

   _____

   _____

C SUBJECT/PREDICATE

Circle the subject and underline the predicate. Rewrite each sentence by moving part of the predicate.

1. Lupe was tired when she went to bed.

   _____

   _____

2. Mike paints in his spare time.

   _____

   _____

3. Your nervous system is working when you think or feel.

   _____

   _____

   _____

4. We played tennis while the sun was out.

   _____

   _____

D BODY RULES

Draw in the arrows. Shade in each tube that carries dark blood. Write **vein** or **artery** in each blank.

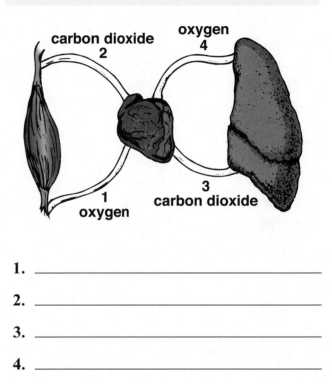

1. _____

2. _____

3. _____

4. _____

E REWRITING PARAGRAPHS

Rewrite the paragraph by combining the sentences that are joined with an underline. If one of the sentences tells **why,** combine the sentences with **because.**

Vitamins are one of the six nutrients. Vitamins can be found in many foods. Your body needs vitamins. Vitamins help keep you well. Vitamin A is an important vitamin. Vitamin A comes from carrots. Night blindness is a bad eye disease. Vitamin A can prevent night blindness.

_____

_____

_____

_____

_____

_____

_____

_____

_____

_____

_____

F DEFINITIONS

Write a word that comes from **consume** in each blank. Then write **verb, noun,** or **adjective** after each item.

1. Your body digests the food you

   _____.

   _____

2. Bob's work _____ all of

   his time yesterday. _____

3. Wood is a _____

   product. _____

4. That office is _____ too

   much paper. _____

5. _____ need
   protection from bad chemicals in food.

   _____

G CONTRADICTIONS

Underline the contradiction.
Circle the statement it contradicts.

Fred had an accident yesterday. He only hurt nerves in his little toe, but the doctor gave him a big cast. It was hard for Fred to walk with the cast on. *Fred asked the doctor why he needed such a big cast. The doctor said, "Anytime you hurt nerves in your central nervous system, you are in big trouble. Be happy that it wasn't any worse."

H SENTENCE COMBINATIONS

You do 2 things for each item.
- **A.** Underline the common part that is at the **end** of one sentence and the **beginning** of another. Then combine those sentences with **who** or **which.**
- **B.** Circle the common part that is at the **beginning** of two sentences. Then combine those sentences with **who** or **which.**

1. His older brother consumed grapes with zest.
   His older brother liked jelly.
   Jelly is made from grapes.

   A. _____

   _____

   _____

   B. _____

   _____

   _____

2. His food was very soft.
   The man had trouble chewing his food.
   The man has no teeth.

   A. _____

   _____

   _____

   B. _____

   _____

   _____

3. His sister played with her cats.
   Her cats liked to roll in mud.
   His sister liked to roll in mud.

   A. _____

   _____

   _____

   B. _____

   _____

   _____

A INFERENCE

Use the facts to fill out the form.

> **Facts:** Your name is Anita Anderson. You are applying for a gas credit card. You make $3,200 a month. Your rent and heat bills add up to $800 a month. You own a car, which is paid for. You are 25 years old. You are a plumber, and you live at 160 Oak St., Danville, Texas.

A. Write your monthly income on line 1.
B. Write the total of your monthly rent and heat bills on line 2.
C. Subtract line 2 from line 1 and write the answer on line 3.
D. State what kind of credit card you want on line 6.
E. Tell your age on line 4.
F. Write your full name, last name first, on line 5.
G. On line 7, write the first sentence above that gives information you didn't use in filling out the form.

1. _____
2. _____
3. _____
4. _____
5. _____
6. _____
7. _____
   _____

B SUBJECT/PREDICATE

Circle the subject and underline the predicate. Rewrite each sentence by moving part of the predicate.

1. Ducks were swimming under the dock.

   _____
   _____

2. He solved the problem without help.

   _____
   _____

3. Blood turns dark when it loses oxygen.

   _____
   _____

4. Apples are ready to eat in the fall.

   _____
   _____

C BODY RULES

Tell what gas each tube carries. Shade in each tube that carries dark blood. Tell if each tube is a vein or an artery.

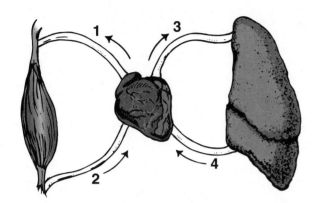

1. _____

2. _____

3. _____

4. _____

D CONTRADICTIONS

Tell which fact each statement relates to. Make each contradiction true.

A. The nerve went from the thumb to the spinal cord.

B. The artery went from the heart to the lungs.

---

1. It was part of the peripheral nervous system. _____

2. It was carrying carbon dioxide. _____

3. It carried messages such as "Move thumb." _____

E BODY SYSTEMS

Fill in each blank.

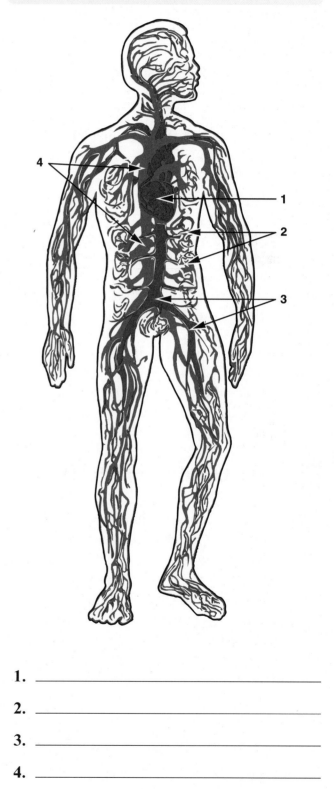

1. _____

2. _____

3. _____

4. _____

F DEFINITIONS

Write a word that comes from **protect** or **consume** in each blank. Then write **verb, noun,** or **adjective** after each item.

1. _____ need to know more

   about products. _____

2. Some liquids give your stomach a

   _____ coating.

   _____

3. The fat cat has _____ a

   lot of food._____

4. The bone that _____
   your brain is called the skull.

   _____

5. That burning candle is _____

   oxygen. _____

G SENTENCE COMBINATIONS

You do 2 things for each item.
- **A.** Underline the common part that is at the **end** of one sentence and the **beginning** of another. Then combine those sentences with **who** or **which.**
- **B.** Circle the common part that is at the **beginning** of two sentences. Then combine those sentences with **who** or **which.**

1. Sensory nerves let you feel.
   The brain can do many things.
   Sensory nerves carry messages to the brain.

A. _____

_____

_____

_____

B. _____

_____

_____

2. Motor nerves carry messages from
   the brain.
   The man hurt his motor nerves.
   The man was in an accident.

A. _____

_____

_____

_____

B. _____

_____

_____

3. Jim was a baseball player.
   Jim spoke with his father.
   His father had strong biceps.

A. _____

_____

_____

B. _____

_____

_____

_____

H EVIDENCE

Write **R** for each fact that is **relevant** to what happened. Write **I** for each fact that is **irrelevant** to what happened.

> Sam wants to modify his car.

1. His car leaks gas. _____

2. He paid for his car with cash. _____

3. Sam likes cars that are different. _____

4. He parks his car in the driveway. _____

I WRITING DIRECTIONS

Write the instructions.

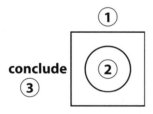

1. (what) _____

   _____

2. (what and where) _____

   _____

3. (what and where) _____

   _____

   _____

J REWRITING PARAGRAPHS

Rewrite the paragraph by combining the sentences that are joined with an underline. If one of the sentences tells **why,** combine the sentences with **because.**

> The brain is the most complex organ in the body. The brain belongs to the nervous system. The brain is very complicated. We do not fully understand the brain. The brain has three parts. The three parts are the cerebrum, the cerebellum, and the brain stem. The cerebrum is larger than the cerebellum. The cerebellum is larger than the brain stem.

_____

_____

_____

_____

_____

_____

_____

_____

_____

_____

_____

_____

_____

_____

_____

_____

K WRITING STORIES

Write a story about this picture of Juan, who is blind. Your story should tell what happened
before the picture, what happened **in** the picture, and what happened **after** the picture.

blind	cane	school	darkness	hearing	touch

A SUBJECT/PREDICATE

Circle the subject and underline the predicate. Rewrite each sentence by moving part of the predicate.

1. You take in oxygen when you breathe.

   _____

   _____

2. They whistled as they worked.

   _____

   _____

3. Many crops are planted in the spring.

   _____

   _____

4. She reads books for the fun of it.

   _____

   _____

B SENTENCE COMBINATIONS

Underline the common part. Combine the contradictory sentences with **but.** Combine the other sentences with **who** or **which.**

1. Pete went to school.
   Pete wanted to stay home.

   _____

   _____

2. Pete went to school.
   Pete had red hair.

   _____

   _____

3. A watch is very small.
   A watch has more than two hundred parts.

   _____

   _____

4. A watch is very small.
   A watch tells time.

   _____

   _____

5. Fred likes to read.
   Fred is a good student.

   _____

   _____

6. Fred likes to read.
   Fred doesn't have any books.

   _____

   _____

C INFERENCE

Read the passage and answer the questions.
- Circle the **W** if the question is answered by words in the passage, and underline those words.
- Circle the **D** if the question is answered by a deduction.

> Your brain has three parts: the **cerebrum,** the **cerebellum,** and the **brain stem.** Your cerebrum, which is by far the largest part of your brain, fills the top half of your skull. You use your cerebrum to think and feel. Your cerebellum is under the back part of your cerebrum. Your cerebellum does a lot of things. One thing is to help you keep your balance. Your brain stem connects your cerebrum to your spinal cord. The brain stem controls your digestive, circulatory, and respiratory systems.

1. Name the three parts of your brain.

   _____

   _____

2. Which part is the largest?

   _____

3. Where is your cerebrum?

   _____

   _____

4. What does your cerebellum do?

   _____

   _____ **W** **D**

5. Where is your cerebellum?

   _____

   _____ **W** **D**

6. Which brain part do you use when you make a deduction?

   _____

   _____ **W** **D**

7. Which brain part regulates your heartbeat?

   _____

   _____ **W** **D**

D WRITING DIRECTIONS

Write the instructions.

1. (what) _____

   _____

2. (what and where) _____

   _____

   _____

3. (what and where) _____

   _____

   _____

E   DEFINITIONS

Write a word that comes from **predict** or **modify** in each blank. Then write **verb, noun,** or **adjective** after each item.

1. Your digestive system _____ food. _____

2. The weather _____ for today were right. _____

3. The heart does not _____ the blood. _____

4. Her remarks were boring and _____. _____

5. Some products could be better with _____. _____

F   EVIDENCE

Write **R** for each fact that is **relevant** to what happened. Write **I** for each fact that is **irrelevant** to what happened.

> The woman's brain sent out this message: "Bend elbow."

1. She had just stubbed her toe. _____

2. She was trying to catch a baseball. _____

3. She was bringing her hand to her eyes. _____

4. Her team was winning the game. _____

G   FOLLOWING DIRECTIONS

Follow the instructions about the sentence in the box.

> This word means "a place where someone lives." _____

1. Cross out the words that are in quotes.
2. Over the words you crossed out, print the word that means **a place where someone lives.**
3. At the end of the sentence, print the verb that the new word comes from.
4. Circle **means.**

H   CONTRADICTIONS

Make each statement mean the same thing as the statement in the box.

> That factory regulates its production daily.

1. That factory controls its production every day.

2. What that factory makes is criticized daily.

3. That factory controls its selection every day.

4. What that factory makes is regulated daily.

❚ BODY RULES

Draw in the arrows. Shade in each tube that
carries dark blood. Tell what gas each tube
carries.

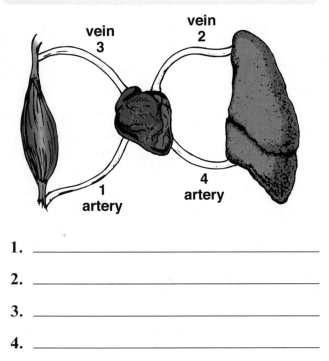

1. _____

2. _____

3. _____

4. _____

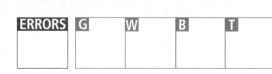

ERRORS G W B T

A SENTENCE COMBINATIONS

Underline the common part. Combine the contradictory sentences with **but.** Combine the other sentences with **who** or **which.**

1. These regulations are fair.
   These regulations have always been ignored.

   _____

   _____

   _____

2. Ken modified his car.
   His car still doesn't run.

   _____

   _____

3. Ken modified his car.
   His car is red.

   _____

   _____

4. The barn was full of hay.
   The barn had red doors.

   _____

   _____

5. Jennifer wanted to construct a house.
   Jennifer didn't have any tools.

   _____

   _____

   _____

6. Jennifer wanted to construct a house.
   Jennifer was six feet tall.

   _____

   _____

   _____

B CONTRADICTIONS

In each passage, underline the contradiction and circle the statement it contradicts. Then tell **why** the underlined statement contradicts the circled statement.

> The aorta is the biggest artery in your body. It is almost an inch wide. The blood in the aorta carries oxygen to all parts of the body. *This blood looks almost black. The aorta is protected by your ribs. If it were ever cut, you probably would die.

1. _____

   _____

> Lester and Shirley were walking around town. They went to the park and to the zoo. Finally they came to a residential district. *They sat down on the curb. Lester said, "This place has almost no residences. It's not very exciting. Let's go back to the park."

2. _____

   _____

   _____

Lesson **23**

C INFERENCE

Read the passage and answer the questions.
• Circle the **W** if the question is answered by words in the passage, and underline those words.
• Circle the **D** if the question is answered by a deduction.

> There are only two kinds of things you can obtain: things you need in order to live and things you don't need in order to live. Things you need are called **needs.** Things you don't need are called **luxuries.** Here are some **needs:** food, so you won't get hungry; clothes, so you won't get cold; a home, so you'll be protected from rain and snow. Here are some **luxuries:** a fancy food like lobster, a fancy boat, a 50-room vacation home on a lake.
>
> Here's a rule about luxuries: The richer you are, the more luxuries you can obtain. A rich person can have a fancy boat; a poor person probably can't. A rich person can have a 50-room vacation home; a poor person probably can't.

1. What do we call things you don't need?

   _____

2. What do we call things you need?

   _____

3. List three kinds of clothes that you need.

   _____

   _____

4. List three kinds of clothes that you don't need.

   _____

   _____

5. What's the rule about the richer you are?

   _____

   _____

   _____ **W   D**

6. Ms. Smith has diamond earrings, an expensive sports car, and three homes. Ms. Jones has plastic earrings, a small car, and a one-room apartment. Which person is probably richer?

   _____ **W   D**

7. Mr. Coltrane earns $1,200 a month. Mr. Thomas earns $1,200 a week. Which person can get more luxuries?

   _____ **W   D**

8. How do you know?

   _____

   _____ **W   D**

D BODY RULES

Draw arrows that show which way messages move in each nerve.

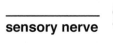

sensory nerve   **motor nerve**

E CONTRADICTIONS

Make each statement mean the same thing as the statement in the box.

> Cars consume gas and produce smoke.

1. Cars use up gas and consume smoke.

2. Cars make smoke and use up gas.

3. Cars consume smoke and use up gas.

4. Cars, which produce smoke, use up gas.

F BODY RULES

Draw in the arrows. Write **vein** or **artery** in each blank. Also write **oxygen** or **carbon dioxide** in each blank.

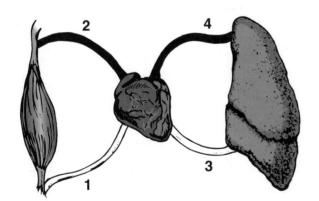

1. _____

2. _____

3. _____

4. _____

G PARTS OF SPEECH

Underline the nouns. Draw **one** line over the adjectives. Draw **two** lines over the articles. Circle the verbs.

1. Sensory nerves carry messages to the brain.

2. Consumers were complaining to the store manager.

3. The store consumes many paper products.

4. Motor nerves let people move.

H BODY SYSTEMS

Fill in each blank.

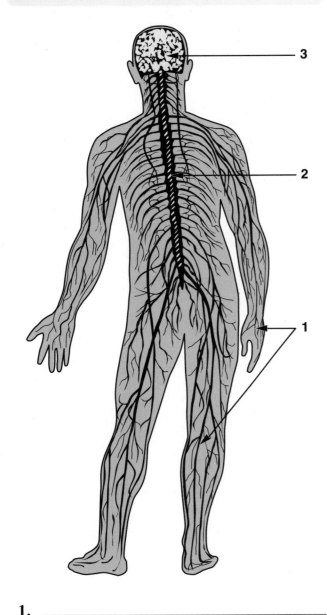

1. _____

2. _____

3. _____

1. _____ nervous system

2 and 3. _____ nervous system

I ANALOGIES

Complete the analogies.

1. Tell what verb each word comes from.

   Conclusion is to _____

   as **conclusive** is to _____.

2. Tell what part of speech each word is.

   Conclusion is to _____

   as **conclusive** is to _____.

3. Tell what ending each word has.

   Conclusion is to _____

   as **conclusive** is to _____.

J FOLLOWING DIRECTIONS

Follow the directions.

[empty box]

1. In the box, draw a line that slants up to the right.
2. Draw a line that slants down to the right from the top of the slanted line.
3. Draw a horizontal line between the bottom ends of the two slanted lines.
4. Below the shape, write the verb that means change.

K WRITING STORIES

Write a story about this picture of Raul and Anita. Your story should tell what happened **before** the picture, what happened **in** the picture, and what happened **after** the picture.

dress	prom	flowers	suit	high school	stairs

_____

_____

_____

_____

_____

_____

_____

_____

_____

_____

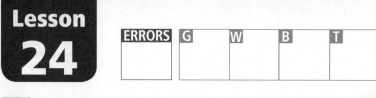

A SENTENCE COMBINATIONS

Underline the common part. Combine the contradictory sentences with **but.** Combine the other sentences with **who** or **which.**

1. Linda has a broken femur.
Linda can walk fast.

_____

_____

2. Modify is a verb.
Modify means change.

_____

_____

3. John paid a lot for that radio.
That radio doesn't work.

_____

_____

4. John paid a lot for that radio.
That radio is green.

_____

_____

5. Sally was happy.
Sally wore a red dress.

_____

_____

6. Sally was happy.
Sally didn't smile.

_____

_____

B REWRITING PARAGRAPHS

Rewrite the paragraph in four sentences. If one of two sentences tells **why,** combine the sentences with **because.** If two sentences seem contradictory, combine them with **but.**

Many animals are faster than people. People can run 100 meters in 10 seconds. A horse is faster. An antelope is faster. A good horse can run one hundred meters in six seconds. One hundred meters in six seconds is pretty fast. Horses seem very fast to us. Horses are much slower than some other animals.

_____

_____

_____

_____

_____

_____

_____

_____

_____

_____

_____

_____

110 *Lesson 24*

C CONTRADICTIONS

Underline the contradiction and circle the statement it contradicts in each passage. Then tell **why** the underlined statement contradicts the circled statement.

The doctor was giving a talk on the nervous system. He showed many slides of body parts. One slide showed the brain. *The doctor said, "This body part may not look like much, but it is very important. It is part of the peripheral nervous system. It controls everything your body does."

---

1. _____

_____

_____

Your brain regulates everything you do. It tells your heart when to beat. It tells your eyes how to read. *It tells your feet how to move. You couldn't do anything without it. It is controlled by your intestines.

---

2. _____

_____

_____

D DEFINITIONS

Write a word that comes from **explain** in each blank. Then write **verb, noun,** or **adjective** after each item.

1. Last week, he _____ his

reasons for leaving. _____

2. That _____ talk was very

clear. _____

3. The teacher criticized my only

_____.

_____

4. She gave several _____

for being late._____.

5. He needs someone to

_____ math to him.

_____

E BODY RULES

Tell if each nerve is a **sensory** nerve or a **motor** nerve. Draw an arrow to show which way the message moves.

1. "Hand feels cold."   2. "Move hand."

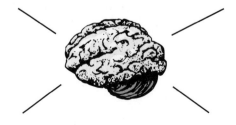

3. "Turn head."   4. "Throat is sore."

F **SIMILES**

Tell **two** ways that the things compared are **not** the same. Tell one way that the things compared **are** the same.

His voice was like a knife.

1. _____

_____

2. _____

_____

3. _____

_____

G **BODY RULES**

Draw in the arrows. Shade in each tube that carries dark blood. Write **vein** or **artery** in each blank.

carbon dioxide   oxygen
        1   2

                4
            carbon dioxide
        3
     oxygen

1. _____

2. _____

3. _____

4. _____

H **DEDUCTIONS**

Use the rule to answer the questions.

The bigger the fire, the more carbon dioxide it produces..

1. What produces more carbon dioxide, a campfire or a candle?

_____

2. Mary's campfire produced a lot of carbon dioxide. Tom's campfire didn't produce much carbon dioxide. Whose fire was bigger?

_____

3. How do you know?

_____

_____

4. Tom lit a match. Mary lit a pile of rags. Whose fire produced more carbon dioxide?

_____

5. How do you know?

_____

_____

▌ INFERENCE

Read the passage and answer the questions.
- Circle the **W** if the question is answered by words in the passage. Then underline those words.
- Circle the **D** if the question is answered by a deduction.

> Here's a rule about needs and luxuries: Over time, some luxuries become needs.
>
> Thousands and thousands of years ago, people didn't need much. They just lived in caves and ate raw meat. Then somebody discovered how to make fire. The cave people didn't really **need** fire, but they liked it. Now they could cook meat and warm their caves at night. Over time, the cave people got so used to cooking meat and keeping warm that they couldn't live without fire. Fire had become a need.
>
> The same thing happened with shoes, cups, plates, chairs, beds, and many other objects. All these objects started out as **luxuries** but ended up as **needs.**

1. What are luxuries?

   _____

   _____

2. What's the rule about what happens over time?

   _____

   _____

   _____ **W   D**

3. Did people need fire at first? _____

4. Did people need fire later? _____

5. Name two new things that people could do with fire.

   _____

   _____

   _____ **W   D**

6. Here are some luxuries that became needs: shoes, cups, plates, and chairs. Name three more.

   _____

   _____

7. Here are some luxuries that will probably never become needs: pet snakes, gold plates, and silver spoons. Name two more.

   _____

   _____

J FOLLOWING DIRECTIONS

Follow the directions.

1. Draw a vertical line in the box.

2. Draw a horizontal line that goes to the right from the top of the vertical line.

3. To the left of the vertical line, write the name of the gas that burning things need.

4. Above the horizontal line, write the name of the gas that burning things produce.

K PARTS OF SPEECH

Underline the nouns. Draw **one** line **over** the adjectives. Draw **two** lines **over** the articles. Circle the verbs.

1. A motor nerve is carrying a message from the brain.

2. A teacher will explain those new rules.

3. The central nervous system is a complex body system.

4. Most new cars come with explanatory booklets.

WORD LIST

conclusion (n) the end or something that is concluded

conclusive (a) that something is true without any doubt

construction (n) something that is constructed

consumable (a) that something can be consumed

consume (v) to use up or to eat

consumer (n) something that consumes

modification (n) a change

modify (v) to change

motor nerve (n) a nerve that lets you move

obtain (v) to get

predictable (a) that something is easy to predict

prediction (n) a statement that predicts

sensory nerve (n) a nerve that lets you feel

A REWRITING PARAGRAPHS

Rewrite the paragraph in four sentences. If one of two sentences tells **why,** combine the sentences with **because.** If two sentences seem contradictory, combine them with **but.**

The cheetah is much faster than the horse. The cheetah has the strongest legs of any land animal. The cheetah lives in Africa. The cheetah lives in parts of Asia. The cheetah doesn't start as fast as some animals. The cheetah can run 100 meters in only three seconds. The cheetah eats only meat. The cheetah is a member of the cat family.

_____

_____

_____

_____

_____

_____

_____

_____

_____

_____

_____

_____

B SENTENCE COMBINATIONS

Underline the common part. Combine the contradictory sentences with **but.** Combine the other sentences with **who** or **which.**

1. **Digestive** comes from the word **digest.**
   Digestive is an adjective.

   _____

   _____

2. Fran was tired.
   Fran didn't sleep.

   _____

   _____

3. Fran was tired.
   Fran had black hair.

   _____

   _____

4. Felipe eats a lot.
   Felipe lives next door.

   _____

   _____

5. Felipe eats a lot.
   Felipe doesn't get fat.

   _____

   _____

6. **Digestive** comes from the word **digest**.
   Digest is a verb.

   _____

   _____

   _____

C   CONTRADICTIONS

In each passage, underline the contradiction
and circle the statement it contradicts. Then
tell **why** the underlined statement contradicts
the circled statement.

> The vena cava is the biggest vein in
> your body. It is very close to your heart.
> The vena cava carries blood from all the
> muscle cells to the heart. *The vena cava
> carries a lot of oxygen. It looks almost
> black. Every bit of blood passes through
> the vena cava at some time.

1. _____

   _____

   _____

> Linda and Jim went to a film. The film
> concluded with a shot of people kissing.
> Jim did not like the film.* He was happy
> when the film was over. He said, "I dislike
> films that begin with kissing." Linda
> thought that Jim was being silly.

2. _____

   _____

D   BODY RULES

Tell if each nerve is a **sensory** nerve or a
motor nerve. Draw an arrow to show which
way the message moves.

1. "Knee hurts."   2. "Sneeze."

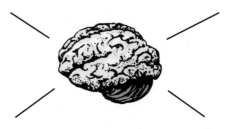

3. "Bend knee."   4. "Nose itches."

E   SUBJECT/PREDICATE

Circle the subject and underline the
predicate. Rewrite the sentence by moving
the predicate.

1. Don was happy because he passed the test.

   _____

   _____

2. That strong old woman will grin if she
   wins.

   _____

   _____

3. You can't go to Spain without a passport.

   _____

   _____

4. She wore her mittens because it was
   snowing.

   _____

   _____

F INFERENCE

Read the passage and answer the questions.
- Circle the **W** if the question is answered by words in the passage, and underline those words.
- Circle the **D** if the question is answered by a deduction.

Here's a rule about ads: **Some ads try to make luxuries a need.**

Let's say a woman sells watches, which are a luxury. She has to sell a lot of watches because she wants to get rich. So, she puts an ad on TV that says, "Everybody needs a watch. It tells you the time all day long. You'll never be late to class. You'll never be late to work. A watch feels good on your wrist, and it doesn't cost much."

Some people who see the woman's ad will think they really do need a watch, and they will buy one from her. If lots of people feel the same way, the woman will get rich. Remember, her ad tried to make a luxury a need.

1. What's the rule about some ads?

   _____

   _____

2. Why does the woman have to sell a lot of watches?

   _____

   _____ **W D**

3. What will some people who see the ad think?

   _____

   _____ **W D**

4. What will they do next? _____

   _____ **W D**

5. Which luxury do you think is easier to make into a need: a microwave oven or a toy train?

   _____

   _____ **W D**

6. Here's an ad: "This balloon is only for the very rich. It takes a long time to fill with air, and you can only use it in the summer." Does this ad try to make a luxury a need?

   _____

7. Do you think the ad will sell many balloons?

   _____

8. Why?

   _____

   _____

   _____

G WRITING DIRECTIONS

Write the instructions.

① _____

explanatory
③

② _____

1. (what) _____

_____

2. (what and where) _____

_____

_____

3. (what and where) _____

_____

_____

_____

H DEFINITIONS

Write a word that comes from **explain** in each blank. Then write **verb, noun,** or **adjective** after each item.

1. She put _____

   notes at the end of her paper.

   _____

2. The traffic police asked her for an

   _____ .

   _____

3. Can you _____ this

   problem? _____

4. I will _____ these critical

   remarks. _____

5. His _____ was very

   conclusive. _____

I WRITING STORIES

Write a story about this picture of Mrs. Peng and her grandson Ming. Your story should tell what happened **before** the picture, what happened **in** the picture, and what happened **after** the picture.

grandson	toddler	visit	pathway	sandals

_____

_____

_____

_____

_____

_____

_____

_____

_____

_____

_____

_____

_____

_____

_____

_____

_____

Fact Game
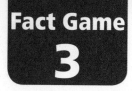

FACT GAME SCORECARD

1	2	3	4	5	6	7	8	9	10	11	12	13	14	15
16	17	18	19	20	21	22	23	24	25	26	27	28	29	30

FG	B	T

2. Combine the sentences in the box with **but.**

> Jill was very hungry. Jill didn't eat dinner.

3. Complete each sentence with a word that comes from **explain.**

  a. The teacher's ▮▮▮▮ comments helped us solve the problem.

  b. The student's ▮▮▮▮ was hard to understand.

4. Complete each sentence.

  a. The nerves that let you feel are called ▮▮▮▮ nerves.

  b. The nerves that let you move are called ▮▮▮▮ nerves.

5. Combine the sentences in the box with **but.**

> These chairs cost a lot of money. These chairs are falling apart.

6. Complete each sentence.

  a. The nerves that carry messages **to** the brain are called ▮▮▮▮ nerves.

  b. The nerves that carry messages **from** the brain are called ▮▮▮▮ nerves.

7. Say each sentence with part of the predicate moved.

  a. His older brother writes books to make money.

  b. She put on her hat because it was raining.

8. Tell if each message would be carried by a **sensory** nerve or a **motor** nerve.

  a. "Hand itches."

  b. "Move hand."

  c. "Shoes are tight."

9. Name the part of speech for each underlined word.

  a. I agreed with his <u>explanation</u>.

  b. These <u>consumers</u> are buying toys.

10. Complete each sentence with a word that comes from **consume.**

  a. If you buy products in a store, you are a ▮▮▮▮.

  b. If something can be consumed, it is ▮▮▮▮.

11. Say each sentence with part of the predicate moved.

  a. Nothing can grow on the moon.

  b. My sister stayed up all night to finish the project.

12. Name the part of speech for each underlined word.

  a. She will <u>explain</u> her selection.

  b. These <u>consumable</u> items are not meant to last.

A INFERENCE

Use the facts to fill out the form.

> **Facts:** Your name is Jeff Miller. You were born on May 26, 1984. You are applying for a job at the post office. For your last job, you drove a truck for the Ace Trucking Company. You worked there for two years, but you had to quit when you got scarlet fever. Your address is 16 Ward Avenue, Springfield, Ohio.

1. Name (last name first):

    _____

2. Date of birth: _____

3. Today's date: _____

4. Address: _____

    _____

5. Which company did you last work for?

    _____

    _____

6. For how long? _____

7. Reasons for leaving: _____

    _____

B CONTRADICTIONS

Underline the contradiction and circle the statement it contradicts in each passage. Then tell **why** the underlined statement contradicts the circled statement.

> Kit wrote a sentence. It was very long. It had six adjectives. *It was about her father. It had only a predicate. It was a pretty good sentence.

1. _____

    _____

    _____

> The man came home on a cold winter night. He started a fire in his fireplace, but his chimney was clogged. He took off his coat and hat. *Pretty soon, he noticed that something was wrong. His house was beginning to fill up with oxygen. He had to open the window, which let the cold air in.

2. _____

    _____

    _____

Lesson 26

C WRITING DIRECTIONS

Write the instructions.

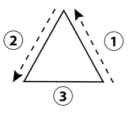

1. (what and where) _____

   _____

   _____

2. (what and where) _____

   _____

   _____

   _____

   _____

3. (what and where) _____

   _____

   _____

D DEDUCTIONS

Write the middle part of each deduction.

1. Blood that is red carries oxygen.

   _____

   _____

   So, blood in the pulmonary vein carries oxygen.

2. Some bones do not support the body.

   _____

   So, maybe the scapula does not support the body.

3. Fred has every kind of artery.

   _____

   So, Fred has an aorta.

E CONTRADICTIONS

Tell which fact each statement relates to. Make each contradiction true.

> **A.** People have arteries in their cheeks.
> **B.** People have sensory nerves in their cheeks.

1. They carry dark blood. _____

2. They carry messages from the brain. _____

3. They carry oxygen. _____

4. They carry messages like "Move cheek." _____

F SUBJECT/PREDICATE

Circle the subject and underline the predicate. Rewrite the sentence by moving part of the predicate.

1. Her bones get stronger as she grows older.

_____

_____

_____

2. Sally sees better when she wears her glasses.

_____

_____

_____

3. He turned the dial to regulate the heat.

_____

_____

4. Those animals let out carbon dioxide when they breathe.

_____

_____

_____

G BODY SYSTEMS

Fill in each blank.

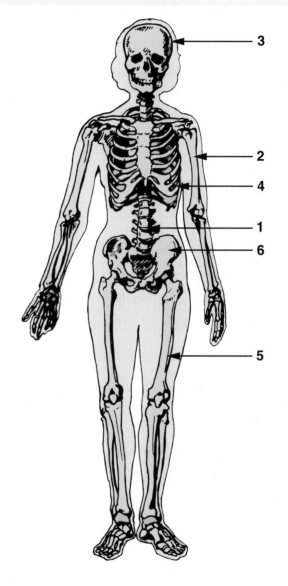

1. _____

2. _____

3. _____

4. _____

5. _____

6. _____

H SENTENCE COMBINATIONS

Underline the common part. Circle the word that combines the sentences correctly. Combine the sentences with that word.

1. The femur is the upper leg bone.
   The quadriceps covers part of the femur.
   which   and   but

   _____

   _____

   _____

   _____

2. That car has red stripes.
   This wagon has red stripes.
   which   and   because

   _____

   _____

   _____

3. A thick book was on the table.
   Ten pens were on the table.
   and   but   because

   _____

   _____

   _____

4. Whales are not fish.
   Whales live in the water.
   who   but   because

   _____

   _____

   _____

5. His wide-brimmed hat is white.
   Her new long dress is white.
   and   but   because

   _____

   _____

   _____

I BODY RULES

Tell if each nerve is a **sensory** nerve or a **motor** nerve. Draw an arrow to show which way the message moves.

1. "Finger hurts."   2. "Bend leg."

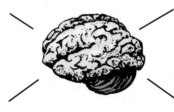

3. "Scratch arm."   4. "Strong smell."

A WRITING DIRECTIONS

Write the instructions.

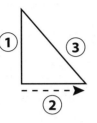

1. (what) _____

   _____

2. (what and where) _____

   _____

   _____

   _____

3. (what and where) _____

   _____

   _____

   _____

B CONTRADICTIONS

Underline the contradiction and circle the statement it contradicts. Then tell **why** the underlined statement contradicts the circled statement.

Sam hurt his arm, so he went to see a doctor. The doctor examined Sam and took some X-rays. *Then she gave Sam some pills that would reduce the pain. The doctor told Sam, "You have a sore femur. It should feel better in a few days."

_____

_____

C INFERENCE

Use the facts to fill out the form.

Facts: You are applying for a driver's license. You live at 1605 Willow Boulevard, Bellingham, Washington. Your phone number is 725-1020. You have never had a driver's license before. You took a driver training class in high school. You wear glasses. Your name is Cristina Lopez.

1. Phone number: _____

2. Have you had any driver training? _____

3. If so, where? _____

4. Full address: _____

   _____

   _____

5. Last name: _____

6. Sex: _____

7. Do you wear glasses? _____

D SIMILES

Make up a simile for each item.

1. A man had bright eyes.

_____

_____

2. A woman was smart.

_____

_____

E BODY RULES

Tell if each nerve is a **sensory** nerve or a **motor** nerve. Draw an arrow to show which way the message moves.

1. "Curl toes."   2. "Food smells good."

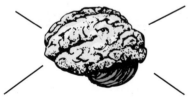

3. "Lie down."   4. "Feel tired."

F SENTENCE COMBINATIONS

Underline the common part. Circle the word that combines the sentences correctly. Combine the sentences with that word.

1. John studied hard.
John did not pass the test.

because   **but**   **which**

_____

_____

_____

2. The mouth belongs to the digestive system. The esophagus belongs to the digestive system.

but   **and**   **which**

_____

_____

_____

3. His mother is explaining the rules.
Her father is explaining the rules.

and   **but**   **which**

_____

_____

_____

4. This stream was moving fast.
That river was moving fast.

because   **who**   **and**

_____

_____

_____

5. Oregon is covered with trees.
Oregon has many lumber mills.

who   **but**   **because**

_____

_____

_____

G DEDUCTIONS

Write the conclusion of each deduction.

1. Some blood vessels go to the heart.
   Venules are blood vessels.

   _____

   _____

2. Some bones support your body.
   The scapula is a bone.

   _____

   _____

3. Blood that is almost black carries carbon
   dioxide.
   Blood in the arm veins is almost black.

   _____

   _____

   _____

H DEFINITIONS

Write a word that comes from **predict** or
digest in each blank. Then write **verb, noun,**
or **adjective** after each item.

1. Andy is _____ the winner

   of the game. _____

2. Her _____ system makes

   strange sounds. _____

3. She drank milk to help her

   _____.

   _____

4. Games that are _____

   are dull. _____

5. The fortune-teller loved to make

   _____ .

   _____

I SUBJECT/PREDICATE

Circle the subject and underline the
predicate. Rewrite the sentence by moving
part of the predicate.

1. This big green truck is fast when it works.

   _____

   _____

2. Your body needs all six nutrients to stay
   healthy.

   _____

   _____

   _____

3. Pete is working longer to increase his
   production.

   _____

   _____

   _____

4. All cups are containers because they can
   hold things.

   _____

   _____

   _____

J BODY SYSTEMS

Fill in each blank.

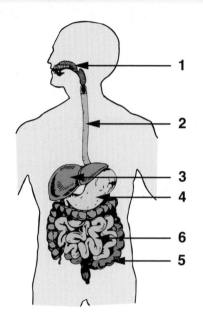

1. _____

2. _____

3. _____

4. _____

5. _____

6. _____

K ANALOGIES

Write what each analogy tells.

> • what each kind of nerve lets you do
> • what body system each nerve belongs to
> • what each nerve carries
> • which direction messages move in each kind of nerve

1. **Sensory nerves** are to **to the brain** as **motor nerves** are to **from the brain.**

   _____

   _____

   _____

2. **Sensory nerves** are to **feeling** as **motor nerves** are to **moving.**

   _____

   _____

3. **Sensory nerves** are to the **nervous system** as **motor nerves** are to the **nervous system.**

   _____

   _____

L WRITING STORIES

Write a story about this picture of Mr. Willis, his son Leon, and his daughter Alissa. Your story should tell what happened **before** the picture, what happened **in** the picture, and what happened **after** the picture.

| giraffe | peacock | zoo | weekend | cages | visit |

_____

_____

_____

_____

_____

_____

_____

_____

_____

_____

_____

_____

A SIMILES

Make up a simile for each item.

1. A man ran fast.

_____

_____

2. A woman's arms were thin.

_____

_____

B BODY RULES

Label each nerve. Write a message for each nerve.

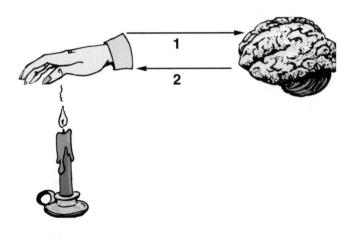

1. _____

2. _____

C EVIDENCE

Write **R** for each fact that is **relevant** to what happened. Write **I** for each fact that is **irrelevant** to what happened.nerve.

> The man's brain sent out this message: "Biceps hurts."

1. The man was wearing tall boots. _____

2. The man's upper arm had just been stung by a bee. _____

3. The man had hit his arm to kill the bee. _____

4. The man was six feet tall. _____

D DEFINITIONS

Fill in each blank with the word that has the same meaning as the word or words under the blank.

1. We stayed until the _____ of the concert.
   (end)

2. Dentists _____ many teeth every day. (look at)

3. Some things are very easy to

   _____.
   (find fault with)

4. People cannot _____ storms.
   (make)

5. To save gas, this car must be

   _____.
   (changed)

E WRITING DIRECTIONS

Write the instructions.

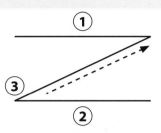

1. (what) _____

   _____

2. (what and where) _____

   _____

   _____

3. (what and where) _____

   _____

   _____

   _____

   _____

   _____

F ANALOGIES

Complete the analogies.

1. **Tell what each kind of nerve lets you do.**
   Sensory nerves are to letting you

   _____ as motor nerves are to

   letting you _____.

2. **Tell what body system each nerve belongs to.**

   Sensory nerves are to the _____
   system as motor nerves are to the

   _____ system.

3. **Tell which direction each kind of nerve message moves in.**

   Sensory nerves are to _____
   the brain as motor nerves are to

   _____ the brain.

G CONTRADICTIONS

Underline the contradiction and circle the statement it contradicts. Then tell **why** the underlined statement contradicts the circled statement.

One day, Ellen fell down the stairs. She hurt one of the nerves in her spinal cord. She broke three ribs. *The doctor said that Ellen would have to stay in bed for a long time. He told her that she had hurt a nerve in her peripheral nervous system. He also told her that she had broken a part of her skeletal system.

_____

_____

_____

Lesson 28

H SENTENCE COMBINATIONS

Underline the common part. Circle the word that combines the sentences correctly. Combine the sentences with that word.

1. Ohio is in the Midwest.
   Ohio borders Lake Erie.

   which   **because**   **who**

   _____

   _____

   _____

2. A body has many parts.
   An engine has many parts.

   because   **and**   **who**

   _____

   _____

3. Mary has big biceps.
   Mary can't lift heavy things.

   because   **which**   **but**

   _____

   _____

   _____

4. Plants are living things.
   Plants produce oxygen.

   which   **but**   **who**

   _____

   _____

5. His tall uncle runs every morning.
   Her slim aunt runs every morning.

   and   **who**   **but**

   _____

   _____

   _____

I BODY RULES

Draw in the arrows. Shade in each tube that carries dark blood. Tell what gas each tube carries.

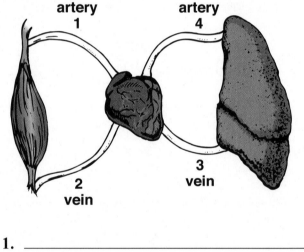

1. _____

2. _____

3. _____

4. _____

J INFERENCE

Read the passage and answer the questions.
- Circle the **W** if the question is answered by words in the passage. Then underline those words.
- Circle the **D** if the question is answered by a deduction.

> Cars as we know them were first made around 1900. They cost a lot, and only rich people could buy them. A man named Henry Ford thought he could make a lot of money if he produced cheap cars that anybody could buy. He started the Ford Motor Company in 1903 and sold his first cars for $850, which was a lot cheaper than any other car. But Ford wanted to make his cars even cheaper. He followed one rule: **The lower the price, the bigger the sales.** Each year more people bought Fords. By 1914, a Ford cost only $500, and one half of all cars made were Fords.

1. About how many years ago were the first cars made?

   _____

   _____ **W D**

2. How did Henry Ford think he could make a lot of money?

   _____

   _____

   _____ **W D**

3. How much cheaper was a 1914 Ford than a 1903 Ford?

   _____ **W D**

4. What rule did Ford follow?

   _____

   _____ **W D**

5. Car A and Car B are very much alike. Car A costs $13,000. Car B costs $18,000. Which car will have bigger sales?

   _____

6. How do you know?

   _____

   _____

7. How much do you think a Ford costs now?

   _____

   _____

A SENTENCE COMBINATIONS

Combine the sentences with **particularly.**

1. Your blood moves fast.
   Your blood moves fastest when you run.

   _____

   _____

   _____

2. John reads books.
   John reads the most books when he is
   at home.

   _____

   _____

   _____

3. The sun is bright.
   The sun is brightest in the summer.

   _____

   _____

   _____

4. They have a lot of fun.
   They have the most fun when they play
   darts.

   _____

   _____

   _____

B BODY RULES

Label each nerve. Then write a message for
each nerve.

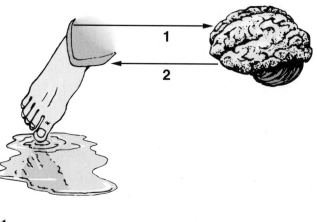

1. _____

2. _____

C DEFINITIONS

Write a word that comes from **manufacture**
in each blank. Then write **verb, noun,** or
adjective after each item.

1. That car _____ makes

   a lot of money. _____

2. He is _____ buttons

   for coats. _____

3. Some _____
   products fall apart quickly.

   _____

4. That _____ will modify

   his line of cars. _____

5. That factory _____

   toys every day. _____

D INFERENCE

Read the passage and answer the questions.
- Circle the **W** if the question is answered by words in the passage. Then underline those words.
- Circle the **D** if the question is answered by a deduction.

Henry Ford made cars a need. Before 1900, cars were a luxury. People didn't need cars to get places because they walked or took a train. But when some people started buying Fords, other people would say, "If you own a Ford, you don't have to walk or take a train. I like that." And then they would buy Fords too.

Pretty soon, lots of people had Fords. Cities had to construct new streets for all the cars. Some people with cars moved from apartments in the city to houses in the suburbs. They could drive to their jobs in the city in the same amount of time that they used to spend walking to their jobs from city apartments. By 1920, cities and suburbs had changed so much that many people really needed a car to live. What had started out as a luxury was now a need.

1. What did Henry Ford make cars?

_____ **W**　**D**

2. Why were cars a luxury before Ford?

_____

_____

3. What did some people do so they wouldn't have to walk everywhere?

_____

4. Where did some people move after they got cars?

_____

_____ **W**　**D**

5. Did it take any longer to get to work if you lived in the suburbs and had a car?

_____

6. About how many years did it take to make cars a need?

_____ **W**　**D**

7. Name two other luxuries that have been made needs since the car.

_____

_____

E PARTS OF SPEECH

Underline the nouns. Draw **one** line over the adjectives. Draw **two** lines over the articles. Circle the verbs.

1. Poets write many similes.

2. Her boss runs six miles every day.

3. Bicycles are manufactured products.

4. The factory manufactured bicycles and motorcycles.

F BODY RULES

Draw in the arrows. Write **vein** or **artery** in each blank. Also write **oxygen** or **carbon dioxide** in each blank.

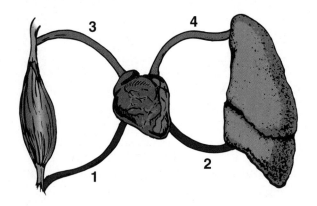

1. _____

2. _____

3. _____

4. _____

G DEDUCTIONS

Write the middle part of each deduction.

1. Feelings go to the brain.

   _____

   So, pain goes to the brain.

2. Commands travel on motor nerves.

   _____

   _____

   So, "Nod head" travels on a motor nerve.

3. Some animals have no bones.

   _____

   So, maybe a snail has no bones.

H FOLLOWING DIRECTIONS

Follow the directions about the sentence in the box.

> The digestive system changes food into fuel.

1. Circle the articles.

2. Cross out the nouns.

3. Underline the words that tell what the digestive system does.

4. Draw a line over the words that tell what body system the large intestine is in.

I CONTRADICTIONS

Underline the contradiction and circle the statement it contradicts. Then tell why the underlined statement contradicts the circled statement.

> The pulmonary vein is the only vein in the body that carries oxygen. It is also one of the biggest veins in the body. *It goes from the lungs to the heart. It looks black. It is part of the circulatory system.

_____

_____

J FOLLOWING DIRECTIONS

Follow the directions.

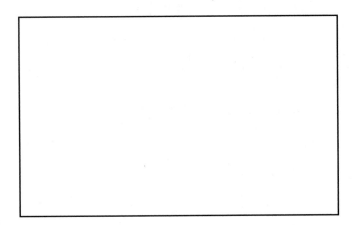

1. Draw a horizontal line in the box.

2. Draw another horizontal line below the first line.

3. Draw a line that slants from the right end of the top line to the left end of the bottom line.

4. To the right of the slanted line, write the verb that means **end.**

K SIMILES

Tell **two** ways that the things compared are **not** the same. Tell **one** way that the things compared **are** the same.

The coach talked like a machine gun.

1. _____

   _____

2. _____

   _____

3. _____

   _____

WORD LIST

arteries (n) the tubes that carry blood away from the heart

capillaries (n) the very small tubes that connect the arteries and veins

circulatory system (n) the body system that moves blood around the body

consume (v) to use up or eat

critical (a) that something criticizes

digestion (n) the act of digesting

explain (v) to make something easier to understand

explanation (n) something that explains

explanatory (a) that something explains

heart (n) the pump that moves the blood

productive (a) that something produces a lot of things

protect (v) to guard

simile (n) a statement that tells how things are the same

veins (n) the tubes that carry blood back to the heart

L WRITING STORIES

Write a story about this picture of Mr. Hopkins. Your story should tell what happened **before** the picture, what happened **in** the picture, and what happened **after** the picture.

businessman	briefcase	garbage can	stress	suit	relax

_____

_____

_____

_____

_____

_____

_____

_____

_____

_____

_____

_____

_____

_____

_____

_____

_____

_____

_____

A SENTENCE COMBINATIONS

Combine the sentences with **particularly**.

1. He cooks good food.
   He cooks the best food when people come for dinner.

   _____

   _____

   _____

2. Your bones are strong.
   Your bones are strongest if you drink lots of milk.

   _____

   _____

   _____

3. She gets angry.
   She gets the angriest when people criticize her.

   _____

   _____

   _____

4. That dog is noisy.
   That dog is the noisiest when it is outside.

   _____

   _____

   _____

B SIMILES

Tell **two** ways that the things compared are **not** the same. Tell **one** way that the things compared **are** the same.

His hands were like spider legs.

1. _____

   _____

2. _____

   _____

3. _____

   _____

C BODY RULES

Draw in the arrows. Shade in each tube that carries dark blood. Tell what gas each tube carries.

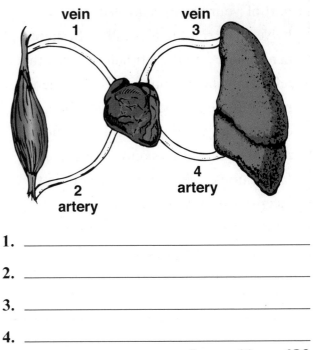

1. _____

2. _____

3. _____

4. _____

D PARTS OF SPEECH

Underline the nouns. Draw **one** line over the adjectives. Draw **two** lines over the articles. Circle the verbs.

1. The woman's sensory nerves let her feel.

2. The store sells many different manufactured goods.

3. A factory was manufacturing tires.

4. People think and feel with their brains.

E INFERENCE

Read the passage and answer the questions.
- Circle the **W** if the question is answered by words in the passage. Then underline those words.
- Circle the **D** if the question is answered by a deduction.

Your cerebrum, which is the top part of your brain, is divided into two halves. The right half is called the **right hemisphere** and the left half is called the **left hemisphere.** Your right hemisphere regulates the muscles on the **left** side of your body, and your left hemisphere regulates the muscles on your **right** side. For example, when you move your left biceps, that movement is controlled by your right hemisphere. And when you move your right quadriceps, that movement is controlled by your left hemisphere.

This same left-right switch happens with many other parts of your body. Sights you see with your left eye go to your right hemisphere, and sounds you hear with your right ear go to your left hemisphere. Both hemispheres work together to help you move, see, hear, think, and talk.

1. What are the two parts of the cerebrum?

    _____

    _____

2. Which muscles does your right hemisphere regulate?

    _____

    _____ W D

3. Which hemisphere controls the muscles on your right side?

    _____ W D

4. When somebody whispers into your right ear, to which hemisphere does the sound go?

    _____

    _____

F BODY RULES

Label each nerve. Then write a message for each nerve.

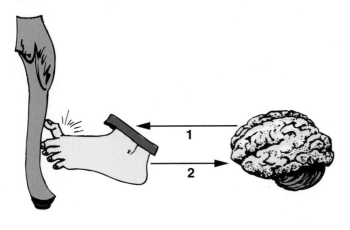

1. _____

2. _____

G DEFINITIONS

Write a word that comes from **manufacture** in each blank. Then write **verb, noun,** or **adjective** after each item.

1. Doctors cannot _____

   a human brain. _____

2. Pat predicts that the cheaply

   _____ product will be

   popular. _____

3. Big companies _____

   TVs every day. _____

4. Some companies

   _____ chairs.

   _____

5. That factory has

   _____ a new line of

   dresses. _____

H FOLLOWING DIRECTIONS

Follow the directions.

1. Draw a horizontal line in the box.

2. Draw a line that slants up to the right from the right end of the horizontal line.

3. At the left end of the horizontal line, draw an arrow that points up.

4. Draw the muscle that will move the horizontal line in the direction of the arrow.

▌ CONTRADICTIONS

Underline the contradiction and circle the
statement it contradicts. Then tell **why** the
underlined statement contradicts the circled
statement.

> John was wandering around a dark
> room. He stubbed his toe on a chair leg.
> The message "Toe hurts" went to his
> brain. *John jumped up and down. The
> message went on a motor nerve. John was
> in great pain for a long time. Finally, he
> stopped jumping up and down.

_____

_____

_____

A SENTENCE COMBINATIONS

Combine the sentences with **particularly.**

1. Cheetahs are fast. Cheetahs are fastest when they are hunting.

2. Mary writes well. Mary writes the best when she is alone.

3. Pete talks a lot.
Pete talks the most at parties.

4. Muscles get sore.
Muscles get sorest after you work hard.

B SIMILES

Make up a simile for each item.

1. A man's hands were smooth.

2. A woman's shirt had a lot of holes.

C REWRITING PARAGRAPHS

Rewrite the paragraph in four sentences. If one of the sentences tells **why,** combine the sentences with **because.** If two sentences seem contradictory, combine them with **but.**

Fred wanted to read a book. Fred turned on the light. The book had a coffee stain on the first page. Fred could not read the book. Fred drank coffee. Fred had not made the stain. He went to see his mother. His mother was in the next room.

D WRITING DIRECTIONS

Write the instructions.

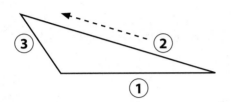

1. (what) _____

    _____

2. (what and where) _____

    _____

    _____

    _____

3. (what and where) _____

    _____

    _____

E CONTRADICTIONS

Make each statement mean the same thing as the statement in the box.

> Her explanatory talk was hard to understand.

1. Her talk that explained was hard to understand.

2. It was easy to understand her explanatory talk.

3. It was hard to understand her talk that explained.

4. Her talk, which was explanatory, was difficult to understand.

F BODY RULES

Label each nerve.
Then write a message for each nerve.

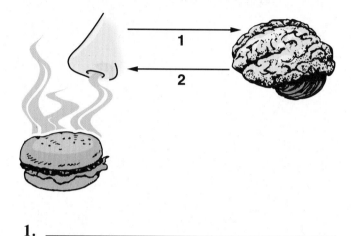

1. _____

2. _____

G SUBJECT/PREDICATE

Circle the subject and underline the
predicate. Rewrite each sentence by moving
part of the predicate.

1. The man was tired by noon.

   _____

   _____

2. The cat came home after three o'clock.

   _____

   _____

3. She wore a coat because the weather was
   cold.

   _____

   _____

   _____

4. He won the race by running the fastest.

   _____

   _____

   _____

H CONTRADICTIONS

Underline the contradiction and circle the
statement it contradicts. Then tell **why** the
underlined statement contradicts the circled
statement.

   From the outside, your upper arm looks
pretty simple. But inside, many complex things
are happening. Arteries are carrying blood to
your biceps. Sensory nerves are sending
feelings to the brain.* The nerves carry little
bits of electricity. The arteries carry carbon
dioxide. All this is going on, but you never have
to think about it.

   _____

   _____

   _____

I BODY SYSTEMS

Fill in each blank.

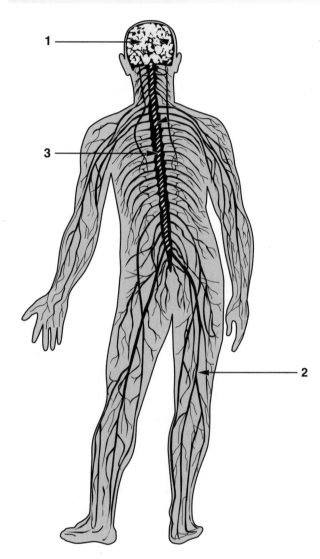

1. _____

2. _____

3. _____

1 and 3. _____ nervous system

2. _____ nervous system

J DEFINITIONS

Write a word that comes from **produce** or **explain** in each blank. Then write **verb, noun,** or **adjective** after each item.

1. The factory tried to increase

_____ by combining some

jobs.

_____

2. An _____ would help me

understand.

_____

3. Most businesses try to be more

_____ .

_____

4. She has _____ herself very

well.

_____

5. Some digestive organs

_____ chemicals.

_____

K INFERENCE

Read the passage and answer the questions.
- Circle the **W** if the question is answered by words in the passage. Then underline those words.
- Circle the **D** if the question is answered by a deduction.

When you walk, your body is doing thousands of things every minute. Your heart is beating; your leg muscles are pulling; your blood is moving. If your cerebrum had to think about doing all those things, it wouldn't have much time for anything else. This is why you have the cerebellum and the brain stem. They regulate all the body parts you never think about. The cerebellum helps you keep your balance. The brain stem controls the digestive, circulatory, and respiratory systems.

1. When you walk, your heart is beating, your leg muscles are pulling, and your blood is moving. Name three other things that your body is doing.

_____

_____

_____

_____

2. Why doesn't your cerebrum think about all those things?

_____

_____

_____

_____ **W   D**

3. What does the cerebellum help you do?

_____

_____ **W   D**

4. Which systems does the brain stem regulate?

_____

_____ **W   D**

5. Tell which part of the brain you use for the following things:

   a. breathing _____

   b. reading _____

   c. thinking _____

   d. keeping your balance _____

   e. pumping blood _____

L WRITING STORIES

Write a story about this picture of Ashley. Your story should tell what happened **before** the picture, what happened **in** the picture, and what happened **after** the picture.

basketball	uniform	bench	frustrated	team player

A INFERENCE

Use the facts to fill out the form.

> Facts: Your name is Mack Johnson. You are applying for a bank loan. You have worked for the Maxwell Pen Company for five years. You make $3,000 a month. You own a 2005 compact car. You are married and have two children. You had to take out a loan to pay for the car. You want this bank loan to construct a house.

A. Print your full name, last name first, on line 5.
B. Enter the name of the company you work for on line 2.
C. On line 3, describe the type of car you drive.
D. State your monthly income on line 1.
E. Enter the total number of people in your family on line 4.
F. On line 6, tell why you want the loan.
G. On line 7, write the second sentence above that gives information you didn't use in filling out the form.

1. _____

2. _____

3. _____

4. _____

5. _____

6. _____

7. _____

_____

_____

B SIMILES

Make up a simile for each item.

1. The town was busy.

_____

_____

2. She talked in a sweet way.

_____

_____

C SENTENCE COMBINATIONS

Combine the sentences with **particularly.**

1. Your digestive system works hard.
   Your digestive system works hardest after you eat.

_____

_____

_____

_____

2. Tony swims fast.
   Tony swims fastest in races.

_____

_____

3. Claire is a productive person.
   Claire is the most productive when she works alone.

   _____

   _____

   _____

   _____

4. Stars look bright.
   Stars look brightest outside the city.

   _____

   _____

   _____

D CONTRADICTIONS

Underline the contradiction and circle the statement it contradicts. Then tell **why** the underlined statement contradicts the circled statement.

   If you are losing a foot race, your brain sends out the message "Move faster" to your legs. Whether or not your legs will move faster depends on many things. All your body systems must work together.* The heart must pump more blood to the gastrocnemius and the quadriceps. The lungs must take in more air. The message must go over a sensory nerve.

   _____

   _____

   _____

   _____

E DEFINITIONS

Write a word that comes from **select** or **regulate** in each blank. Then write **verb, noun,** or **adjective** after each item.

1. The careful shopper tried to

   _____ the best apples.

   _____

2. New stop signs will _____

   the traffic.

   _____

3. The boss was very _____

   in hiring new people.

   _____

4. They did not _____ enough

   fruit for lunch.

   _____

5. The army has _____ about

   everything.

   _____

F BODY RULES

Draw in the arrows. Shade in each tube that carries dark blood. Tell what gas each tube carries.

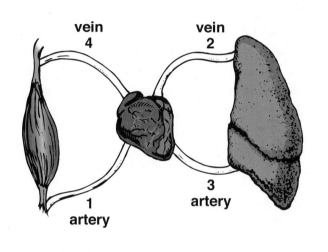

vein 4 vein 2

1 artery

3 artery

1. _____
2. _____
3. _____
4. _____

G SUBJECT/PREDICATE

Circle the subject and underline the predicate. Rewrite each sentence by moving part of the predicate.

1. The halls are white upstairs.

_____

_____

2. She goes to the store every morning.

_____

_____

3. They rolled down the hill for the fun of it.

_____

_____

4. He went to the beach to swim.

_____

_____

H WRITING DIRECTIONS

Write the instructions.

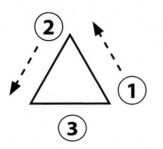

1. (what and where) _____

_____

_____

2. (what and where) _____

_____

_____

_____

_____

3. (what and where) _____

_____

_____

I REWRITING PARAGRAPHS

Rewrite the paragraph in four sentences. If one of the sentences tells **why,** combine the sentences with **because.** If two sentences seem contradictory, combine them with **but.**

Cape Horn is on Horn Island. Horn Island is below the southern tip of South America. Sailors are afraid of sailing around the cape. The cape has dangerous waves. The waves get big. The waves get biggest in the winter. The cape is near the South Pole. The cape gets very cold.

_____

_____

_____

_____

_____

_____

_____

_____

_____

_____

_____

_____

_____

A CONTRADICTIONS

Underline the contradiction and circle the statement it contradicts. Then tell **why** the underlined statement contradicts the circled statement. Make the underlined statement true.

Ted was sick, so he went to see a doctor. The doctor shot some medicine into one of Ted's veins. The doctor said, "This medicine will make you well again.* It will kill the germs in your circulatory system that are making you sick. Right now, the medicine is going away from your heart. You should be feeling better by tomorrow."

_____

_____

_____

B SIMILES

Make up a simile for each item.

1. The man's voice was very sharp.

_____

_____

2. The woman talked very fast.

_____

_____

_____

C INFERENCE

Use the facts to fill out the form.

Facts: Your name is Alice Brown. You are applying for a credit card at the Paris Department Store. You are making payments of $200 a month on your car. You have lived at 144 Stone Avenue, Atlanta, Georgia, for one year. You have worked as a bookkeeper for Jones Manufacturing for three years. You make $2,000 a month, and you spend about $1,400 a month, including your car payments.

1. Last name _____

2. Street address _____

_____

3. Monthly income _____

4. Place of work _____

_____

5. Monthly expenses _____

6. Are you making payments on a car? _____

7. Subtract expenses from income and write the number on line 1.

D BODY RULES

Tell if each nerve is a **sensory** nerve or a **motor** nerve. Draw an arrow to show which way the message moves.

1. "Head hurts."   **2.** "Toes are cold."

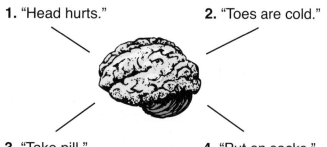

3. "Take pill."   **4.** "Put on socks."

E SENTENCE COMBINATIONS

Circle the word that combines the sentences correctly. Combine the sentences with that word.

1. Gwen was older than Jim.
Patrick was older than Jim.

    but   which   and

_____

_____

2. John is very sick.
John won't go to the doctor.

    particularly   which   but

_____

_____

3. Milk contains vitamin D.
Cheese contains vitamin D.

    particularly   because   and

_____

4. That stream moves fast.
That stream moves fastest down Rose Hill.

    and   particularly   who

_____

_____

5. Smokers have poor circulation.
Smokers don't breathe well.

    and   which   but

_____

_____

F BODY RULES

Shade in each tube that carries dark blood. Write **vein** or **artery** in each blank. Also write **oxygen** or **carbon dioxide** in each blank.

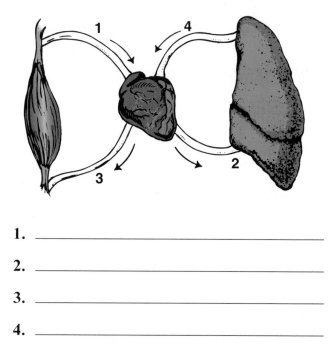

1. _____

2. _____

3. _____

4. _____

G DEDUCTIONS

Write the middle part of each deduction.

1. Ruth has had some diseases.

_____

So, maybe Ruth has had the mumps.

2. Commands come from the brain.

_____

So, "move leg" comes from the brain.

3. Some plants cannot be eaten.

_____

So, maybe ferns cannot be eaten.

H WRITING DIRECTIONS

Write the instructions.

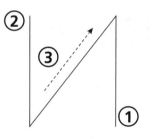

1. (what) _____

_____

2. (what and where) _____

_____

_____

3. (what and where) _____

_____

_____

I BODY SYSTEMS

Fill in each blank.

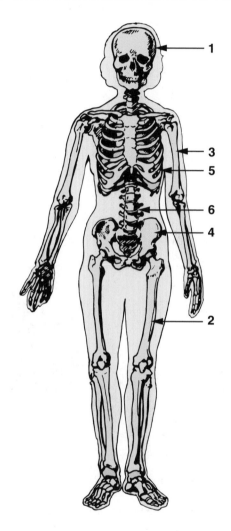

1. _____

2. _____

3. _____

4. _____

5. _____

6. _____

J WRITING STORIES

Write a story about this picture of the jet, the rescue party, and the snow monster. Your story should tell what happened **before** the picture, what happened **in** the picture, and what happened **after** the picture.

rescue	icicles	monster	mountain	crashed	winter

_____

_____

_____

_____

_____

_____

_____

_____

_____

A CONTRADICTIONS

Underline the contradiction and circle the statement it contradicts. Then tell **why** the underlined statement contradicts the circled statement. Make the underlined statement true.

A woman was in a bad car accident, and she blacked out. When she came to, she couldn't feel anything in her left hand. She was in a hospital bed. * A doctor told her that she was going to be operated on. She had cut a motor nerve. The woman felt lucky to be alive.

_____

_____

B DEFINITIONS

Write a word that comes from **participate** in each blank. Then write **verb, noun,** or **adjective** after each item.

1. Last year he _____ in

   the production. _____

2. Volleyball is a _____

   sport. _____

3. Teachers regulate classroom

   _____.

   _____

4. He doesn't want to

   _____ in plays.

   _____

5. They asked for Ann's

   _____ in the game.

   _____

C WRITING DIRECTIONS

Write the instructions.

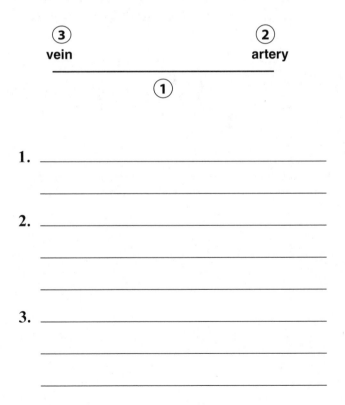

③ vein   ② artery
         ①

1. _____

   _____

2. _____

   _____

3. _____

   _____

   _____

Lesson 34

D SIMILES

Make up a simile for each item.

1. She swims very well.

   _____

   _____

2. The man had a bald head.

   _____

   _____

E INFERENCE

Read the passage and answer the questions.
* Circle the **W** if the question is answered by words in the passage. Then underline those words.
* Circle the **D** if the question is answered by a deduction.

Here's a rule about demand and supply: **When the demand is greater than the supply, prices go up.**

Mr. Jones runs the only dairy farm near Mudville. In January, his cows produce just as much milk as Mudville needs. Mr. Jones makes $1,000 from milk sales that month. In February, his cows produce a lot less milk than Mudville needs. If Mr. Jones sells the milk at the old price, he won't make $1,000 because he doesn't have as much milk to sell. But Mr. Jones wants to make $1,000, so he raises his prices.

Mudville's demand for milk is much greater than Mr. Jones's supply, and he has no trouble selling his milk at the higher price. People in Mudville may not like the higher price, but they know that they need milk and that Mr. Jones's farm is the only place where they can get milk.

1. What's the rule about demand and supply?

   _____

   _____

   _____

2. Was the demand greater than the supply in January?

   _____ **W D**

3. Which was greater in February, the demand or the supply?

   _____ **W D**

4. If Mr. Jones sells his milk at the old price, why won't he make $1,000?

_____

_____

_____ **W   D**

5. Why did he raise his prices?

_____

_____

_____

6. Why didn't he have any trouble selling the milk at the higher price?

_____

_____

_____

_____ **W   D**

7. Give two reasons why the people of Mudville pay the higher price, even though they don't like it.

a. _____

_____

b. _____

_____

_____

8. Did the demand become greater than the supply because the supply went down or because the demand went up?

_____

_____ **W   D**

F BODY SYSTEMS

Fill in each blank.

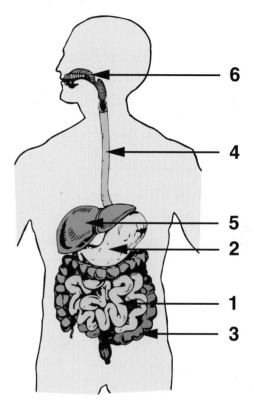

1. _____

2. _____

3. _____

4. _____

5. _____

6. _____

Lesson 34

G SENTENCE COMBINATIONS

Circle the word that combines the sentences correctly. Combine the sentences with that word.

1. Trees need carbon dioxide.
   Bushes need carbon dioxide.

   who   **particularly**   **and**

   _____

   _____

2. Animals are living things.
   Animals produce carbon dioxide.

   which   **but**   **particularly**

   _____

   _____

   _____

3. Venus is near the sun.
   Mercury is near the sun.

   particularly   **which**   **and**

   _____

   _____

4. She jogs a lot.
   She jogs the most before races.

   and   **because**   **particularly**

   _____

   _____

5. That lime has vitamin C.
   These lemons have vitamin C.

   because   **but**   **and**

   _____

   _____

H BODY RULES

Circle each bone that will move. Then draw an arrow that shows which way the bone will move.

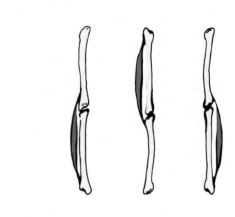

I BODY RULES

Draw in the arrows. Shade in each tube that carries dark blood. Tell if each tube is a **vein** or an **artery**.

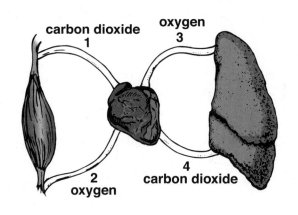

carbon dioxide
1

oxygen
3

4
carbon dioxide

2
oxygen

1. _____

2. _____

3. _____

4. _____

J DEDUCTIONS

Write the conclusion of each deduction.

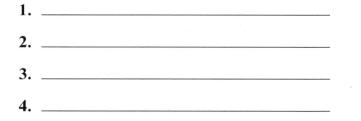

1. Feelings travel on sensory nerves.
   Pain is a feeling.

   _____

   _____

2. Commands go on motor nerves.
   "Move arm" is a command.

   _____

   _____

3. Some diseases damage nerves.
   Polio is a disease.

   _____

   _____

WORD LIST

bronchial tubes (n) the tubes inside the lungs

conclude (v) to end or figure out

conclusion (n) the end or something that is concluded

examine (v) to look at

explain (v) to make something easier to understand

lung (n) a large organ that brings air into contact with the blood

manufacture (v) to make in a factory

manufactured (a) that something has been made in a factory

manufacturer (n) something that manufactures

regulate (v) to control

reside (v) to live somewhere

respiratory system (n) the body system that brings oxygen to the blood

select (v) to choose

trachea (n) the tube that brings outside air to the lungs

A CONTRADITIONS

Underline the contradiction and circle the statement it contradicts. Tell **why** the underlined statement contradicts the circled statement. Make the underlined statement true.

The Smiths had a wood stove in their kitchen. One night, their electricity went out. They huddled together in the kitchen because the house was so cold. Mrs. Smith closed the doors and lit a fire in the stove. * Pretty soon, everybody was toasty warm. The kitchen air began to fill with carbon dioxide, so Ms. Smith opened the doors. Then she turned on the lights.

_____

_____

_____

B WRITING DIRECTIONS

Write the instructions.

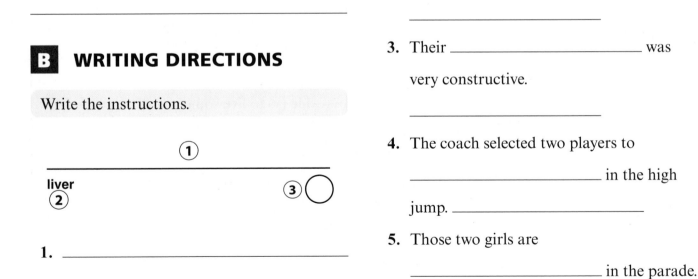

① _____

liver
②   ③ ◯

1. _____

_____

2. _____

_____

_____

3. _____

_____

_____

C DEFINITIONS

Write a word that comes from **participate** in each blank. Then write **verb, noun,** or **adjective** after each item.

1. He had a _____ role in the meeting.

   _____

2. Fran does not like to

   _____ in picnics.

   _____

3. Their _____ was very constructive.

   _____

4. The coach selected two players to

   _____ in the high

   jump. _____

5. Those two girls are

   _____ in the parade.

   _____

D CONTRADICTIONS

Tell which fact each statement relates to.
Make each contradiction true.

> A. The demand for pens was high.
> B. The supply of pens was low.

1. Not very many people wanted pens. _____

2. The warehouse had only a few
   boxes of pens. _____

3. Stores had lots of pens. _____

E BODY SYSTEMS

Fill in each blank.

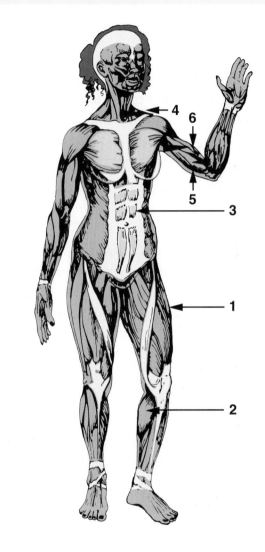

1. _____
2. _____
3. _____
4. _____
5. _____
6. _____

F SENTENCE COMBINATIONS

Circle the word that combines the sentences correctly. Combine the sentences with that word.

1. The Bing Company manufactures baseballs.
    Smashers Unlimited manufactures baseballs.
    which   and   particularly

    _____

    _____

    _____

2. Mr. Brown is very critical.
    Mr. Brown is most critical when he is hungry.
    and   because   particularly

    _____

    _____

    _____

3. Diane is participating in the play.
    Vernon is participating in the play.
    particularly   but   and

    _____

    _____

    _____

4. Hector is wearing a hat.
    Hector doesn't like his haircut.
    but   which   because

    _____

    _____

    _____

5. The cheetah was faster than the truck.
    The lion was faster than the truck.
    which   and   particularly

    _____

    _____

    _____

G SIMILES

Tell **two** ways that the things compared are **not** the same. Tell **one** way that the things compared **are** the same.

> Her criticism was like a razor.

1. _____

    _____

2. _____

    _____

3. _____

    _____

H **INFERENCE**

Read the passage and answer the questions.
- Circle the **W** if the question is answered by words in the passage. Then underline those words.
- Circle the **D** if the question is answered by a deduction.

Here's a rule about demand and supply: **When the demand is greater than the supply, prices go up.**

Ms. Lopez runs the only chicken farm near Mudville. In March, her chickens produce just as many eggs as Mudville needs, which is 1,000 dozen a month. Ms. Lopez sells the eggs for $1 a dozen, so she makes $1,000 that month.

In April, a big group of people moves into Mudville, and Mudville's demand for eggs goes up to 1,500 dozen a month. But Ms. Lopez's chickens are still producing only 1,000 dozen a month, and it becomes very hard for the people of Mudville to get all the eggs they need. People start to offer Ms. Lopez more for her eggs, just so they can be sure of getting some. Ms. Lopez, who likes the idea of making extra money, decides to raise the price to $1.25 a dozen. Because the demand is so high, she has no trouble selling the eggs at the new price.

1. What's the rule about demand and supply?

_____

_____

_____

2. In March, was the demand for eggs greater than the supply of eggs?

_____ **W** **D**

3. Why did the demand for eggs increase in April?

_____

_____

_____

4. Why do people start offering Ms. Lopez more for her eggs?

_____

_____

_____ **W** **D**

5. Why doesn't Ms. Lopez have any trouble selling eggs at a new price?

_____

_____ **W** **D**

6. Would prices have gone up if the chickens had laid 1,500 dozen eggs in April?

_____ **W** **D**

1 WRITING STORIES

Write a story about this picture of Mr. Minh and his grandson Cam. Your story should tell what happened **before** the picture, what happened **in** the picture, and what happened **after** the picture.

grandfather	bicycle	summer	short pants	backyard

_____

_____

_____

_____

_____

_____

_____

_____

_____

_____

_____

_____

_____

_____

_____

_____

_____

_____

_____

_____

FACT GAME SCORECARD

1	2	3	4	5	6	7	8	9	10	11	12	13	14	15
16	17	18	19	20	21	22	23	24	25	26	27	28	29	30

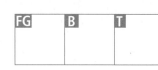

Fact Game 4

2. Complete each sentence with a word that comes from **participate.**

   a. She wanted to ▓▓▓▓ in the play.
   b. That school has no ▓▓▓▓ sports.

3. Name the part of speech for each underlined word.

   a. They asked for his <u>participation</u> at the meeting.
   b. The city tried to get the <u>manufacturer</u> to move her factory.

4. Combine the sentences in the box with **particularly.**

   > Your circulatory system works hard. Your circulatory system works hardest when you exercise.

5. Name the part of speech for each underlined word.

   a. They <u>participated</u> in the contest.
   b. The store carried only <u>manufactured</u> products.

6. Tell if each statement is about **demand** or **supply.**

   a. The bakery produces 200 loaves of bread every day.
   b. Cars were lined up for gas.

7. Combine the sentences in the box with **but.**

   > Tom had to cut the grass.
   > Tom didn't have a lawn mower.

8. Tell if each statement is about **demand** or **supply.**

   a. People buy fewer bikes in the winter.
   b. More new homes were bought last year.

9. Answer the questions.

   a. What color is blood that carries carbon dioxide?
   b. What color is blood that carries oxygen?

10. Combine the sentences in the box with **particularly.**

    > Pete watches TV. Pete watches the most TV on weekends.

11. Answer the questions.

    a. What do we call nerves that carry messages **to** the brain?
    b. What do we call nerves that carry messages **from** the brain?

12. Complete each sentence with a word that comes from **manufacture.**

    a. That new factory will ▓▓▓▓ laptop computers.
    b. Cars are a good example of a ▓▓▓▓ product.

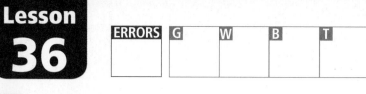

A INFERENCE

Read the passage and answer the questions.
- Circle the **W** if the question is answered by words in the passage. Then underline those words.
- Circle the **D** if the question is answered by a deduction.

Here's another rule about demand and supply: **Manufacturers always try to make the demand greater than the supply.**

Mr. Franklin runs the only lightbulb factory in Mudville. In May, he produces just as many lightbulbs as Mudville needs, which is 1,000 a month. Mr. Franklin makes 50 cents for each light bulb he sells in May.

In June, Mr. Franklin decides that he wants to make more than 50 cents for each lightbulb he sells. He knows that if he can make the demand greater than the supply, the price of lightbulbs will go up. So he puts an ad in the paper that says, "If you have more lamps in your house, you will be able to see better. You won't stub your toes in dark corners, you will be able to read anywhere, and your house will be cheery." The ad works, and the demand for lightbulbs goes up. Because the demand is so high, Mr. Franklin raises the price of his lightbulbs, and he sells all 1,000 of them.

1. What's another rule about demand and supply?

_____

_____

_____

_____

2. How much money did Mr. Franklin make in May?

_____ **W**   **D**

3. What did the ad try to make people think?

_____

_____ **W**   **D**

4. Why is Mr. Franklin able to sell all 1,000 of his lightbulbs in June at the higher price?

_____

_____ **W**   **D**

5. Name another way that Mr. Franklin could have increased the demand.

_____

_____

6. What would happen to the demand if the ad did not work?

_____

_____ **W**   **D**

7. If Mr. Franklin makes 60 cents for each lightbulb he sells in June, how much money will he make that month?

_____

B SENTENCE ANALYSIS

For each sentence, write **two** sentences that have the underlined common part.

1. <u>Randy</u>, who likes participatory sports, broke his leg playing basketball.

a. _____

_____

b. _____

_____

2. <u>Ted</u> has poor circulation because he smokes.

a. _____

_____

b. _____

_____

3. <u>The woman</u> felt bad, but she didn't go to the doctor.

a. _____

_____

b. _____

_____

4. <u>Those new regulations</u> are stupid and unfair.

a. _____

_____

b. _____

_____

C REWRITING PARAGRAPHS

Rewrite the paragraph in four sentences. If one of the sentences tells **why**, combine the sentences with **because**. If two sentences seem contradictory, combine them with **but**.

> Magellan tried to sail around the world. Magellan was born in 1480. He lived in Portugal. Portugal is next to Spain. Magellan tried to obtain ships in Portugal. Magellan did not have any luck. So Magellan went to see the Spanish king. The Spanish king gave him five ships.

_____

_____

_____

_____

_____

_____

_____

_____

_____

_____

_____

_____

_____

_____

_____

_____

Lesson 36

D CONTRADICTIONS

Underline the contradiction and circle the statement it contradicts. Then tell **why** the underlined statement contradicts the circled statement. Make the underlined statement true.

Gina did many exercises every day. In her first exercise, she bent her arms to pick up big boxes. In her second exercise, she stood on her toes. In her third exercise, she turned her head. * She said, "These exercises are only good for my triceps, my gastrocnemius, and my trapezius. I need to start working on my abdominal muscles and my quadriceps." So she got an exercise book from the library.

_____

_____

_____

E BODY RULES

Label each nerve.
Then write a message for each nerve.

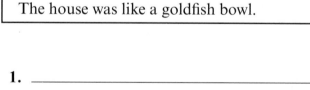

1._____

2. _____

F SIMILES

Tell two ways that the things compared are **not** the same. Tell one way that the things compared **are** the same.

The house was like a goldfish bowl.

1. _____

_____

2. _____

_____

3. _____

_____

G SUBJECT/PREDICATE

Circle the subject and underline the predicate. Rewrite each sentence by moving part of the predicate.

1. You should wear big boots to go hiking.

   _____

   _____

   _____

2. They can play if they finish their homework.

   _____

   _____

   _____

3. Her dad drank milk before he went to work.

   _____

   _____

   _____

4. A plane was flying over the house.

   _____

   _____

H BODY SYSTEMS

Fill in each blank.

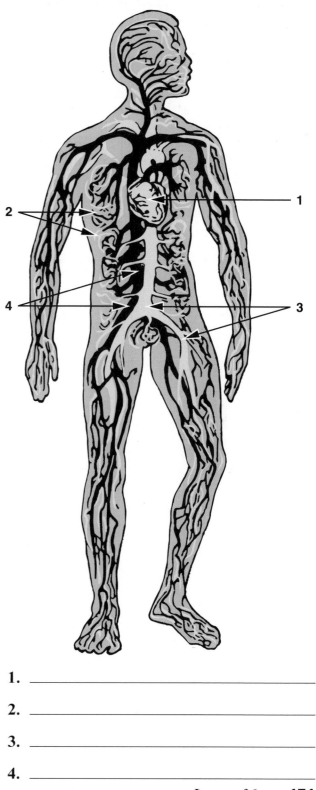

1. _____

2. _____

3. _____

4. _____

Lesson 36

I **PARTS OF SPEECH**

Underline the nouns. Draw **one** line **over** the adjectives. Draw **two** lines **over** the articles. Circle the verbs

1. Participatory sports are played in every country.

2. Students are participating in that assembly.

3. A manufacturer in town was modifying some smokestacks.

4. The government regulates many manufacturers.

J **DEFINITIONS**

Fill in the blank with the word that has the same meaning as the word or words under the blank.

1. Some _____ are
   (things that are constructed)
   more than one hundred stories high.

2. Your body is always _____
   (making)
   new blood cells.

3. Meat takes a long time to be

   _____.

   (changed into fuel for the body)

4. Earthquakes are hard to _____.
   (say that they will happen)

A SIMILES

Make up a simile for each item.

1. Her teeth were very white.

_____

_____

2. Her hair was very red.

_____

_____

B SENTENCE ANALYSIS

For each sentence, write **two** sentences that have the underlined common part.

1. <u>Water</u> is hard to find, particularly in deserts.

a. _____

_____

b. _____

_____

2. Tom and Roberto are <u>skating on the pond</u>.

a. _____

_____

b. _____

_____

3. You must follow <u>this regulation</u>, which states that you cannot shout.

a. _____

_____

b. _____

_____

4. The man and the woman have <u>been running for ten minutes</u>.

a. _____

_____

b. _____

_____

C SUBJECT/PREDICATE

Circle the subject and underline the predicate. Rewrite each sentence by moving part of the predicate.

1. They planted a garden next to their residence.

_____

_____

2. Participation in sports is not important if you're sick.

_____

_____

_____

3. He opened the tool chest by using a hammer.

_____

_____

4. She took out her wallet as she got on the bus.

_____

_____

D INFERENCE

Read the passage and answer the questions.
- Circle the **W** if the question is answered by words in the passage. Then underline those words.
- Circle the **D** if the question is answered by a deduction.

You use both your cerebrum and your cerebellum whenever you move. Let's say you want to walk across a room to open a door. First your **cerebrum** tells your leg muscles to start walking. Then your **cerebellum** makes sure that all your leg muscles are working together as you walk. If you trip over something, your cerebellum helps you find your balance again.

When you get to the door, your cerebrum tells your arm muscles to turn the doorknob. Then your cerebellum helps guide your muscles as you reach for the knob and turn it.

Remember, your cerebrum tells your muscles what to do, and your cerebellum helps your muscles work together.

---

1. What two parts of your brain do you use whenever you move?

   _____

   _____

2. Which part tells your muscles what to do?

   _____ **W** **D**

3. Which part helps your muscles work together?

   _____ **W** **D**

4. If someone has trouble keeping their balance, what part of their brain might have a problem?

   _____

   _____ **W** **D**

5. Pretend the different parts of your brain could talk. Which part might say, "Arm muscles, start bending"?

   _____

E BODY SYSTEMS

Fill in each blank.

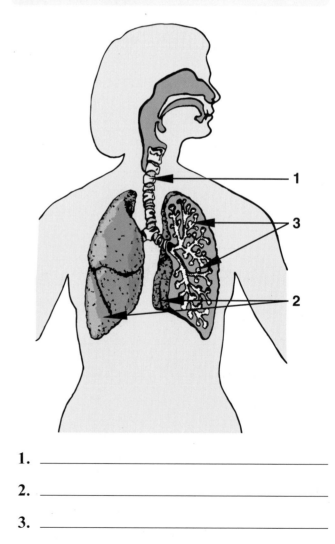

1. _____

2. _____

3. _____

F REWRITING PARAGRAPHS

Rewrite the paragraph in four sentences. If one of two sentences tells **why**, combine the sentences with **because**. If two sentences seem contradictory, combine them with **but**.

Magellan left Spain in 1519. Magellan crossed the Atlantic Ocean. In 1520, Magellan sailed into the Pacific Ocean through what is now the Strait of Magellan. The Strait of Magellan is a channel at the southern tip of South America. Magellan's crew began to get restless. Magellan's crew got the most restless when they were crossing the Pacific. Magellan's ships took several months to cross the Pacific. Magellan's ships were not very fast.

G CONTRADICTIONS

Underline the contradiction and circle the statement it contradicts. Then tell **why** the underlined statement contradicts the circled statement. Make the underlined statement true.

Your leg has many veins. Some of these veins carry carbon dioxide away from your toe muscles. The farther the veins go up your leg, the bigger they get. * You can see these veins on some people if you look closely. These veins are easiest to see near the ankles. They look red, and some of them are near the skin.

H DEFINITIONS

Fill in each blank with the word that has the same meaning as the word or words under the blank.

1. Many schools have fewer

   _____ now than
   (rules)
   they had ten years ago.

2. Cars _____ fuel.
   (use up)

3. Some businesses

   _____
   (change)
   their products every year.

4. Many companies

   _____ only one
   (make in a factory)
   product.

I PARTS OF SPEECH

Underline the nouns. Draw **one** line **over** the adjectives. Draw **two** lines **over** the articles. Circles the verbs.

1. Manufacturers are controlling the supply of car parts.

2. The teacher supplied his students with pencils for the test.

3. This product has a low demand.

4. The workers demanded some changes at the factory.

J WRITING STORIES

Write a story about this picture of Marcy. Your story should tell what happened **before** the picture, what happened **in** the picture, and what happened **after** the picture.

rabbit	empty	scarf	table	flowers	hiding	reached

_____

_____

_____

_____

_____

_____

_____

_____

_____

_____

A ECONOMICS RULES

Tell if each event changed the **demand** or the **supply.**

> A farmer had 10,000 ripe apples in her barn. A store owner planned to buy 5,000 of the apples for his store.

1. A flood ruined a third of the apples.

   _____

2. Because of the flood, the store owner did not come to the farm.

   _____

3. Another store owner called the farm and said he wanted to buy apples.

   _____

4. The farmer picked another 2,000 ripe apples from her apple trees.

   _____

B SIMILES

Make up a simile for each item.

1. The man was very tall.

   _____

   _____

2. Her skin was smooth.

   _____

   _____

C SENTENCE ANALYSIS

Underline the common part. For each sentence, write **two** sentences with that common part.

1. Blue River floods a lot, particularly in the spring.

   a. _____

   _____

   b. _____

   _____

2. One cup and six plates were on the table.

   a. _____

   _____

   b. _____

   _____

3. Ten dogs and six cats were running in the yard.

   a. _____

   _____

   b. _____

   _____

4. Lillian and James walk to work every day.

   a. _____

   _____

   b. _____

   _____

D BODY RULES

Label each nerve.
Write a message for each nerve.

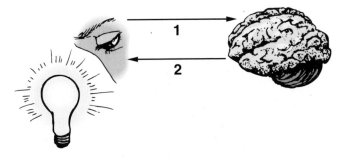

1. _____

2. _____

E WRITING DIRECTIONS

Write the instructions.

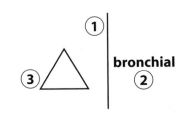

1. _____
   _____

2. _____
   _____
   _____

3. _____
   _____

F INFERENCE

Use the facts to fill out the form.

Facts: Your name is Mickey O'Hara. You
are applying for a loan to buy a house.
You work at the Johnson Carpet
Company. You make $2,800 a month.
You are 28 years old and married. You
rent a house for $800 a month. Your car
payments are $300 a month. Your wife
works in a bakery and makes $2,000 a
month. You drive a 2001 compact car.

1. Type of loan needed _____

2. Total monthly income in your household
   _____

3. Current employer _____
   _____

4. Age _____

5. Model of car _____

6. Year _____

7. Total yearly payments on car _____

8. Cross out the first sentence that gives
   information you didn't use.

G EVIDENCE

Write R for each fact that is **relevant** to what happened. Write I for each fact that is **irrelevant** to what happened.

> She will participate in the swim meet.

1. She wants to win a medal. ____

2. She lives on a busy street. ____

3. She's been swimming every day. ____

4. She wears goggles when she swims. ____

H BODY SYSTEMS

Fill in each blank.

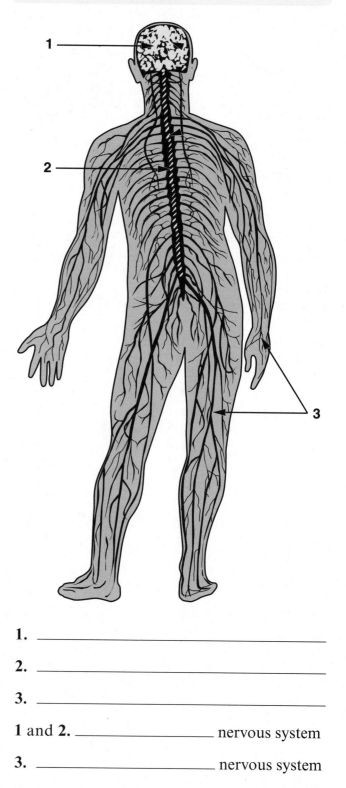

1. _____

2. _____

3. _____

1 and 2. _____ nervous system

3. _____ nervous system

I SENTENCE COMBINATIONS

Circle the word that combines the sentences correctly. Combine the sentences with that word.

1. A pickup truck was having a race.
   A dirt bike was having a race.
   particularly   **which**   **and**

   _____
   _____
   _____

2. Sensory nerves send messages to the brain.
   Sensory nerves let you feel.
   who   **which**   **particularly**

   _____
   _____
   _____

3. That older woman has bad circulation.
   Her youngest son has bad circulation.
   who   **which**   **and**

   _____
   _____
   _____

4. He respires loudly.
   He respires most loudly when he has a cold.
   because   **particularly**   **which**

   _____
   _____
   _____

5. Tom predicts snow tonight.
   His brothers predict snow tonight.
   but   **because**   **and**

   _____
   _____

J CONTRADICTIONS

Underline the contradiction and circle the statement it contradicts. Then tell why the underlined statement contradicts the circled statement. Make the underlined statement true.

Sam resided in the suburbs and worked in the city. One day, he tripped over a wire at work. His lower leg was badly hurt. * Sam went to a doctor, who took X-rays of Sam's leg. The doctor said that Sam had pulled his gastrocnemius, but that it wouldn't take long to heal. Sam went back to his home, which was in the city.

_____
_____

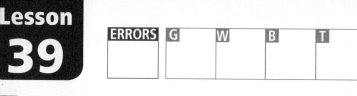

A EDITING

Underline the redundant sentences.

> Some people read magazines. Some people don't. The store had many different kinds of magazines. John wanted to acquire a magazine, so he went to the store. The store had a wide selection of magazines. John looked for a magazine about cars. The store had ten different car magazines. John tried to decide which one to buy. The store had more than one car magazine. John didn't know which one he wanted.

B DEFINITIONS

Write a word that comes from **circulate** or **respire** in each blank. Then write **verb, noun,** or **adjective** after each item.

1. The _____ system moves blood around the body.

   _____

2. The _____ system brings oxygen to the blood.

   _____

3. Your heart _____ blood.

   _____

4. He is _____ through his nose.

   _____

5. Her _____ is bad because her capillaries are clogged.

   _____

C SENTENCE ANALYSIS

Underline the common part. For each sentence, write **two** sentences with that common part.

1. People get many diseases, particularly in the winter.

   a. _____

   _____

   b. _____

   _____

2. The demand for gas, which is large, increases each year.

   a. _____

   _____

   b. _____

   _____

3. The doctor checked the man's respiration, which was loud.

   a. _____

   _____

   b. _____

   _____

4. Her mother and father are talking about money.

   a. _____

   _____

   b. _____

   _____

D ECONOMIC RULES

Tell if each event changed the demand or the supply.

> The factory manufactured 1,000 cars a week. The factory sold 1,000 cars a week.

1. The power went out at the factory, and no cars were made for a week.

_____

2. For two weeks, people did not buy cars.

_____

3. The factory made 2,000 cars in one week.

_____

4. People started buying the factory's cars again.

_____

E WRITING DIRECTIONS

Write the instructions.

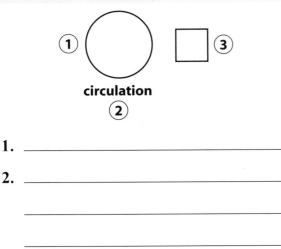

1. _____

2. _____

_____

_____

3. _____

_____

F REWRITING PARAGRAPHS

Rewrite the passage in four sentences. If one of the sentences tells **why,** combine the sentences with **because.** If the sentences seem contradictory, combine them with **but.**

> Finally, Magellan came to an island called Cebu. Cebu is in the southern Philippine Islands. Magellan thought his trip was almost over. Magellan was still very far from home. Magellan was killed on a nearby island. Magellan got into a battle. His crew fled the island. His crew kept on sailing.

_____

_____

_____

_____

_____

_____

_____

_____

_____

_____

_____

_____

_____

G SUBJECT/PREDICATE

Circle the subject and underline the predicate. Rewrite each sentence by moving part of the predicate.

1. She respired deeply because she felt dizzy.

   _____

   _____

2. Everyone was cold last winter.

   _____

   _____

3. Many people walk quickly in New York City.

   _____

   _____

4. The Golden Gate Bridge must be painted every few years.

   _____

   _____

   _____

H SIMILES

Make up a simile for each item.

1. His body was limp.

   _____

   _____

2. The dancer could spin very fast.

   _____

   _____

I CONTRADICTIONS

Make each statement mean the same thing as the statement in the box.

> Jenny, who participated in many sports, was very strong.

1. Jenny, who took part in many sports, wasn't very strong.

2. Jenny, who had lots of strength, took part in many sports.

3. Jenny participated in many sports and was very strong.

4. Jenny was very strong, and she didn't take part in many sports.

J INFERENCE

Use the facts to fill out the form.

Facts: You are applying for a job in a department store. You want to sell dresses, but you will also work as a cashier. You have worked as a cashier for three years at Snappy Burger, and you are bored with the job. You have never had a serious illness. You live at 22 Madrona Court in Los Angeles, California. Your social security number is 123-12-0888. Your name is Susan Thompson.

A. On line 8, write your social security number.

B. On line 4, state how many years you have held your present job.

C. Write your first name on line 3.

D. On line 2, tell what state you live in.

E. List any serious illnesses you have had on line 7.

F. Print your street address on line 6.

G. Tell what job you want most on line 5.

H. Print the name of your current employer on line 1.

1. _____
2. _____
3. _____
4. _____
5. _____
6. _____

7. _____
8. _____

K BODY RULES

Draw in the arrows. Shade in each tube that carries dark blood. Tell what gas each tube carries.

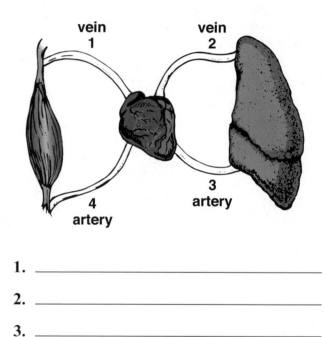

1. _____
2. _____
3. _____
4. _____

WORD LIST

construct (v) to build

consumable (a) that something can be
  consumed

consumer (n) something that consumes

demand (n) how well something sells

manufacture (v) to make in a factory

modified (a) that something is changed

obtain (v) to get

participate (v) to take part in something

participation (n) the act of participating

participatory (a) that something
  involves participation

predicate (n) the part of a sentence that
  tells more

predict (v) to say that something will
  happen

subject (n) the part of a sentence that
  names

supply (n) how much there is of
  something

L WRITING STORIES

Write a story about this picture of Megan. Your story should tell what happened **before** the picture, what happened **in** the picture, and what happened **after** the picture.

graveyard	sorrow	gravestone	American flag	soldier	autumn

_____

_____

_____

_____

_____

_____

_____

_____

_____

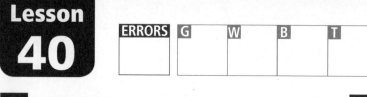

ERRORS | G | W | B | T

A SENTENCE ANALYSIS

Underline the common part. For each sentence, write **two** sentences with that common part.

1. The movie was predictable, but it was funny.

a. _____

_____

b. _____

_____

2. The teacher and his students have gone home.

a. _____

_____

b. _____

_____

3. She participated in the play and produced a film.

a. _____

_____

b. _____

_____

4. Fred respires loudly because he has a cold.

a. _____

_____

b. _____

_____

B ECONOMICS RULES

Answer the questions.

1. What's the rule about when the demand is greater than the supply?

_____

_____

_____

In the winter, the demand for grapes is greater than the supply of grapes.

2. What will happen to the price of grapes?

_____

3. How do you know?

_____

_____

_____

Last summer, the price of bikes went up.

4. Which was greater, the demand or the supply?

_____

5. How do you know?

_____

_____

This year, the demand for gas is greater than the supply of gas.

6. What will happen to the price of gas?

_____

7. How do you know?

_____

_____

_____

C EDITING

Underline the redundant sentences.

A bell rang. Sam put on his firefighter's hat and his firefighter's coat. He jumped on the fire truck as it roared out of the station. Sam was a firefighter. The truck sped down Oak Street and screeched around the corner of Oak and First. The truck was going sixty miles an hour. The truck was going fast. At First and Elm, the truck screamed to a stop, and Sam jumped off to look for a fire hydrant. The fire was at First and Elm.

D SIMILES

Make up a simile for each item.

1. She can sing very well.

_____

_____

2. His voice is very loud.

_____

_____

E REWRITING PARAGRAPHS

Rewrite the paragraph in four sentences. If one of the sentences tells **why,** combine the sentences with **because.** If two sentences seem contradictory, combine them with **but.**

In 1522, Magellan's crew arrived in Spain. Spain looked good to them. Five ships had started the trip. Only one ship finished the trip. The crew had acquired many things. The crew acquired mostly spices. People paid a lot of money for the spices. The spices were rare.

_____

_____

_____

_____

_____

_____

_____

_____

_____

_____

_____

F INFERENCE

Read the passage and answer the questions.
- Circle the **W** if the question is answered by words in the passage. Then underline those words.
- Circle the **D** if the question is answered by a deduction.

> When you stub your toe, the message "toe hurts" goes from your toe to your brain. Your nerves don't really carry the words "toe hurts." What they do carry is a little bit of electricity. The electricity comes in very short bursts called **impulses**. If the toe doesn't hurt too much, the message may have just a few impulses per second. If the toe hurts a lot, the message may have many impulses per second. The greater the pain, the more impulses per second.

1. Which system carries the message "toe hurts" to your brain?

   _____ **W** **D**

2. How is a nerve like a lamp cord?

   _____

   _____

   _____ **W** **D**

3. What are impulses?

   _____

   _____

4. If a message has 10 impulses per second, how many impulses will it have in 5 seconds?

   _____

5. Pain Message A has 50 impulses per second. Pain Message B has 120 impulses per second. Which message describes more pain?

   _____ **W** **D**

6. Which gives more impulses per second: banging your knee against a door or touching your knee with a glove?

   _____

   _____

G WRITING DIRECTIONS

Write the instructions.

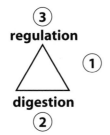

3 regulation

1

digestion

2

1. _____

_____

_____

2. _____

_____

_____

3. _____

_____

_____

H DEFINITIONS

Write a word that comes from **circulate** or **respire** in each blank. Then write **verb, noun,** or **adjective** after each item.

1. You have to _____ to get

air into your lungs. _____

2. _____ is the act of

breathing. _____

3. Publishers _____ many

books. _____

4. Your lungs are in your

_____ system.

_____

5. Some people enjoy _____

at parties. _____

I CONTRADICTIONS

Underline the contradiction and circle the statement it contradicts. Then tell **why** the underlined statement contradicts the circled statement. Make the underlined statement true.

Joan was a productive painter. She had more than 100 pictures ready for an art show, and she was excited. One day when she was working, a pot of paint fell on her hand and hurt the motor nerves in her fingers. * Joan went to see a doctor. He knew she was an artist who made lots of paintings. He told her she would still be able to move her fingers, but she wouldn't feel anything with them for a while. Joan felt lucky.

_____

_____

A ECONOMICS RULES

Answer the questions.

1. What's the rule about when the demand is greater than the supply?

   _____

   _____

   _____

> In the fall, the demand for warm coats is greater than the supply of warm coats.

2. What will happen to the price of warm coats?

   _____

3. How do you know?

   _____

   _____

   _____

> Last year, the price of gasoline went up.

4. Which was greater, the supply or the demand?

   _____

5. How do you know?

   _____

   _____

> Fifty people want to buy swimsuits. The seller has thirty swimsuits.

6. Which is greater, the supply or the demand?

   _____

7. What will happen to the price of swimsuits?

   _____

8. How do you know?

   _____

   _____

B EDITING

Underline the redundant sentences.

> Jane was on a low-calorie diet. She ate only fruit. Jane wanted to lose weight. Jane became weak and sick because she wasn't getting all the vitamins and minerals she needed. Her doctor gave Jane some vitamin pills and told her to eat more kinds of food. Jane took the pills and ate more kinds of food. The pills were full of vitamins. She felt better and lost ten pounds. After she started taking the vitamin pills, Jane lost weight.

C INFERENCE

Read the passage and answer the questions.
- Circle the **W** if the question is answered by words in the passage. Then underline those words.
- Circle the **D** if the question is answered by a deduction.

> Here's another rule about demand and supply: **When the demand is less than the supply, prices go down.**
>
> Ms. Thomas runs the only dairy farm near Newton. In July, her cows produce just as much milk as Newton needs, which is 1,000 gallons a month. In August, a big group of people moves out of Newton, and Newton's demand for milk drops to 600 gallons a month. But Ms. Thomas's cows are still producing 1,000 gallons a month.
>
> Ms. Thomas sells 600 gallons at the old price, and then she is stuck with 400 gallons that will soon go bad. She thinks she can get people to buy the 400 gallons if she lowers the price. Her idea works, and she sells all 400 gallons at the lower price.

1. What rule about demand and supply is this passage about?

   _____

   _____

   _____

2. What would have happened to the price of milk if a big group of people had moved into Newton in July?

   _____

   _____ **W D**

3. Was the demand smaller than the supply in August because the demand went down or because the supply went up?

   _____

   _____

4. What did Ms. Thomas do to get people to buy the 400 gallons she had left over?

   _____

   _____ **W D**

5. What will Ms. Thomas have to do to the demand for milk to sell 1,000 gallons at the old price in September?

   _____

   _____ **W D**

6. Name one way she could do that.

   _____

7. Did Ms. Thomas lose money in August?

   _____ **W D**

D SENTENCE COMBINATIONS

Combine the sentences with **although.**

1. John went to school.
   John wanted to stay at home.

   _____

   _____

   _____

2. Sam constructs many things.
   Sam doesn't have any tools.

   _____

   _____

   _____

3. Jane was hungry.
   Jane didn't want to eat.

   _____

   _____

   _____

E SENTENCE ANALYSIS

Underline the common part. For each
sentence, write two sentences with that
common part.

1. The United States and Japan manufacture
   cars.

   A. _____

   _____

   B. _____

   _____

2. A goat and its kids are consuming those
   bushes.

   A. _____

   _____

   B. _____

   _____

3. Cats have soft fur, particularly when
   they're young.

   A. _____

   _____

   B. _____

   _____

4. Six women and a boy were constructing a
   swimming pool.

   A. _____

   _____

   _____

   B. _____

   _____

F DEFINITIONS

Write a word that comes from **manufacture** or **participate** in each blank. Then write **verb, noun,** or **adjective** after each item.

1. A car _____ has to

follow regulations.

_____

2. Some companies don't

_____ many

products. _____

3. You don't have to

_____ in this game.

_____

4. Many _____

products are advertised.

_____

5. Some classes are not very

_____.

_____

G CONTRADICTIONS

Underline the contradiction and circle the statement it contradicts. Then tell **why** the underlined statement contradicts the circled statement. Make the underlined statement true.

When Mel finished high school, he left Columbus for a year. While he was away, construction workers modified every building on Main Street. Many people moved into town, and the mayor had to make new regulations. Most people predicted that Columbus would keep growing.* When Mel came back, he hardly recognized the place. All kinds of new people were walking in the streets. His friends were saying that Columbus would get bigger. There were many new rules to follow. At least the barber shop on Main Street was the same.

_____

_____

H CONTRADICTIONS

Tell which fact each statement relates to.
Make each contradiction true.

> A. The demand for bottles was low.
> B. The supply of bottles was high.

1. Many people wanted bottles. _____

2. Stores had very few bottles. _____

3. It was easy to find bottles. _____

I DEDUCTIONS

Write the conclusion of each deduction.

1. Commands come from the brain.
"Bend knee" is a command.

_____

_____

2. Some diseases damage your heart.
Measles is a disease.

_____

_____

_____

3. Feelings go to the brain.
Cold is a feeling.

_____

_____

J FOLLOWING DIRECTIONS

Follow the directions.

1. Draw a big circle in the box.

2. Draw a horizontal line from the left side
of the circle to the right side of the circle.

3. Draw a vertical line from the top of the
circle to the bottom of the circle.

4. In the top right part of the circle, write the
word that means **use up** or **eat.**

K SIMILES

Tell **two** ways that the things compared are **not** the same. Tell **one** way that the things compared **are** the same.

| The field was like a pancake. |

1. _____

   _____

2. _____

   _____

3. _____

   _____

L WRITING STORIES

Write a story about this picture of Paula and Jasper. Your story should tell what happened **before** the picture, what happened **in** the picture, and what happened **after** the picture.

deaf	hearing aid	sign language	silence	happy

_____

_____

_____

_____

_____

_____

_____

_____

_____

_____

A EDITING

Cross out the wrong word and write the correct word above it. (4)

Last year, Mike have three rabbits. He kept them in a cage. One night, the rabbits got out of the cage. It hopped under the house and wouldn't come out. Mike had to crawl under the house to grab her rabbits. He pulled them out and put it back in the cage.

B SENTENCE COMBINATIONS

Combine the sentences with **although.**

1. That car is new.
   That car is not running.
   _____
   _____

2. She consumed lots of food.
   She did not get fat.
   _____
   _____
   _____

3. Tod likes to go fast.
   Tod dislikes jets.
   _____
   _____

C DEDUCTIONS

Write the middle part of each deduction.

1. The company manufactured products.
   _____
   So, maybe the company manufactured tires.

2. Feelings go to the brain.
   _____
   So, heat goes to the brain.

3. Muscles do not push.
   _____
   So, the trapezius does not push.

D DEFINITIONS

Write a word that comes from **predict** or **digest** in each blank. Then write **verb, noun,** or **adjective** after each item.

1. He _____ that we would have a cold winter. _____

2. The way she acts is always _____. _____

3. Some people get tired when they _____ lots of food. _____

4. Being well helps your _____. _____

5. _____ sometimes come true. _____

E   ECONOMICS RULES

Answer the questions.

1. What's the rule about when the demand is greater than the supply?

    _____

    _____

    _____

> Chong's Meat Market raised the price of turkey yesterday.

2. Which was greater, the supply or the demand?

    _____

3. How do you know?

    _____

    _____

> Twenty people want turkeys. Chong's Meat Market has ten turkeys.

4. Which is greater, the supply or the demand?

    _____

5. What will happen to the price of turkey?

    _____

> Last week, turkeys cost 40 cents a pound. This week, turkeys cost 50 cents a pound.

6. What happened to the price of turkeys?

    _____

7. Which was greater, the supply or the demand?

    _____

8. How do you know?

    _____

    _____

F   EDITING

Underline the redundant sentences.

> Donna was a paper clip manufacturer. She made paper clips in a factory. Every day Donna got up at 6 and went to her factory. She made sure that the factory workers were doing their jobs. She got up very early in the morning. Donna liked her factory. It was clean and modern. Her workers were happy because she paid them a lot of money. Every two hours, her workers got a break. Then they went back to work. The factory workers were happy because they got good pay checks. Donna was happy because her workers were happy.

Lesson 42

G FOLLOWING DIRECTIONS

Follow the directions.

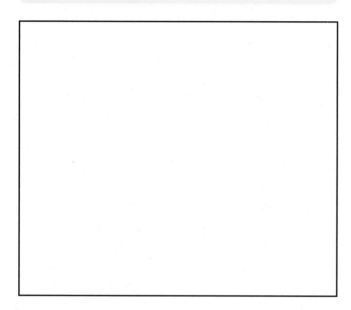

1. Write a big **T** in the box.

2. On the right side of the **T,** write the word that means **make something in a factory.**

3. On the left side of the **T,** write what part of speech that word is.

4. Draw a horizontal line under the **T.**

H SENTENCE ANALYSIS

Underline the common part. For each sentence, write two sentences with that common part.

1. Redwoods get very big, particularly in California.

A. _____

_____

B. _____

_____

2. Mike and Kim have many secrets.

A. _____

_____

B. _____

_____

3. That company, which manufactures paper, hires a lot of people.

A. _____

_____

B. _____

_____

4. Gloria modified her stereo, which had large speakers.

A. _____

_____

B. _____

_____

I INFERENCE

Read the passage and answer the questions.
- Circle the **W** if the question is answered by words in the passage. Then underline those words.
- Circle the **D** if the question is answered by a deduction.

You know that **when the demand is less than the supply, prices go down.**

Mr. Hightower runs the only chicken farm near Newton. In September, his chickens produce just as many eggs as Newton needs, which is 1,000 dozen a month. Mr. Hightower sells the eggs for $2 a dozen, so he makes $2,000 that month.

The people of Newton think that $2 a dozen is too much to pay for eggs. In October, they all get together and decide not to buy eggs from Mr. Hightower. This action is called a **boycott.**

Mr. Hightower, whose chickens are still producing eggs, is stuck with 1,000 dozen eggs that will soon go bad. The only way he can make any money in October is to lower the price of eggs and hope that people will like the new price. So he lowers the price to $1 a dozen. The people of Newton like this new price, and they buy all the eggs.

---

1. What's one rule about demand and supply?

   _____

   _____

   _____

2. Why did people in Newton decide not to buy eggs in October?

   _____

   _____

   _____

   _____

3. Why is Mr. Hightower stuck with 1,000 dozen eggs?

   _____

   _____

   _____ **W**   **D**

4. In October, was the demand smaller than the supply because the demand went down or because the supply went up?

   _____

   _____

   _____ **W**   **D**

5. Why did Mr. Hightower lower the price?

   _____

   _____

   _____

6. How much did Mr. Hightower make in October?

   _____

7. What does a boycott do to the demand?

   _____ **W**   **D**

J ANALOGIES

Write what each analogy tells.

> - what each word means
> - what part of speech each word is
> - what adjective comes from each word
> - what noun comes from each word

1. **Manufacture** is to **make in a factory** as **participate** is to **take part in something.**

   _____

   _____

2. **Manufacture** is to **manufacturer** as **participate** is to **participation.**

   _____

   _____

3. **Manufacture** is to **manufactured** as **participate** is to **participatory.**

   _____

   _____

A WRITING DIRECTIONS

Write the instructions.

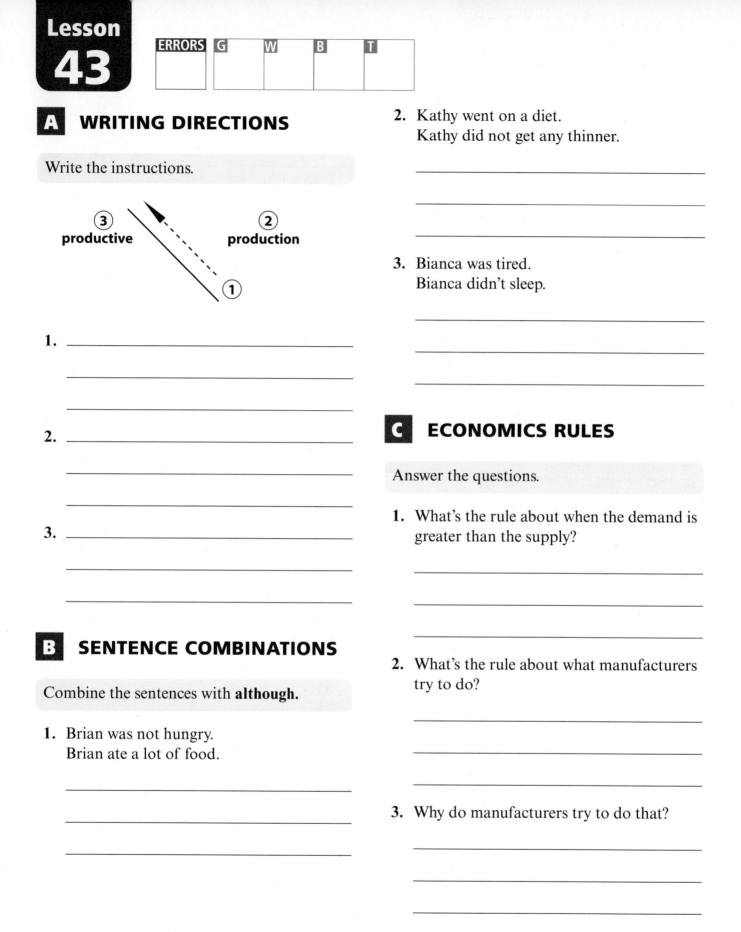

3 productive   2 production   1

1. _____

_____

2. _____

_____

3. _____

_____

B SENTENCE COMBINATIONS

Combine the sentences with **although.**

1. Brian was not hungry.
   Brian ate a lot of food.

_____

_____

2. Kathy went on a diet.
   Kathy did not get any thinner.

_____

_____

_____

3. Bianca was tired.
   Bianca didn't sleep.

_____

_____

_____

C ECONOMICS RULES

Answer the questions.

1. What's the rule about when the demand is greater than the supply?

_____

_____

_____

2. What's the rule about what manufacturers try to do?

_____

_____

_____

3. Why do manufacturers try to do that?

_____

_____

_____

> A car manufacturer makes 1,000 cars a week and sells 1,000 cars a week.

4. Is the demand greater than the supply?

_____

5. So what will the manufacturer try to do?

_____

_____

_____

> Name two ways that the manufacturer can do that.

6. _____

7. _____

D EVIDENCE

For each sentence followed by a blank, write the number of the rule that relates to that sentence.

> **1.** Hot air holds more water than cold air.
> **2.** When hot air rises, it cools off.

Hot air often blows across the Pacific Ocean toward the West Coast of the United States. When it reaches the West Coast, this air is carrying a great deal of water. _____ The air is then forced up by mountains along the coast. By the time it reaches the mountaintops, the air is quite cool. _____ The air can no longer hold all its water. _____ As a result, the west side of the mountains gets a lot of rain. When the air goes down the east side of the mountains, it gets warmer. _____

E EDITING

Cross out the wrong word and write the correct word above it. (4)

That company manufacture animal crackers every day. The people who work there make cookie batter in big vats. Then they pour the batter into little molds of lions, tigers, and bears. After the batter is cooked, the animal crackers is rolled down a big belt. Workers stands at the belt. They throw away all the crackers that doesn't look like animals.

F DEFINITIONS

Fill in each blank with the word that has the same meaning as the word or words under the blank.

1. They _____ a car with a large
   (chose)
   trunk.

2. Some people tried to figure out the

   _____ of that book.
   (end)

3. The worker _____ the
   (found fault with)
   company's plan.

4. Teachers should be able to

   _____.
   (make things easier to understand)

G BODY RULES

Label each nerve as a **sensory** nerve or a **motor** nerve. Draw an arrow to show which way the message moves.

1. "Hand itches."   2. "Rub towel on leg."

3. "Shoes are tight."   4. "Lips are chapped."

H REWRITING PARAGRAPHS

Rewrite the paragraph in four sentences. If one of the sentences tells **why,** combine the sentences with **because.** If two sentences seem contradictory, combine them with **but.**

> Diamonds and coal are made of the same mineral. The same mineral is carbon. Diamonds are used for jewelry. Diamonds are used in industry. Diamonds can cut any other material in the world. Diamonds are very hard. Some colored diamonds are quite rare. Red diamonds are the rarest.

_____

_____

_____

_____

_____

_____

_____

_____

_____

_____

_____

_____

206   *Lesson 43*

I BODY SYSTEMS

Fill in each blank.

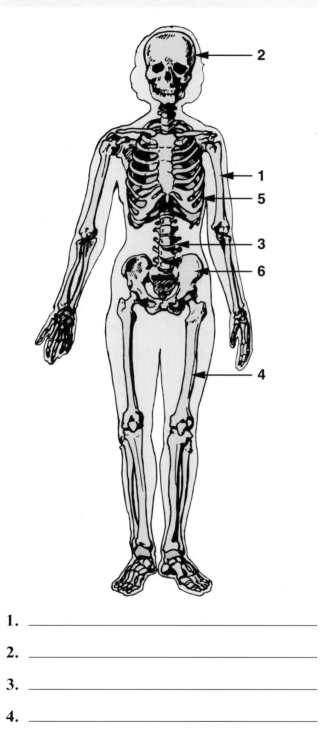

1. _____

2. _____

3. _____

4. _____

5. _____

6. _____

J INFERENCE

Read the passage and answer the questions.
- Circle the **W** if the question is answered by words in the passage. Then underline those words.
- Circle the **D** if the question is answered by a deduction.

> You know that **when the demand is greater than the supply, prices go up.**
>
> Mr. Jones runs the only dairy farm near Mudville. In January, his cows produce just as much milk as Mudville needs. Mr. Jones makes $1,000 from milk sales that month. In February, his cows produce a lot less milk than Mudville needs. If Mr. Jones sells the milk at the old price, he won't make $1,000 because he doesn't have as much milk to sell. But Mr. Jones wants to make $1,000, so he raises his prices.
>
> Mudville's demand for milk is much greater than Mr. Jones's supply, and he has no trouble selling his milk at the higher price. People in Mudville may not like the higher price, but they know that they need milk and that Mr. Jones's farm is the only place where they can get milk.

1. What's the rule about demand and supply?

_____

_____

_____

2. Was the demand greater than the supply in January?

_____ **W   D**

3. Which was greater in February, the demand or the supply?

_____ **W D**

4. If Mr. Jones sells his milk at the old price, why won't he make $1000?

_____
_____
_____ **W D**

5. Why did he raise his prices?

_____
_____
_____

6. Why didn't he have any trouble selling the milk at the higher price?

_____
_____
_____
_____ **W D**

7. Give two reasons why the people of Mudville pay the higher price, even though they don't like it.

a. _____
_____
_____

b _____
_____
_____

8. Did the demand become greater than the supply because the supply went down or because the demand went up?

_____
_____

K EDITING

Underline the redundant sentences.

Only one of Jack's many friends had red hair. Most of Jack's friends did not have red hair. Jack's best friend, Bert, who had red hair, came over to Jack's home. Jack was downtown, looking for Bert. But Bert was at Jack's residence. Jack decided to go back to his home, and Bert decided to go downtown. They were changing places. Finally, Jack ran into Hector. Hector was not Jack's best friend. Hector did not have red hair.

L   WRITING STORIES

Write a story about this picture of Stacey. Your story should tell what happened **before** the picture, what happened **in** the picture, and what happened **after** the picture.

lifeguard	cliff	beach	lake	swimming	suddenly

_____

_____

_____

_____

_____

_____

_____

_____

_____

_____

_____

ERRORS | G | W | B | T

A EVIDENCE

For each sentence followed by a blank, write the number of the rule that relates to that sentence.

> 1. When the demand is greater than the supply, prices go up.
> 2. Manufacturers try to make the demand greater than the supply.

Not long ago, people did not want to buy bikes. They liked their cars, and they did not see any reason to own a bike. But when gas got expensive, the bike makers said, "A bike never needs gas." _____ Many people liked the idea of not paying for gas, and the demand for bikes skyrocketed. Prices soared. _____ Bike manufacturers had to work overtime just to meet the demand.

When gas became cheap again, bike makers said, "If you buy a bike now, you will get a free lock." _____ The bike makers hoped that the lock gimmick would work. If enough people wanted the lock, the manufacturers could raise the price. _____

B EDITING

Underline the redundant sentences.

Most people like to play sports. Some people don't. People who lived thousands of years ago had footraces. They had games to see who could throw a spear the farthest. They had games to see who could run the fastest. Today, we play basketball, football, and many other games. People played sports thousands of years ago. People will still be playing and watching sports thousands of years from now. There will be sports fans in the future.

C WRITING DIRECTIONS

Write the instructions.

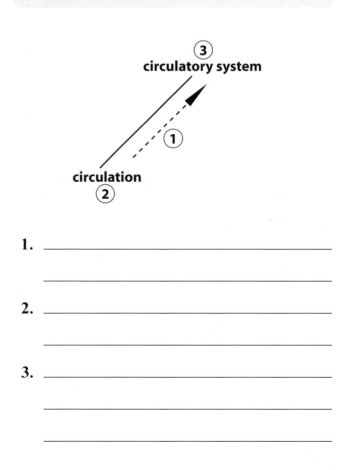

1. _____

   _____

2. _____

   _____

3. _____

   _____

   _____

D ECONOMICS RULES

Answer the questions.

1. What's the rule about when the demand is greater than the supply?

_____

_____

_____

2. What's the rule about what manufacturers try to do?

_____

_____

_____

3. Why do manufacturers try to do that?

_____

_____

> A purse manufacturer makes 5,000 purses a month and sells 4,000 purses a month.

4. Is the demand greater than the supply?

_____

5. So what will the manufacturer try to do?

_____

_____

_____

> Name two ways that the manufacturer can do that.

6. _____

_____

7. _____

_____

E SENTENCE COMBINATIONS

Combine the sentences with **although.**

1. He didn't have all the facts.
   His conclusion was correct.

   _____

   _____

   _____

2. That regulation is not fair.
   That regulation has to be followed.

   _____

   _____

   _____

3. Clarence modified his engine.
   His engine still doesn't run well.

   _____

   _____

   _____

F   SIMILES

Make up a simile for each item.

1. His feet are big.

   _____

   _____

2. Her hair was red.

   _____

   _____

G   EDITING

Cross out the wrong word and write the correct word above it. (4)

One day, Tom were in a race and hurt his gastrocnemius. It hurt so badly that Tom can't walk. They had to stay in a hospital for two days. Then Tom got a cast on their leg. He couldn't run in any races for two months.

H   REWRITING PARAGRAPHS

Rewrite the paragraph in four sentences. If one of the sentences tells **why,** combine the sentences with **because.** If sentences seem contradictory, combine them with **but.**

The Amazon River is the second longest river in the world. The Amazon River runs through South America. It is almost 4,000 miles long. It is up to 300 feet deep. Many places along the river have bad floods. Many places along the river have the worst floods between January and June. You must be very careful when you fish in the Amazon River. The Amazon River has many alligators and dangerous fish.

_____

_____

_____

_____

_____

_____

_____

_____

_____

_____

_____

_____

_____

_____

_____

I PARTS OF SPEECH

Underline the nouns. Draw **one** line **over** the adjectives. Draw **two** lines **over** the articles. Circle the verbs.

1. The local paper has a large circulation.
2. Ten running women were respiring at a rapid rate.
3. Her heart is being examined.
4. Every written sentence must have an end mark.

J INFERENCE

Use the facts to fill out the form.

Facts: Your name is Brian Ozaki. You have just graduated from State University in Rushville with a B.A. degree in journalism. You are applying for a job with a newspaper. You were editor of your high school and college newspapers. You are 22 years old. You are single and unemployed. Your address is 22 W. Main, Farmington, NM. You want to write for the sports page.

1. Name, last name first (please print)

   _____

2. Colleges or universities attended

   _____

   _____

3. Degrees, if any

   _____

4. Journalism experience, if any

   _____

   _____

   _____

5. Current employer

   _____

6. Are you married? _____

7. Address

   _____

   _____

8. What section do you prefer to write for?

   _____

WORD LIST

carbon dioxide (n) the gas that burning things produce
circulate (v) to move around
circulation (n) the act of circulating
circulatory (a) that something involves circulation
criticize (v) to find fault with
digestive (a) that something involves digestion
explanation (n) something that explains
oxygen (n) the gas that burning things need
participate (v) to take part in something
produce (v) to make
redundant (a) that something repeats what has already been said
respiration (n) the act of respiring
respiratory (a) that something involves respiration
respire (v) to breathe

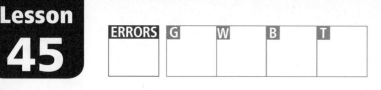

A EDITING

Underline the redundant sentences.

Carla was writing a story. Her first sentence said, "The woman ran like the wind." Carla showed that the woman ran fast. Then she wrote five more sentences about the woman. Her story was six sentences long. Carla liked her story, so she let Dan read it. Dan read Carla's story. He said, "This is good, Carla. You should let other people read it." Carla liked her story, too. She told Dan that she would work on the story some more.

B EVIDENCE

For each sentence followed by a blank, write the number of the rule that relates to that sentence.

1. Unlike magnetic poles attract one another.
2. Like magnetic poles repel one another.

All magnets have two poles, one on each end of the magnet. The two poles of the magnet are called the north pole and the south pole. If the magnet is shaped like a bar, one end of the bar is the north pole, and the other end is the south pole.

If you hold the north pole of one magnet near the north pole of another magnet, the magnets will try to move away from each other. _____ And if you hold the south pole of one magnet against the south pole of another magnet, the magnets will also try to move away from each other. _____ But if you hold the south pole of one magnet near the north pole of another magnet, the magnets will move toward each other. _____ The magnets will stick together, and you will have to pull hard to separate them. _____

C SIMILES

Complete the items about the words in the box.

fist	rock

1. Tell how the objects could be the same.

   _____

   _____

2. Write a simile about the objects.

   _____

   _____

D ECONOMICS RULES

Answer the questions.

1. What's the rule about when the demand is less than the supply?

   _____

   _____

   _____

2. What's the rule about what manufacturers try to do?

   _____

   _____

   _____

3. What's the rule about when the demand is greater than the supply?

   _____

   _____

   _____

> In the summer, the demand for grapes is less than the supply of grapes.

4. What will happen to the price of grapes?

   _____

5. How do you know?

   _____

   _____

   _____

> Last winter, the price of bikes went down.

6. Which was greater, the demand or the supply?

   _____

7. How do you know?

   _____

   _____

8. What will the bike manufacturer try to do?

   _____

   _____

> Name two ways that the manufacturer can do that.

9. _____

   _____

10. _____

   _____

E SUBJECT/PREDICATE

Circle the subject and underline the predicate. Rewrite each sentence by moving the predicate.

1. Many birds fly south every year.

   _____

   _____

2. Winters are drier in the Southwest.

   _____

   _____

3. She explained her criticism when Terry got mad.

   _____

   _____

   _____

4. He ate lots of carrots because he had night blindness.

   _____

   _____

F SENTENCE ANALYSIS

Underline the common part. For each sentence, write two sentences with that common part.

1. Although that manufacturer resides in a big house, she drives an old car.

   A. _____

   _____

   B. _____

   _____

2. Cops and dogs protected the residence from robbers.

   A. _____

   _____

   B. _____

   _____

3. A cop and his dog are protecting the home.

   A. _____

   _____

   B. _____

   _____

4. Jane consumed a lot of water because she was thirsty.

   A. _____

   _____

   B. _____

   _____

G SENTENCE COMBINATIONS

For each item, circle the word that combines the sentences correctly. Then combine the sentences with that word.

1. Margie obtained a watch.
   Margie can't tell time.

   particularly   **although**   **which**

   _____

   _____

2. Blood circulates in your arteries.
   Nutrients circulate in your arteries.

   who   **and**   **but**

   _____

   _____

   _____

3. Jupiter has many moons.
   Saturn has many moons.

   although   **because**   **and**

   _____

   _____

   _____

4. Supply is related to prices.
   Demand is related to prices.

   although   **and**   **which**

   _____

   _____

   _____

5. Ms. Ortega was digging for gold.
   Her crew was digging for gold.

   and   **who**   **particularly**

   _____

   _____

   _____

H EDITING

Cross out the wrong word and write the correct word above it. (5)

Last Monday, three men was running a race. They all had sneakers on. The man in the lead were wearing red shorts. Her hair was red also. He said to himself, "If I wins this race, I will get lots of money." So she ran faster. He won the race, but not by much.

I INFERENCE

Use the facts to fill out the form.

Facts: Your name is Edna Vacek. You are
applying for unemployment benefits. You
were laid off last week by the Bunyan
Lumber Company, where you worked the
saw. You started working there five years
ago, right after you finished high school.
Your social security number is 999-42-
6857. You want to get another job with a
lumber company, and you will not take
less than $500 a week. You are 23 years
old.

1. Name and age _____

2. Social security number _____

3. Circle highest school grade completed:

   1 2 3 4 5 6 7 8 9 10 11 12

4. What kind of work are you looking for?

   _____

   _____

5. What is the minimum starting wage you
   will accept on your next job?

   _____

6. Who was your last employer?

   _____

7. How long did you work there?

   _____

8. How long have you been out of work?

   _____

   _____

J WRITING STORIES

Write a story about this picture of Coach Hendrix and Daryl. Your story should tell what happened **before** the picture, what happened **in** the picture, and what happened **after** the picture.

| football | helmet | big game | touchdown | defeat | unhappy |

_____

_____

_____

_____

_____

_____

_____

_____

_____

_____

_____

Fact Game
5

FACT GAME SCORECARD

1	2	3	4	5	6	7	8	9	10	11	12	13	14	15
16	17	18	19	20	21	22	23	24	25	26	27	28	29	30

FG	B	T

2. Complete each sentence with a word that comes from **circulate.**

   a. When you exercise, your ▒▒▒▒▒▒ increases.
   b. The cows ▒▒▒▒▒▒ around the pasture yesterday.

3. Make two sentences from the sentence in the box.

   > Jessie and Len are going to the party.

4. Combine the sentences in the box with **although.**

   > He doesn't exercise.
   > He is in good shape.

5. Name the part of speech for each underlined word.

   a. The newspaper tried to increase its <u>circulation</u> by advertising.
   b. The tired man <u>respired</u> deeply and sat down.

6. Complete the sentence in the box.

   > When the demand is greater than the supply, prices go ▒▒▒▒▒▒.

7. Answer the question about the sentence in the box.

   > In the winter, the demand for ice skates is greater than the supply of ice skates.

   What will happen to the price of ice skates?

8. Complete each sentence with a word that comes from **respire.**

   a. Asthma is a ▒▒▒▒▒▒ disease.
   b. Your body is ▒▒▒▒▒▒ all the time.

9. Complete the sentence in the box.

   > Manufacturers try to make the ▒▒▒▒▒▒ greater than the supply.

10. Combine the sentences in the box with **although.**

    > She modified her explanation.
    > Her explanation was still unclear.

11. Make two sentences from the sentence in the box.

    > Doris runs every day because she's in training.

12. Answer the question about the sentence in the box.

    > In the summer, the demand for ice skates is less than the supply of ice skates.

    What will happen to the price of ice skates?

A ECONOMICS RULES

Answer the questions.

1. What's the rule about when the demand is greater than the supply?

   _____

   _____

   _____

2. What's the rule about when the demand is less than the supply?

   _____

   _____

   _____

3. What's the rule about what manufacturers try to do?

   _____

   _____

   _____

   _____

In the winter, the demand for mittens is greater than the supply of mittens.
---

4. What will happen to the price of mittens?

   _____

5. How do you know?

   _____

   _____

   _____

This spring, mittens cost $1 a pair. Last winter, mittens cost $2 a pair.
---

6. What happened to the price of mittens?

   _____

7. Which was greater in the spring, the demand or the supply?

   _____

8. How do you know?

   _____

   _____

9. What will mitten manufacturers try to do?

   _____

   _____

   _____

Name two ways that the manufacturers can do that.
---

10. _____

    _____

11. _____

    _____

B SIMILES

Complete the items about the words in the box.

neck   tree trunk

1. Tell how the objects could be the same.

_____

_____

2. Write a simile about the objects.

_____

_____

C EVIDENCE

For each sentence followed by a blank, write the number of the rule that relates to that sentence.

1. Vibrating objects produce sound.
2. Metals conduct sound better than air.

Even when a train doesn't blow its whistle, it makes a lot of noise. It makes noise because all its parts are moving back and forth.____ If you put a microphone next to the tracks, it can hear a train that is a mile away. If you put the microphone on the tracks, it can hear a train that is many miles away.____ Sometimes the track, which is shaking, makes a little hum of its own.____ In the old days, train robbers needed to know when a train was coming. Instead of listening for the sound in the air, they would put their ears on the track.____ They were always ready for the train when it came.

D EDITING

Cross out the wrong word and write the correct word above it. (5)

Only a few years ago, people don't think it was important for girls to play sports. Schools had sports programs for boys, but not for girls. Today, people know that it are important for girls to play sports, too. Girls has basketball teams and baseball teams. Them run track and play volleyball. Playing sports is as good for girls as it are for boys.

E CONTRADICTIONS

Underline the contradiction and circle the statement it contradicts. Then tell **why** the underlined statement contradicts the circled statement. Make the underlined statement true.

Corn farmers have to protect their crops from many different bugs. Many times in the past, bugs have wiped out corn crops. Last year, bugs ate a lot of corn, and there was not enough corn for everybody who wanted it. The farmers tried everything to get rid of the bugs.* They sprayed powder from planes. They tried to find animals that would eat the bugs. Corn prices began to go down. One company started manufacturing seeds that were bugproof. All in all, it was a very bad year for farmers.

_____

_____

_____

_____

F EDITING

Underline the redundant sentences.

Last summer, everybody in Coal City wanted a pair of sandals. Mr. Poole ran the only shoe store in town. There was a big demand for sandals. Mr. Poole got lots of sandals from a manufacturer. No other place in town sold sandals. Mr. Poole made $1 on each pair of sandals that he sold. One day, Mr. Poole sold 90 pairs of sandals. He made $90 from sandal sales that day. Every person in town wanted sandals.

G INFERENCE

Read the passage and answer the questions.
- Circle the **W** if the question is answered by words in the passage. Then underline those words.
- Circle the **D** if the question is answered by a deduction.

You know that **when the demand is greater than the supply, prices go up.**

Ms. Lopez runs the only chicken farm near Mudville. In March, her chickens produce just as many eggs as Mudville needs, which is 1,000 dozen a month. Ms. Lopez sells the eggs for $1 a dozen, so she makes $1,000 that month.

In April, a big group of people moves into Mudville, and Mudville's demand for eggs goes up to 1,500 dozen a month. But Ms. Lopez's chickens are still producing only 1,000 dozen a month, and it becomes very hard for the people of Mudville to get all the eggs they need. People start to offer Ms. Lopez more for her eggs, just so they can be sure of getting some. Ms. Lopez, who likes the idea of making extra money, decides to raise the price to $1.25 a dozen. Because the demand is so high, she has no trouble selling the eggs at the new price.

1. What's the rule about demand and supply?

   _____

   _____

   _____

2. In March, was the demand for eggs greater than the supply of eggs?

   _____ **W D**

3. Why does the demand for eggs increase in April?

   _____

   _____

   _____

4. Why do people start offering Ms. Lopez more for her eggs?

   _____

   _____

   _____ **W D**

5. Why doesn't Ms. Lopez have any trouble selling eggs at a new price?

   _____

   _____ **W D**

6. Would prices have gone up if the chickens had laid 1,500 dozen eggs in April?

   _____ **W D**

H SENTENCE ANALYSIS

Underline the common part. For each sentence, write two sentences with that common part.

1. Although Don hurt his gastrocnemius, he can still run.

   A._____

   _____

   B._____

   _____

2. Frank and Martha participate on the volleyball team.

   A._____

   _____

   _____

   B._____

   _____

   _____

3. Her circulation, which is slow, is being checked by a doctor.

   A._____

   _____

   _____

   B._____

   _____

   _____

4. Roller coasters are fun, particularly when they are scary.

   A._____

   _____

   _____

   B._____

   _____

   _____

I BODY RULES

Shade in each tube that carries dark blood. Write **vein** or **artery** in each blank. Also write **oxygen** or **carbon dioxide** in each blank.

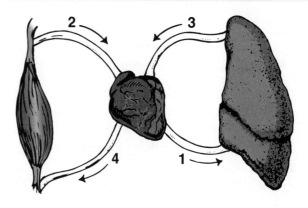

1. _____

   _____

2. _____

3. _____

4. _____

J SENTENCE COMBINATIONS

Circle the word that combines the sentences correctly. Combine the sentences with that word.

1. Tom has been playing tennis.
   Bob has been playing tennis.

   which   **and**   **but**

   _____

   _____

2. Mary cut herself.
   Mary did not bleed.

   who   **because**   **although**

   _____

   _____

   _____

3. A captain is modifying that boat.
   His first mate is modifying that boat.

   although   **but**   **and**

   _____

   _____

   _____

4. The beginning of the film was predictable.
   The end of the film was predictable.

   who   **particularly**   **and**

   _____

   _____

   _____

5. Frank is selective.
   Frank is the most selective when he goes to restaurants.

   and   **which**   **particularly**

   _____

   _____

   _____

A SENTENCE ANALYSIS

Rewrite the passage in six sentences.

> A boy and his cat were sitting on the porch. The cat looked content, but it was unhappy. It wanted to catch mice and chase after birds.

_____

_____

_____

_____

_____

_____

B SIMILES

Complete the items about the words in the box.

> eyes   emeralds

1. Tell how the objects could be the same.

_____

_____

2. Write a simile about the objects.

_____

_____

C ECONOMICS RULES

Answer the questions.

1. What's the rule about when the demand is less than the supply?

_____

_____

_____

2. What's the rule about when the demand is greater than the supply?

_____

_____

_____

3. What's the rule about what manufacturers try to do?

_____

_____

_____

> Pete's Shoe Store can't sell all its shoes.

4. Which is greater, the supply or the demand?

_____

5. What will happen to the price of shoes?

_____

6. How do you know?

_____

In the spring, Pete's Shoe Store lowers its prices on boots.

7. Which is greater, the supply or the demand?

   _____

8. How do you know?

   _____

   _____

9. What will the boot manufacturer try to do?

   _____

   _____

   _____

Name two ways the manufacturer can do that.

10. _____

    _____

11. _____

    _____

D EVIDENCE

For each sentence followed by a blank, write the number of the rule that relates to that sentence.

> 1. When the demand is greater than the supply, prices go up.
> 2. When the demand is less than the supply, prices go down.

The demand for gas is always growing. When there is a surplus of gas, consumers are happy because their bills are low. _____ But when there is a shortage of gas, consumers' wallets are hit hard. _____ Some dishonest companies have tried to create fake shortages. They have made consumers believe that there is almost no gas left, which means that prices will have to change. _____ When the price gets up to where the companies want it, they "find" more gas and sell it for the new price.

E EDITING

Underline the redundant sentences.

The zoo owned a giant ape named Gog. Gog was so big that he could jump over houses and lift cars with one hand. One day, Gog broke out of his cage and started walking around town, crushing mailboxes and fire hydrants with his feet. Gog belonged to the zoo. He saw men loading bananas onto a truck and roared with joy. The men ran away. Gog wasn't very small, and he could lift men with a single hand. He grabbed six hundred bananas and took them back to his cage. His cage was broken.

F DEDUCTIONS

Use the rule in the box to answer the questions.

> The hotter the liquid, the faster it evaporates.

1. The water in the cup is 80 degrees. The water in the glass is 50 degrees.

   a. Which water is hotter?

   _____

   b. Which water will evaporate faster?

   _____

   c. How do you know?

   _____

   _____

2. Gene's lemonade evaporated in 30 minutes. Lin's lemonade evaporated in 60 minutes.

   a. Whose lemonade evaporated faster?

   _____

   b. Whose lemonade was hotter?

   _____

   c. How do you know?

   _____

   _____

G DEFINITIONS

Fill in each blank with the word that has the same meaning as the word or words under the blank.

1. The basketball player _____
   her shot.   (changed)

2. The play has a very strange

   _____.
            (end)

3. Companies do not

   _____ live trees.
      (make in a factory)

4. A good swimmer can _____ very
   slowly.   (breathe)

H EDITING

Cross out the wrong word and write the correct word above it. (4)

Last year, Mr. Jeter decided to modify his house, because his house were too small. He wanted to build an extra bedroom and a family room. Mr. Jeter had tools, but he have no wood. She went to the lumber yard and bought some pine. When Mr. Jeter are building the extra rooms he hit his hand with the hammer. Mr. Jeter yelled so loudly that all his neighbors heard him.

I INFERENCE

Read the passage and answer the questions.
- Circle the **W** if the question is answered by words in the passage. Then underline those words.
- Circle the **D** if the question is answered by a deduction.

You know that **manufacturers always try to make the demand greater than the supply.**

Mr. Franklin runs the only lightbulb factory in Mudville. In May, he produces just as many lightbulbs as Mudville needs, which is 1,000 a month. Mr. Franklin makes 50 cents for each lightbulb he sells in May.

In June, Mr. Franklin decides that he wants to make more than 50 cents for each lightbulb he sells. He knows that if he can make the demand greater than the supply, the price of lightbulbs will go up. So he puts an ad in the paper that says, "If you have more lamps in your house, you will be able to see better. You won't stub your toes in dark corners, you will be able to read anywhere, and your house will be cheery." The ad works, and the demand for lightbulbs goes up. Because the demand is so high, Mr. Franklin raises the price of his light bulbs, and he sells all 1,000 of them.

1. What's another rule about demand and supply?

_____

_____

_____

_____

2. How much money did Mr. Franklin make in May?

_____ **W D**

3. What did the ad try to make people think?

_____

_____

_____ **W D**

4. Why is Mr. Franklin able to sell all 1,000 of his light bulbs in June at the higher price?

_____

_____ **W D**

5. Name another way that Mr. Franklin could have increased the demand.

_____

_____

6. What would happen to the demand if the ad did not work?

_____

_____ **W D**

7. If Mr. Franklin makes 60 cents for each lightbulb he sells in June, how much money will he make that month?

_____

J BODY SYSTEMS

Fill in each blank.

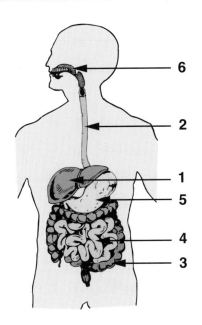

1. _____

2. _____

3. _____

4. _____

5. _____

6. _____

K FOLLOWING DIRECTIONS

Follow the directions

1. Draw a horizontal line in the box.

2. Draw a line that slants down to the left from the left end of the horizontal line.

3. At the bottom of the slanted line, draw an arrow that points to the right.

4. Draw the muscle that will move the slanted line in the direction of the arrow.

L WRITING STORIES

Write a story about this picture of Roberta and Belinda. Your story should tell what happened **before** the picture, what happened **in** the picture, and what happened **after** the picture.

factory	daydream	necklace	horse	flowers

_____

_____

_____

_____

_____

_____

_____

_____

_____

_____

_____

A INFERENCE

Read the passage and answer the questions.
- Circle the **W** if the question is answered by words in the passage. Then underline those words.
- Circle the **D** if the question is answered by a deduction.

Ms. Jackson runs the only flour mill in Zork City. In October, her mill produces only 1,000 pounds, which is half as much flour as Zork City needs each month. Because the demand is so much greater than the supply, Ms. Jackson charges $1 a pound for her flour.

Mr. Ross thinks he can make money if he starts another flour mill in Zork City that will compete with Ms. Jackson's mill. In November, he puts 1,500 pounds of flour up for sale at 75 cents a pound. Everybody starts buying Mr. Ross's flour. Then Ms. Jackson, who needs to sell her flour, lowers her price to 50 cents a pound. Everybody starts buying Ms. Jackson's flour again.

Each mill keeps lowering the price of flour until the price is as low as it can be. This lowering of prices is called a **price war.** It's a war that uses prices instead of soldiers.

1. Why can Ms. Jackson charge so much for flour in October?

_____

_____

_____ W D

2. Which was greater in November, the supply or the demand?

_____ W D

3. Why did Mr. Ross sell his flour for less than Ms. Jackson's flour?

_____

_____ W D

4. What did Mr. Ross do after Ms. Jackson lowered her price to 50 cents a pound?

_____

_____

5. Flour prices went down in November because of the price war. Give another reason why they went down.

_____

_____

_____ W D

6. If both mills end up charging 40 cents a pound for flour, how can one mill attract more customers?

_____

7. Why might price wars make consumers happy?

_____

_____ W D

B SENTENCE ANALYSIS

Rewrite the passage in six sentences.

> Samuel Clemens, who is better known as Mark Twain, was one of the greatest writers in American history. Although he is best known for his sense of humor, he wrote many serious works. As he grew older, Twain became bitter about many things, particularly American morality.

_____

_____

_____

_____

_____

_____

_____

_____

_____

_____

_____

_____

_____

_____

_____

C EDITING

Underline the redundant sentences.

When Gog got back to his cage, the zookeeper was having a fit. He took away Gog's bananas and made Gog fix the cage. Gog was sad. Gog did what the zookeeper told him to do. The zookeeper was really mad at Gog. He said, "You're lucky you didn't kill anybody today." Gog was not happy. His cage was a mess, but the town was worse. Water was everywhere, and letters blew about like leaves in the wind. Happily, nobody was dead.

D BODY RULES

Label each nerve. Write a message for each nerve.

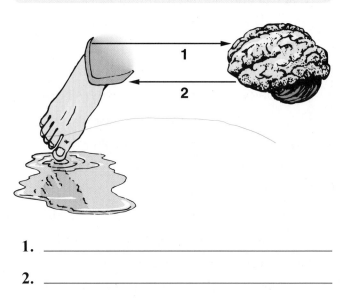

1. _____

2. _____

E CONTRADICTIONS

Make each statement mean the same thing as the statement in the box.

> Although every person produces carbon dioxide, there is not much in the air.

1. All people produce carbon dioxide, but there is not much in the air.

2. Although people use up carbon dioxide, there isn't a lot in the air.

3. Every person makes carbon dioxide, but there's a lot in the air.

4. Although there is not much carbon dioxide in the air, every person consumes it.

F DEDUCTIONS

Write the middle part of each deduction.

1. Some storms generate electricity.

   _____

   So, maybe tornadoes generate electricity.

2. Steve had some Mexican coins.

   _____

   _____

   So, maybe Steve had a peso.

3. Some lakes have salt water.

   _____

   So, maybe Lake Erie has salt water.

G SIMILES

Complete the items about the words in the box.

> words   knives

1. Tell how the objects could be the same.

   _____

   _____

2. Write a simile about the objects.

   _____

   _____

> skin   milk

3. Tell how the objects could be the same.

   _____

   _____

4. Write a simile about the objects.

   _____

   _____

Lesson 48

H EVIDENCE

For each sentence followed by a blank, write the number of the rule that relates to that sentence.

> 1. Like magnetic poles repel one another.
> 2. Unlike magnetic poles attract one another.

Many years ago, a magician amazed people with a "floating magnet" trick. He used two ring magnets and a stick. Holding the stick up in one hand, he would slide the first ring down the stick with the north pole facing up. Then he would slide the second ring down the stick with the north pole facing down. The second ring wouldn't touch the first ring. _____ It "floated" above the first ring. _____

Then the magician would slide the top ring off, turn it around, and slide it back down the stick. This time, the two rings stuck together like glue. _____ When he slid the top ring up, the bottom ring came with it. _____ This trick is easy to understand now, but it took people a long time to figure it out.

I DEFINITIONS

Write a word that comes from **construct** or **consume** in each blank. Then write **verb, noun,** or **adjective** after each item.

1. We need to _____ less gasoline. _____
2. Some _____ cost billions of dollars. _____
3. _____ should know more about supply and demand. _____
4. That town was not _____ ten years ago. _____
5. Food is _____, so people must buy it all the time. _____

J FOLLOWING DIRECTIONS

Follow the directions.

1. Draw a circle in the box.
2. Draw a horizontal line from the left side of the circle to the right side of the circle.
3. Above the line, write the word that means **that something involves participation.**
4. Below the line, write what part of speech that word is.

K ECONOMICS RULES

Answer the questions.

1. What's the rule about when the demand is greater than the supply?

   _____

   _____

   _____

2. What's the rule about when the demand is less than the supply?

   _____

   _____

   _____

Twenty people want to buy wading pools. Jan's Sporting Goods has thirty wading pools.

---

3. Which is greater, the supply or the demand?

   _____

4. What will happen to the price of wading pools?

   _____

5. How do you know?

   _____

   _____

   _____

6. What will the manufacturers try to do?

   _____

   _____

   _____

Name two ways that the manufacturers can do that.

---

7. _____

   _____

8. _____

   _____

In the summer, the price of wading pools goes up.

---

9. Which is greater, the supply or the demand?

   _____

10. How do you know?

    _____

    _____

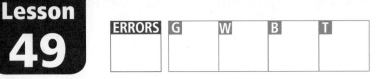

ERRORS G W B T

A SENTENCE ANALYSIS

Rewrite the passage in six sentences.

> One of the rarest bills in the world is the United States $10,000 bill, which was last made in 1946. The bill pictures Salmon P. Chase, who was an important judge and senator. A few collectors still own $10,000 bills, but they cannot use them.

_____

_____

_____

_____

_____

_____

_____

_____

_____

_____

_____

B SENTENCE COMBINATIONS

Combine the sentences with **however.**

1. John made his selection.
    John didn't get what he wanted.

    _____

    _____

    _____

    _____

2. Frogs are born in the water.
    Frogs grow up on the land.

    _____

    _____

    _____

3. He modified the car.
    The car looked the same.

    _____

    _____

    _____

4. Bats are not birds.
    Bats fly.

    _____

    _____

C EDITING

Underline the redundant sentences.

The man went from house to house, trying to get people to buy brushes. He was not having very good luck. The man was a salesman. The man had a standard sales pitch. He told people that their lives would change if they bought his brushes. Not many people fell for this pitch. The man modified his sales pitch. When he tried to sell his brushes, he gave people a different pitch.

D DEFINITIONS

Write a word that comes from **erode** in each blank. Then write **verb, noun,** or **adjective** after each item.

1. Farmers are learning to prevent soil

   _____ . _____

2. Water has a lot of _____

   power. _____

3. The sea will _____ its

   shoreline. _____

4. Wind has _____ rocks in the

   desert. _____

5. Rain is a very _____ force.

   _____

E EVIDENCE

For each sentence followed by a blank, write the number of the rule that relates to that sentence.

1. When the demand is less than the supply, prices go down.
2. Manufacturers try to make the demand greater than the supply.

It was a dry winter, and there was no snow on the mountains. The ski factory was losing a lot of money. ____ The factory owner tried to get the ski resorts to buy a snow-making machine. ____ He said, "If we don't get snow on the slopes soon, we'll all go out of business. ____ We need to put lots of ads on TV to show that machine-made snow is just as good as the real thing." ____ So they did. People tried the new snow, but they did not like it. The ski manufacturer was glad when the winter was over. It had been a very bad year for his company, and he had almost gone broke. ____

F **INFERENCE**

Read the passage and answer the questions.
- Circle the **W** if the question is answered by words in the passage. Then underline those words.
- Circle the **D** if the question is answered by a deduction.

> Mr. Bock runs the only pen factory in Zork City. Mr. Bock makes his pens cheaply, and they are not very good. But he can still sell them because the demand is so high. However, Ms. Flap starts another pen factory in Zork City. Her pens are better made, and they cost the same as Mr. Bock's. Pretty soon, everybody is buying Ms. Flap's pens.
>
> Mr. Bock has to make his pens even better than Ms. Flap's. People start buying his pens again. Each factory keeps improving its pens until the pens are of top quality. The people of Zork City are very happy, except for Mr. Bock, who liked the early days better.

1. Why weren't Mr. Bock's pens very good?

   _____

   _____

2. Why did people in Zork City buy his pens?

   _____

   _____

   _____

3. Why did Ms. Flap make her pens better than Mr. Bock's pens?

   _____

   _____ **W D**

4. What might have happened to Mr. Bock if he had kept on making the same old pens?

   _____

   _____

   _____ **W D**

5. Car manufacturers always compete with each other. Here are some ways that cars have improved because of competition: better gas mileage, more legroom, disk brakes. Name three more.

   _____

   _____

   _____

6. Name another manufactured product that has improved because of competition.

   _____

7. How has that product improved?

   _____

   _____

G CONTRADICTIONS

Tell which fact each statement relates to.
Make each contradiction true.

> A. The demand for gas is greater than the
>   supply of gas.
> B. The gas company is trying to make the
>   demand even bigger.

1. The gas company put an ad on TV that

   told people to use less gas.   _____

2. The price kept going down.   _____

3. They want to make more money.   _____

H WRITING DIRECTIONS

Write the instructions.

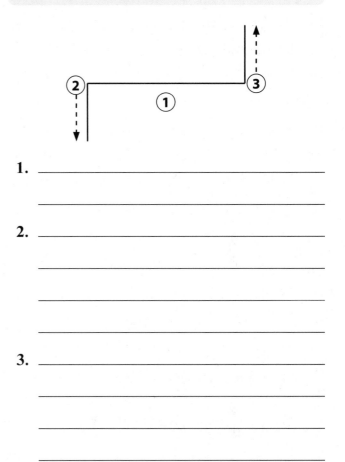

1. _____

   _____

2. _____

   _____

   _____

3. _____

   _____

   _____

   _____

I ECONOMICS RULES

Answer the questions.

1. What's the rule about when the demand is less than the supply?

    _____

    _____

    _____

2. What's the rule about what manufacturers try to do?

    _____

    _____

    _____

Lin's Bakery has 40 loaves of bread. Fifty people want loaves of bread.

3. Which is greater, the supply or the demand?

    _____

4. What will happen to the price of bread?

    _____

5. How do you know?

    _____

    _____

    _____

Last week, a loaf of bread cost $1.50. This week, a loaf of bread costs $1.40.

6. What happened to the price of bread?

    _____

7. Which was greater, the supply or the demand?

    _____

8. What will the manufacturers try to do?

    _____

    _____

    _____

Name two ways that the manufacturers can do that.

9. _____

    _____

10. _____

    _____

J SIMILES

Make up a simile for each item.

1. That football player runs right over everyone.

    _____

    _____

2. His fingers are long and thin.

    _____

    _____

K DEDUCTIONS

Write the conclusion of each deduction.

1. Some minerals help your body. Iron is a mineral.

    _____

    _____

2. Some body cells are long and thin. Bone cells are body cells.

    _____

    _____

3. Tom has every kind of tooth. A molar is a tooth.

    _____

WORD LIST

central nervous system (n) the body system made up of the brain and spinal cord

circulate (v) to move around

conclude (v) to end or figure out

conclusive (a) that something is true without any doubt

manufacturer (n) something that manufactures

nervous system (n) the body system of nerves

peripheral nervous system (n) the body system made up of all the nerves that lead to and from the spinal cord and the brain

protection (n) something that protects

regulation (n) a rule

residence (n) the place where someone resides

residential (a) that a place has many residences

respire (v) to breathe

selection (n) something that is selected

simile (n) a statement that tells how things are the same

L WRITING STORIES

Write a story about this picture of Olivia. Your story should tell what happened **before** the picture, what happened **in** the picture, and what happened **after** the picture.

accident	rear bumper	inspect	repair	costly

_____

_____

_____

_____

_____

_____

_____

_____

_____

_____

244 *Lesson 49*

A SENTENCE COMBINATIONS

Combine the sentences with **however.**

1. She ate a big lunch.
   She still felt hungry.

   _____

   _____

   _____

2. Mike went to the store.
   Mike didn't buy anything.

   _____

   _____

   _____

3. Pat has a broken femur.
   Pat can walk fast.

   _____

   _____

   _____

4. That woman makes many criticisms.
   That woman is very kind.

   _____

   _____

   _____

   _____

B CONTRADICTIONS

Underline the contradiction. Circle the statement it contradicts. Then tell **why** the underlined statement contradicts the circled statement. Make the underlined statement true.

The Popper Company was a large toaster manufacturer. Most of the people in Popsville worked for the Popper Company. Joyce worked for the advertising department, and she liked her job. Every day, she participated in basketball games at the factory. * Besides taking part in basketball games, Joyce predicted what kinds of toasters people wanted. The Popper Company always tried to make people want fewer toasters than it could make. Joyce was very good at writing ads for the toasters.

   _____

   _____

   _____

   _____

C SIMILES

Make up a simile for each item.

1. Her skin was tough and wrinkled.

_____

_____

2. His eyes were very bright.

_____

_____

D INFERENCE

Use the facts to fill out the form.

Facts: Your name is Otis Buckley. You have never had a job. You live with your parents. Your address is 122 Oakway, Charlotte, North Carolina. You graduated from high school last year. You had a C average in school. Your favorite class was art. Your art teacher, Mr. Collins, thought you were very talented. You are applying for a job as a window decorator in a department store.

A. Print your name on line 2.

B. Print the name of your current employer on line 3.

C. On line 1, write the highest grade you have completed in school.

D. Print your full address on line 5.

E. On line 4, list any experience you have had in this position, or reasons why you feel qualified for this position.

F. On line 6, give the name of a person who could recommend you for this position.

G. Cross out the second sentence that gives information you didn't use.

1. _____

2. _____

3. _____

4. _____

5. _____

_____

_____

6. _____

E EDITING

Cross out the wrong word and write the correct word above it. (4)

My dog is a bulldog. Many people is afraid of bulldogs, but my dog is a very nice dog. We goes walking every day in the park. I keep him in the backyard, but sometimes he get loose. If you ever see a bulldog with a green collar, that's my dog. Her name is Sam.

F DEFINITIONS

Write a word that comes from **erode** in each blank. Then write **verb, noun,** or **adjective** after each item.

1. The earth loses a lot of productive land

   through _____.

   _____

2. We can't afford to let good cropland be

   _____.

   _____

3. Wind and water are _____

   forces. _____

4. Rain can swell rivers and

   _____ their banks.

   _____

5. Wind can _____ land in

   hot dry weather. _____

G EDITING

Underline the redundant sentences.

Jeff looked at the catcher's mitt, waiting for the signal. The batter looked like she could really hit, and Jeff was worried. The catcher signaled a fastball. Jeff got ready to throw. He was a pitcher, and he was playing a game. He threw the ball fast. The batter seemed to have the strength to really whack the ball. She swung hard, but the ball whizzed by her. Jeff had thrown a strike. The crowd cheered.

H WRITING DIRECTIONS

Write the instructions.

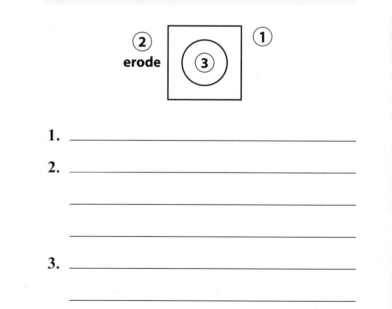

1. _____

2. _____

   _____

   _____

3. _____

   _____

I SENTENCE ANALYSIS

Rewrite the passage in six sentences.

> North and South America have many baseball teams. People on both continents love to go to baseball games, particularly on the weekends. Baseball will always have fans because it is so much fun to watch.

A SENTENCE COMBINATIONS

Combine the sentences with **however.**

1. He likes participatory sports.
   He doesn't like basketball.

   _____

   _____

2. Ted was very happy.
   Ted was frowning.

   _____

   _____

3. Smoking is bad for people's lungs.
   Many people are still smoking.

   _____

   _____

4. She is very productive.
   She has always been lazy.

   _____

   _____

B ECONOMICS RULES

Answer the questions.

1. What's the rule about products that are readier to use?

   _____

   _____

2. Which is readier to use, a cake or a cake mix?

   _____

3. So what else do you know about a cake?

   _____

4. How do you know?

   _____

5. Which costs more, a bike that's put together or a bike that comes in parts?

   _____

6. How do you know?

   _____

> Mr. Marek gets chicken in a restaurant.
> Mr. Montini gets raw chicken in a store and then spends an hour cooking it.

7. Whose chicken costs more?

   _____

8. How do you know?

   _____

C SIMILES

Complete the items about the words in the box.

man	gorilla

1. Tell how the objects could be the same.

   _____

   _____

2. Write a simile about the objects.

   _____

   _____

D CONTRADICTIONS

Underline the contradiction and circle the statement it contradicts. Then tell **why** the underlined statement contradicts the circled statement. Make the underlined statement true.

Before Nelly opened her new dress shop, she put an ad in the paper. Customers filled the shop soon after it opened. They wanted more dresses than Nelly had. * Nelly was very happy. She lowered her prices. Then she called the paper and told them to run the ad for another week.

_____

_____

_____

E DEFINITIONS

Write a word that comes from **produce** or **circulate** in each blank. Then write **verb, noun,** or **adjective** after each item.

1. Smoking may hurt the

   _____ in your legs.

   _____

2. Many things are _____

   by machines. _____

3. Our crop _____went

   down last year. _____

4. She wants to be a more

   _____ writer.

   _____

5. Food sellers often

   _____at ball games.

   _____

F — REWRITING PARAGRAPHS

Rewrite the paragraph in four sentences. If one of the sentences tells **why,** combine them with **because.** If the sentences seem contradictory, combine them with **although.**

Much of the music you hear comes from jazz. Jazz was invented in the United States. Jazz started with slaves. Slaves came from Africa. They led very hard lives. They sang to keep their spirits up. Their first songs were almost all African. Their later songs began to change.

G — EDITING

Underline the redundant sentences.

Pete dribbled the ball down the court. He looked at the scoreboard. Only three seconds were left. Pete was playing basketball. His team had 75 points, but the other team had 76 points. There was less than one minute to play. Pete's team was behind. Pete shot the ball. It circled the rim twice and finally dropped in. Pete's team started cheering. Pete had made the basket.

H — EDITING

Cross out the wrong word and write the correct word above it. (4)

Many people don't like their jobs, but most firefighters is happy with their work. A firefighter's job is a popular job. Most cities has a long list of people waiting to be firefighters. If you are hired as a firefighter, you must spent several months training for the job. You must run, exercise, and climb ropes and ladders. Firefighters mustn't be very strong, because their work is very hard.

Lesson 51

I INFERENCE

Use the facts to fill out the form.

Facts: Your name is Virgil Johnson. You have lived at 112 Bingham Lane in Salem, Oregon, for three years. Your rent is $900 a month, and your car payments are $400 a month. You were born February 2, 1980. Your first job, which you started in 1998, was with American Title Company. Since 2000, you have worked for Juniper Credit, and you make $3,000 a month. You have no credit cards, and you are divorced. You are filling out a credit application to obtain a stereo.

1. Name, last name first _____

_____

2. Age _____

_____

3. Most recent employer _____

_____

4. How long have you worked there? _____

_____

5. Are you married? _____

6. Monthly income _____

7. Total monthly rent and car payments

_____

8. Full address _____

_____

J FOLLOWING DIRECTIONS

Follow the directions.

1. Draw a vertical line in the box.

2. Draw another vertical line to the right of the first line.

3. Draw a horizontal line from the bottom of the first line to the bottom of the second line.

4. Between the vertical lines, write the word that means **how well something sells.**

K SENTENCE ANALYSIS

Rewrite the passage in six sentences.

> Hard balls and wooden bats were used in other sports before baseball. Americans, who love sports, invented a game that made use of hard balls and wooden bats in the 1840s. Although the game was complex, it was soon being played by many people.

_____

_____

_____

_____

_____

_____

_____

_____

_____

_____

_____

_____

_____

_____

L WRITING STORIES

Write a story about this picture of Ethan. Your story should tell what happened **before** the picture, what happened **in** the picture, and what happened **after** the picture.

| fire fighter | helmet | hose | smoke | flames | danger |

_____

_____

_____

_____

_____

_____

_____

_____

_____

_____

_____

_____

_____

_____

_____

_____

_____

_____

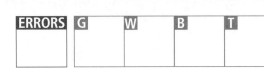

A ECONOMICS RULES

Answer the questions.

1. What's the rule about products that are readier to use?

_____

_____

_____

2. Which is readier to use, a ready-made skirt or material and a pattern?

_____

3. So what else do you know about a ready-made skirt?

_____

4. How do you know?

_____

_____

5. Which costs more, a model that you have to put together or a model that is already put together?

_____

_____

6. How do you know?

_____

_____

Ms. Anderson obtains five pounds of frozen chicken.
Ms. Miller obtains five pounds of cooked chicken.

7. Whose chicken cost more?

_____

8. How do you know?

_____

_____

B SENTENCE COMBINATIONS

Combine the sentences with **however.**

1. The man modified his car.
His car still did not run.

_____

_____

_____

2. Vern hurt his quadriceps.
Vern won the race.

_____

_____

_____

3. They had a big supply of tennis shoes.
They ran out.

_____

_____

_____

4. She concluded her speech.
She kept on talking.

_____

_____

C EDITING

Underline the redundant sentences. Circle and correct the punctuation errors.

A bell rang. Sam put on his firefighter's hat and his firefighter's coat, He jumped on the fire truck as it roared out of the station. Sam was a firefighter. The truck sped down Oak Street and screeched around, the corner of Oak and First. The truck was going sixty miles an hour however it could have gone a lot faster. The truck was speeding along. The truck screamed to a stop at First and Elm. Sam jumped off to look for a fire hydrant which wasn't easy. The fire was at First and Elm.

D PARTS OF SPEECH

Underline the nouns. Draw **one** line **over** the adjectives. Draw **two** lines **over** the articles. Circle the verbs

1. Wind and water were eroding the mountain.

2. That stream has eroded its banks.

3. A large black goat was under a tree.

4. Erosion changes everything on the planet.

E BODY RULES

Draw in the arrows. Write **vein** or **artery** in each blank. Also write **oxygen** or **carbon dioxide** in each blank.

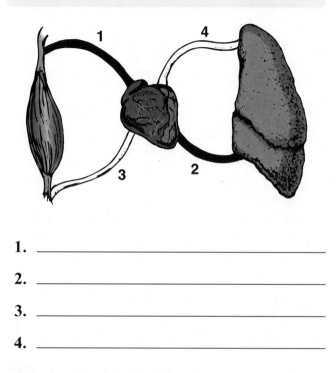

1. _____

2. _____

3. _____

4. _____

F DEFINITIONS

Write a word that comes from **obtain** or **respire** in each blank. Then write **verb, noun,** or **adjective** after each item.

1. She is trying to _____

   new tires. _____

2. After you run, your _____

   is much faster. _____

3. Your bronchial tubes are in your

   _____system.

   _____

4. That country is _____

   new jets. _____

5. You should _____

   slowly if you feel dizzy. _____

G INFERENCE

Read the passage and answer the questions.
- Circle the **W** if the question is answered by words in the passage. Then underline those words.
- Circle the **D** if the question is answered by a deduction.

You know that: **When the demand is less than the supply, prices go down.**

Ms. Thomas runs the only dairy farm near Newton. In July, her cows produce just as much milk as Newton needs, which is 1,000 gallons a month. In August, a big group of people moves out of Newton, and Newton's demand for milk drops to 600 gallons a month. But Ms. Thomas's cows are still producing 1,000 gallons a month.

Ms. Thomas sells 600 gallons at the old price, and then she is stuck with 400 gallons that will soon go bad. She thinks she can get people to buy the 400 gallons if she lowers the price. Her idea works, and she sells all 400 gallons at the lower price.

1. What rule about demand and supply is this passage about?

   _____

   _____

   _____

2. What would have happened to the price of milk if a big group of people had moved into Newton in July?

   _____

   _____ **W D**

3. Was the demand smaller than the supply in August because the demand went down or because the supply went up?

   _____

   _____

4. What did Ms. Thomas do to get people to buy the 400 gallons she had left over?

   _____

   _____ **W D**

5. What will Ms. Thomas have to do to the demand for milk to sell 1,000 gallons at the old price in September?

   _____

   _____ **W D**

6. Name one way she could do that.

   _____

   _____

7. Did Ms. Thomas lose money in August?

   _____ **W D**

H SENTENCE ANALYSIS

Rewrite the passage in six sentences.

> Many great players played for the Los Angeles Dodgers, particularly in the 1960s. One very famous player was Sandy Koufax, who was an amazing pitcher. His style and speed are copied by many pitchers today.

_____

_____

_____

_____

_____

_____

_____

_____

_____

_____

_____

I REWRITING PARAGRAPHS

Rewrite the paragraph in four sentences. If one of the sentences tells **why,** combine the sentences with **because.** If two sentences seem contradictory, combine them with **although.**

> The slaves sang many kinds of songs. The slaves sang mostly work songs and hymns. Most of their music was sung. Some of their music was played on instruments. The music started changing after 1865. 1865 was when the slaves were freed. Sometimes, former slaves played music at dances. Dances were held everywhere.

_____

_____

_____

_____

_____

_____

_____

_____

_____

_____

_____

_____

J SIMILES

Complete the items about the words
in the boxes.

voice   gravel

1. Tell how the objects could be the same.

_____

_____

2. Write a simile about the objects.

_____

_____

lips   cherries

3. Tell how the objects could be the same.

_____

_____

4. Write a simile about the objects.

_____

_____

K FOLLOWING DIRECTIONS

Follow the directions.

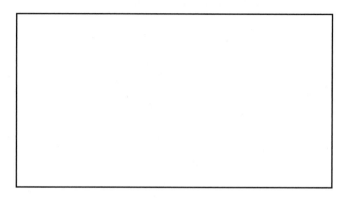

1. Draw a horizontal line in the box.

2. Draw a line that slants down to the right
from the right end of the horizontal line.

3. At the bottom of the slanted line, draw an
arrow that points to the left.

4. Draw the muscle that will move the
slanted line in the direction of the arrow.

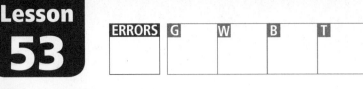
A EDITING

Underline the redundant sentences.
Circle and correct the punctuation errors.

Mr. Alper had a problem. He had ordered a big, supply of sandals in August. Now it was October, and nobody was buying sandals. Mr. Alper started advertising his sandals, but nobody bought them. Advertising didn't work. So Mr. Alper decided to have a big sale. He put a sign on his door; that said, "Two pairs of sandals for the price of one." His store started to fill with customers. Customers were all over his store. Although he sold many sandals he still had some left after the sale.

B ECONOMICS RULES

Answer the questions.

1. What's the rule about products that are readier to use?

_____

_____

_____

2. Which is readier to use, a car that needs repairs or a car that runs perfectly?

_____

_____

3. So what else do you know about that car?

_____

4. How do you know?

_____

_____

> Frozen fish costs less than cooked fish.

5. Which is readier to use when you obtain it?

_____

6. How do you know?

_____

_____

> Andrew and Mike shop at the same store. On Thursday, they both have meat pie for dinner. Andrew's pie costs 50 cents. Mike's pie costs $2.

7. Whose dinner was readier to eat when he obtained it?

_____

8. Who spent more time fixing dinner?

_____

C SENTENCE COMBINATIONS

Circle the word that combines the sentences correctly. Combine the sentences with that word.

1. Those striking workers are circulating leaflets.
   Those striking workers are giving speeches.
   however   **which**   **and**

   _____

   _____

   _____

2. Mary is always late.
   Mary will lose her job.
   however   **particularly**   **because**

   _____

   _____

   _____

3. That person is lazy.
   That person is productive.
   who   **but**   **because**

   _____

   _____

   _____

4. The monkey is consuming carrots.
   A gorilla is consuming carrots.
   and   **however**   **because**

   _____

   _____

   _____

5. The man manufactured spoons.
   Spoons were in low demand.
   because   **however**   **which**

   _____

   _____

   _____

D ANALOGIES

Write what each analogy tells.

- what part of speech each word is
- what verb each word comes from
- what each word means
- what ending each word has

1. **Erosion** is to **ion** as
   respiratory is to **ory.**

   _____

   _____

2. **Erosion** is to **noun** as
   respiratory is to **adjective.**

   _____

   _____

3. **Erosion** is to **erode** as
   respiratory is to **respire.**

   _____

   _____

Lesson 53

E **INFERENCE**

Read the passage and answer the questions.
- Circle the **W** if the question is answered by words in the passage. Then underline those words.
- Circle the **D** if the question is answered by a deduction.

You know that **when the demand is less than the supply, prices go down.**

Mr. Hightower runs the only chicken farm near Newton. In September, his chickens produce just as many eggs as Newton needs, which is 1,000 dozen a month. Mr. Hightower sells the eggs for $2 a dozen, so he makes $2,000 that month.

The people of Newton think that $2 a dozen is too much to pay for eggs. In October, they all get together and decide not to buy eggs from Mr. Hightower. This action is called a **boycott.**

Mr. Hightower, whose chickens are still producing eggs, is stuck with 1,000 dozen eggs that will soon go bad. The only way he can make any money in October is to lower the price of eggs and hope that people will like the new price. So he lowers the price to $1 a dozen. The people of Newton like this new price, and they buy all the eggs.

1. What rule about demand and supply is this passage about?

_____

_____

2. Why did people in Newton decide not to buy eggs in October?

_____

_____

3. Why was Mr. Hightower stuck with 1,000 dozen eggs?

_____

_____

_____ **W** **D**

4. In October, was the demand smaller than the supply because the demand went down or because the supply went up?

_____

_____

_____ **W** **D**

5. Why did Mr. Hightower lower the price?

_____

_____

6. How much did Mr. Hightower make in October?

_____

7. What does a boycott do to the demand?

_____

_____ **W** **D**

F BODY SYSTEMS

Fill in each blank.

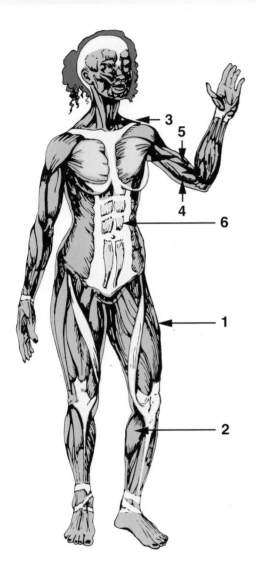

1. _____

2. _____

3. _____

4. _____

5. _____

6. _____

G SUBJECT/PREDICATE

Circle the subject and underline the predicate. Rewrite each sentence by moving part of the predicate.

1. Hank played tennis while the sun was out.

   _____

   _____

2. The weather was very dry last winter.

   _____

   _____

3. Many people ride bikes in China.

   _____

   _____

4. You should have a license to drive a car.

   _____

   _____

H **ECONOMICS RULES**

Answer the questions.

1. What's the rule about when the demand is greater than the supply?

_____

_____

_____

> After a mild winter, the demand for lemons is less than the supply of lemons.

2. What will happen to the price of lemons?

_____

3. How do you know?

_____

_____

_____

4. What will the farmers try to do?

_____

_____

_____

> Name two ways that the farmers can do that.

5. _____

_____

6. _____

_____

> After a bad winter, the demand for lemons is greater than the supply of lemons.

7. What will happen to the price of lemons?

_____

_____

8. How do you know?

_____

_____

> Last winter, lemons cost 89 cents a pound. This winter, lemons cost 39 cents a pound.

9. What happened to the price of lemons?

_____

10. Which was greater, the supply or the demand?

_____

I SENTENCE ANALYSIS

Rewrite the passage in six sentences.

> Babe Ruth could really hit the ball; however, he could not run very fast. For many years, he held the home-run record and the total hit record. His hat and glove are kept in the Baseball Hall of Fame.

_____

_____

_____

_____

_____

_____

_____

_____

_____

_____

J EVIDENCE

Write **R** for each fact that is **relevant** to what happened. Write **I** for each fact that is **irrelevant** to what happened.

> Ms. Nelson buys raw meat because it costs less than cooked meat.

1. Ms. Nelson wants to save money. _____

2. Ms. Nelson goes shopping on

   Saturdays. _____

3. Ms. Nelson can speak Spanish. _____

4. Ms. Nelson doesn't have much

   money. _____

K WRITING STORIES

Write a story about this picture of Miguel, who's waiting to ski, and his friend Sanjay, who's already skiing. Your story should tell what happened **before** the picture, what happened **in** the picture, and what happened **after** the picture.

skiing	steep	nobody	scared	snow

_____

_____

_____

_____

_____

_____

_____

_____

_____

_____

266 *Lesson 53*

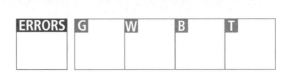

A ECONOMICS RULES

Answer the questions.

1. What's the rule about products that are readier to use?

   _____

   _____

   _____

2. Which is readier to use, a balloon with air in it or a balloon without any air in it?

   _____

3. So what else do you know about that balloon?

   _____

4. How do you know?

   _____

   _____

5. Bob acquires a model plane and spends two months putting it together. Tom obtains a model plane at the store and plays with it that night. Whose model plane cost more?

   _____

6. How do you know?

   _____

   _____

7. If you want to save money, is it better to buy cooked meat or raw meat?

   _____

8. If you want to save time, is it better to buy cooked meat or raw meat?

   _____

B INFERENCE

Put the statements below the story in the right order.

> Before Bill made a kite, he got a book on kite building and studied it for a long time. The first kite Bill constructed was a Chinese snake kite. It had a tail that was ten meters long. The tail got tangled up in a tree, and Bill lost the kite. So he made a box kite. It was the highest-flying kite he made. It went up over two thousand feet. Sadly, the string broke and Bill never found the kite. The last kite Bill made was a diving kite. He could make it dive by letting the string go slack. To pull the kite out of a dive, Bill pulled hard on the string.

He made a kite that went very high. _____

He made a snake kite. _____

He made a diving kite. _____

He got a book. _____

A kite got stuck in a tree. _____

He studied a book. _____

Lesson 54

C DEFINITIONS

Write a word that comes from **acquire** in each blank. Then write **verb, noun,** or **adjective** after each item.

1. Art collectors are _____.

    _____

2. He _____ some tools to

    construct a shed. _____

3. Rosa is _____ a lot of

    money. _____

4. His coat is an expensive

    _____.

    _____

5. Many rich people are very

    _____.

    _____

D ANALOGIES

Complete the analogies.

1. **Tell what part of speech each word is.**

    Participatory is to _____

    as **circulation** is to _____.

2. **Tell what verb each word comes from.**

    Participatory is to _____

    as **circulatory** is to _____.

3. **Tell what each word means.**

    Participatory is to _____

    _____

    _____

    as **circulation** is to _____

    _____.

E BODY RULES

Draw the arrow for each nerve.
Write a message for each nerve.

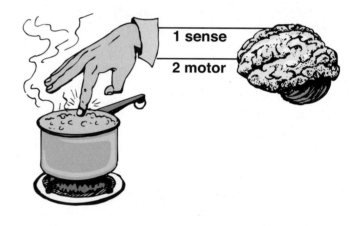

1. _____

2. _____

268   *Lesson 54*

F ECONOMICS RULES

Answer the questions.

1. What's the rule about what manufacturers try to do?

   _____

   _____

   _____

> Mike's Dairy produces 100 pounds of butter a week. Mike's Dairy sells 70 pounds of butter a week.

2. Which is greater, the supply or the demand?

   _____

3. What will happen to the price of butter?

   _____

4. How do you know?

   _____

   _____

   _____

5. What will Mike's Dairy try to do?

   _____

   _____

   _____

> Name two ways that Mike's Dairy can do that.

6. _____

   _____

7. _____

   _____

> Last week, the price of cheese at Mike's Dairy went down.

8. Which was greater, the supply or the demand?

   _____

   _____

9. How do you know?

   _____

   _____

10. Today, the price of milk at Mike's Dairy went up. Which was greater, the supply or the demand?

    _____

G CONTRADICTIONS

Make each statement mean the same thing as the statement in the box.

> Ron was very shy; however, he always participated in class.

1. Although Ron was very shy, he never took part in class.

2. Ron always took part in class, but he was very shy.

3. Ron was very shy, but he never took part in class.

4. Ron, who was very shy, always participated in class.

H DEDUCTIONS

Write the conclusion of each deduction.

1. Some rock comes from volcanoes.
Granite is rock.

_____

_____

2. Burning things produce carbon dioxide.
Fires are burning things.

_____

_____

3. All oceans are made up of salt water.
The Pacific is an ocean.

_____

_____

I SENTENCE COMBINATIONS

Circle the word that combines the sentences correctly. Combine the sentences with that word.

1. The femurs support the pelvis.
The femurs are the longest bones in the body.

who   **which**   **because**

_____

_____

2. That woman has swum across the lake.
Her children have swum across the lake.

although   **and**   **because**

_____

_____

3. Her older brother modifies cars.
My dad modifies cars.

who   **although**   **and**

_____

_____

4. Wind was eroding the mountain.
Rain was eroding the mountain.

which   **however**   **and**

_____

_____

5. The fat cat is hungry.
The fat cat won't eat.

because   **however**   **particularly**

_____

_____

J SENTENCE ANALYSIS

Rewrite the passage in six sentences.

> Hank Aaron, who played for the Atlanta Braves, broke Babe Ruth's home-run record in 1974. Aaron's record looks unbeatable; however, it will probably be broken some day. Batting and pitching records are always falling.

_____

_____

_____

_____

_____

_____

_____

_____

_____

_____

_____

_____

_____

_____

_____

K EDITING

Underline the redundant sentences.
Circle and correct the punctuation errors.

Sally got hit with a baseball, bat in her arm. Her humerus was cracked. When she was injured, the bone in her upper arm was broken. Sally went to a doctor The doctor told Sally that she would have to wear a cast however Sally did not want to wear one. The doctor told Sally that she had no choice. There was nothing else that Sally could do. So the doctor put the cast on Sally's arm, It was so heavy that Sally needed a sling around her neck to hold it up

WORD LIST

constructive (a) that something is helpful
consume (v) to use up or eat
erode (v) to wear things down
erosion (n) what happens when something is eroded
erosive (a) that something erodes
examine (v) to look at
heart (n) the pump that moves the blood
modification (n) a change
nerve (n) a wire in the body that carries messages
obtain (v) to get
participate (v) to take part in something
predictable (a) that something is easy to predict
spinal cord (n) the body part that connects the brain to all parts of the body

Lesson 55

A INFERENCE

Put the statements below the story in the right order.

> Susan got up early in the morning on Saturday and washed her hair. She made coffee and woke up her roommate. "Get up," she said. "It's a sunny day!" Her roommate got up and they drank coffee together. Then Susan's roommate went off to play tennis. Susan dried her hair in the sun and pulled weeds from her garden. Then she went into the house and watered her plants. "I need to obtain new pots for some of these plants," Susan said to herself. So she went to the store. When Susan came home again, her roommate was back from tennis. They made a big salad and ate it outside in the warm sun.

She said, "It's a sunny day!" _____

She watered her plants. _____

She woke up early in the morning. _____

Her roommate went off to play tennis. _____

She dried her hair. _____

She went to the store. _____

B WRITING DIRECTIONS

Write the instructions.

_____ ① _____
③ acquisition

_____ _____
②

1. _____

_____

_____

2. _____

_____

_____

3. _____

_____

_____

C REWRITING PARAGRAPHS

Rewrite the paragraph in four sentences. If one of the sentences tells **why,** combine the sentences with **because.** If two sentences seem contradictory, combine them with **however.** Move part of the predicate in sentences that you don't combine.

Many black jazz musicians started getting famous around 1900. Scott Joplin became very popular for his style of jazz piano. His style of jazz piano was called ragtime. Joplin did not live very long. Joplin wrote many songs. Ragtime piano was played all over the country in only a few years.

_____

_____

_____

_____

_____

_____

_____

_____

_____

_____

_____

_____

D EDITING

Underline the redundant sentences. Circle and correct the punctuation errors.

Gog who was a huge ape was picking his teeth with a pine tree. He had just eaten two million bananas, and bits of banana peel had worked their way between Gog's dainty molars. Gog who was the only ape of his kind in the world had very bad teeth. Gog did not want to go to the dentist; however his teeth felt terrible. There were no other apes like Gog. Gog knew that his dentist, Dr. Painless, would scold Gog for not brushing his teeth more Gog slowly lumbered off to see Dr. Painless. The doctor was going to be mad at Gog. Gog became so afraid that he started to shake, setting off five earthquakes and a tidal wave.

E ECONOMIC RULES

Answer the questions.

1. What's the rule about products that are readier to use?

_____

_____

_____

2. Which costs more, a table that is ready to use or a table that comes in parts?

_____

_____

3. How do you know?

_____

_____

Linda and Sally are wearing the same kind of dress. Linda's was already made when she acquired it. Sally made her dress herself.

---

4. Whose dress cost more?

_____

5. How do you know?

_____

_____

Tom and Rob shop at the same store. On Friday, they both have a glass of lemonade. Tom's lemonade cost him 10 cents. Rob's lemonade cost him 20 cents.

---

6. Whose lemonade was readier to drink when he acquired it?

_____

7. How do you know?

_____

_____

8. Who spent less time fixing his lemonade?

_____

F EDITING

Cross out the wrong word and write the correct word above it. (5)

Mr. Casolini owned a grocery store. Last Thanksgiving, he have a big demand for turkeys. People was in the grocery store all day long, buying turkeys. Mr. Casolini were busy all day. When she went home, Mr. Casolini soaked his feet for two hours. His feet hurts from working all day.

G DEFINITIONS

Write a word that comes from **acquire** in each blank. Then write **verb, noun,** or **adjective** after each item.

1. Some people are more

   _____ than others.

   _____

2. He _____ a predictable

   hat. _____

3. That boat was a cheap

   _____.

   _____

4. Tom is _____ a bunch of

   flowers for Susan. _____

5. Mr. Chong is very _____.

   _____

H SIMILES

Complete the items about the words
in the box.

| woman   tree |

1. Tell how the objects could be the same.

   _____

   _____

2. Write a simile about the objects.

   _____

   _____

I BODY RULES

Draw in the arrows. Shade in each tube that carries dark blood. Tell what gas each tube carries.

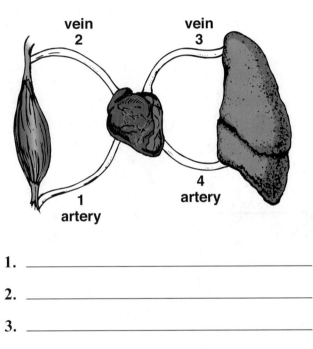

vein 2   vein 3

1 artery   4 artery

1. _____

2. _____

3. _____

4. _____

J WRITING STORIES

Write a story about this picture of Lucia. Your story should tell what happened **before** the picture, what happened **in** the picture, and what happened **after** the picture.

palace	courtyard	statues	travel	waving	handbag

_____

_____

_____

_____

_____

_____

_____

_____

_____

_____

_____

_____

_____

_____

_____

_____

_____

_____

_____

_____

FACT GAME SCORECARD

1	2	3	4	5	6	7	8	9	10	11	12	13	14	15
16	17	18	19	20	21	22	23	24	25	26	27	28	29	30

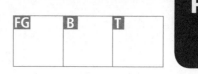

Fact Game

6

2. Complete each sentence with a word that comes from **erode.**

   a. The ocean is ▭ this beach.
   b. Some parts of that mountain have had lots of ▭.

3. Answer the questions.

   a. Which is readier to use, real oatmeal or instant oatmeal?
   b. So which costs more?

4. Name the part of speech for each underlined word.

   a. She did not pay much for that <u>acquisition</u>.
   b. Water and wind are both <u>erosive</u> forces.

5. Combine the sentences in the box with **however.**

> Whales are not fish.
> Whales live in the sea.

6. Make two sentences from the sentence in the box.

> Although she loves to read, she doesn't own any books.

7. Complete the sentence in the box.

> When you buy products in large quantities, you pay ▭ for each unit.

8. Combine the sentences in the box with **especially.**

> She plays basketball.
> She plays the most basketball in the winter.

9. Complete the sentence in the box.

> Products that are readier to use cost ▭.

10. Complete each sentence with a word that comes from **acquire.**

   a. Our team ▭ new hats for the game.
   b. He spends lots of money on ▭.

11. Make two sentences from the sentence in the box.

> Anna made the trip with Yoko, who is her best friend.

12. Answer the questions about the sentences in the box.

> Giant Mart buys 10,000 loaves of bread a day. Mom and Pop Mart buys 100 loaves of bread a day.

   a. Which store buys more loaves of bread?
   b. So which store pays less for each loaf?

Lesson 56

ERRORS | G | W | B | T

A WRITING DIRECTIONS

Write the instructions.

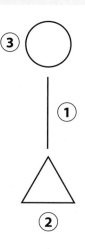

1. _____

2. _____

3. _____

B REWRITING PARAGRAPHS

Rewrite the paragraph in four sentences. If one of the sentences tells **why,** combine the sentences with **because.** If two sentences seem contradictory, combine them with **however.** Move part of the predicate in sentences you don't combine.

Another early jazz musician was William Handy. William Handy played the trumpet. Handy's band played in street parades at first. Later, they toured the country. They mostly toured the South. Handy's band was quite different from John Philip Sousa's band. John Philip Sousa's band was also popular at the time.

C INFERENCE

Put the statements below the passage in the right order.

> Gog the ape is having a hard time cleaning his toenails. Yesterday, he played in his sandbox for a few hours, and little grains of sand stuck to his toenails. Last night, he tried to clean his toenails with a toothbrush, but the brush did not work. This morning, he tried a broom, but the broom fell apart. Right now, he is soaking his feet in water, but nothing is happening. Gog is getting desperate because he wants to look good for his date tonight.

A tool fell apart. _____

A tool did not work. _____

An ape began to play in sand. _____

An ape got his feet wet. _____

Sand stuck to something. _____

An ape used a sweeping tool. _____

D EDITING

Cross out the wrong word and write the correct word above it. (5)

Bob likes to play tennis. Him has a good tennis racket. He have good tennis shoes. Bob has everything he needs to play tennis, but Bob can't hit the ball. Him practice every day, but he never wins a game. Sometimes, Bob are sad, but he keeps playing.

E SUBJECT / PREDICATE

Circle the subject and underline the predicate. Rewrite each sentence by moving part of the predicate.

1. The rivers are low because we've had no rain.

   _____

   _____

2. Many people can't see without glasses.

   _____

   _____

3. Janet plays basketball even though she is short.

   _____

   _____

   _____

F ECONOMICS RULES

Answer the questions.

> Mark works all day and goes to school at night. Jim doesn't work at all, and he doesn't go to school.

1. What's the rule about products that are readier to use?

   _____

   _____

   _____

6. Who has more time to work on dinner?

   _____

7. Who probably buys foods that are readier to use?

   _____

8. Who probably spends less on food?

   _____

> Pam and Sarah got apartments that are alike, and that are in the same part of town. Pam's apartment came with a bed, a couch, and some chairs. Sarah's apartment didn't come with anything.

2. Who spends more on rent?

   _____

3. How do you know?

   _____

   _____

   _____

> Sandwiches you make yourself cost less than sandwiches you get in a restaurant.

4. Which kind of sandwich is readier to use when you obtain it?

   _____

   _____

5. How do you know?

   _____

   _____

G EVIDENCE

For each sentence followed by a blank, write the number of the rule that relates to that sentence.

> 1. When the demand is greater than the supply, prices go up.
> 2. Products that are readier to use cost more.

Beth tried to save money at the supermarket. It was winter, and the store was low on fresh tomatoes, so Beth didn't buy tomatoes. _____ She got regular oatmeal rather than instant oatmeal. _____ She almost got oranges, but oranges were not in season and the store had very few. _____ She got raw beans instead of cooked beans. _____ By the time she finished shopping, she had saved so much money that she bought flowers.

H EDITING

Underline the redundant sentences.
Circle and correct the punctuation errors.

When Gog got to Dr. Painless's office, he told the man, about the bits of banana peel. Dr. Painless sighed and took out his tools. Gog became afraid at the sight of the sharp picks and mean-looking drills. Gog began to shake again. The dental tools scared Gog. He shook so hard that the banana peel bits started to come loose. Now it was Dr. Painless's turn to be afraid. Gog's shaking had loosened the bits. Bits were hurtling across the room like rockets. They landed everywhere, especially on the dental tools. The picks and drills got covered with bits of peel Gog said, "Gog not afraid of tools any more. Now tools appeal to Gog."

I DEFINITIONS

Write a word that comes from **reside** or **acquire** in each blank. Then write **verb, noun,** or **adjective** after each item.

1. She needs to _____

   a winter coat. _____

2. Most people prefer to live in

   _____ areas.

   _____

3. The _____ of

   diamonds is a costly hobby.

   _____

4. Jane wants to _____

   in an apartment. _____

5. She is so _____ that

   her home is bursting with objects.

   _____

J SIMILES

Make up a simile for each item.

1. They jump very high.

   _____

   _____

2. His beard was very scratchy.

   _____

   _____

K CONTRADICTIONS

Underline the contradiction and circle the statement it contradicts. Then tell **why** the underlined statement contradicts the circled statement. Make the underlined statement true.

Bob was in a car wreck. Only the nerves that carried messages from his brain to his body were hurt. Bob was very sad. He asked the doctors when he would be well.* The doctors told Bob that he would walk again, but that he might limp. They told him that it would take a year for his sensory nerves to heal. Bob stayed in bed for a year and read books.

_____

_____

_____

_____

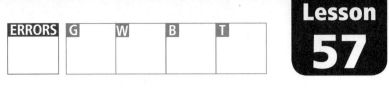

Lesson 57

A INFERENCE

Put the statements below the story in the right order.

> Mrs. Lopez was a cook. One day, she decided to make spaghetti noodles. First she made a dough of eggs and flour. She let the dough sit for two hours, and then she pushed it through a pasta machine. The dough came out in long noodles. Mrs. Lopez let them sit for a long time, until they got hard. While the noodles hardened, she made a sauce of meat and tomatoes. She put many spices in the sauce. When the noodles were hard, Mrs. Lopez put them in boiling water. It took Mrs. Lopez all day to make spaghetti.

She let the dough sit for two hours. _____

She made a meat and tomato sauce. _____

She put the noodles in boiling water. _____

She decided to make spaghetti _____

She put many spices in the sauce. _____

She made a dough. _____

B ECONOMICS RULES

Answer the questions.

1. What's the rule about when you buy products in large quantities?

   _____

   _____

   _____

   _____

> A man buys three pads of paper. A big office buys 5,000 pads of paper.

2. Who buys large quantities of paper?

   _____

3. Who pays less for each pad?

   _____

4. How do you know?

   _____

   _____

   _____

> A big supermarket charges less for pumpkins than a small store.

5. Which store probably pays less for each pumpkin?

   _____

6. So which store probably gets its pumpkins in large quantities?

   _____

> You can buy large quantities of milk from the dairy. You can't buy large quantities of milk from the store.

7. Where could you pay less for each gallon of milk?

_____

8. How do you know?

_____

_____

_____

C   SENTENCE COMBINATIONS

Combine the sentences with **especially.**

1. She worked hard.
She worked hardest in the morning.

_____

_____

_____

2. Days in the desert are hot.
Days in the desert are hottest at noon.

_____

_____

_____

3. Your heart works hard.
Your heart works hardest when you run.

_____

_____

_____

4. The man was mean.
The man was meanest to his dog.

_____

_____

_____

D   EDITING

Underline the redundant sentences.
Circle and correct the punctuation errors.
Cross out and correct the wording errors.

Tom had a sore trapezius from, reading in bed. He read in bed because the light is not good in his living room. Tom's neck hurt. He did some exercises but it still felt stiff. Tom concluded that he have better stop reading in bed. He bought a lamp at the store and he put it in his living room. Tom improved the light in his house.

E WRITING DIRECTIONS

Write the instructions.

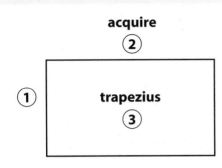

acquire
②

① **trapezius**
③

1. _____

_____

_____

2. _____

_____

_____

3. _____

_____

_____

F SIMILES

Tell **two** ways the things compared are **not** the same. Tell **one** way the things compared **are** the same.

The meat was like leather.

1. _____

_____

2. _____

_____

3. _____

_____

G EVIDENCE

For each sentence followed by a blank, write the number of the rule that relates to that sentence.

1. Products that are readier to use cost more.
2. When the demand is less than the supply, prices go down.

Mr. Bolt manufactured and bottled orange juice. His juice cost a lot more than frozen orange juice. _____ When people started getting low on money, Mr. Bolt's sales dropped. He had to lower his prices. _____ To save money, Mr. Bolt stopped putting real oranges into his juice, and put in just orange flavoring. Mr. Bolt knew that people would still pay more for his juice. _____ And since the juice now cost him less to make, he could still make a lot of money. But people didn't like the way the flavoring tasted. Mr. Bolt's prices dropped again. _____

H DEDUCTIONS

Write the middle part of each deduction.

1. Every plant has roots.

   _____

   So, a coleus has roots.

2. The museum had paintings by some artists.

   _____

   So, maybe the museum had a painting by Turner.

3. The museum did not have any paintings by French artists.

   _____

   So, the museum did not have any paintings by Renoir.

I REWRITING PARAGRAPHS

Rewrite the paragraph in four sentences. If one of the sentences tells **why,** combine the sentences with **because.** If two sentences seem contradictory, combine them with **although.** Move part of the predicate in sentences you don't combine.

New Orleans was the center of jazz for many years. Jazz musicians played everywhere in the city. They played mostly at dances and in bars. Small jazz bands became very popular. Small jazz bands consisted of a trumpet, a clarinet, a bass, a piano, and drums. The most famous band was King Oliver's band. King Oliver's band had a trumpeter named Louis Armstrong.

286 *Lesson 57*

J DEFINITIONS

Write a word that comes from **predict** or acquire in each blank. Then write **verb, noun,** or **adjective** after each item.

1. Hector fell asleep during the

   _____ movie.

   _____

2. That man is _____ that

   food prices will rise even higher.

   _____

3. Last week, the bank

   _____ many stocks.

   _____

4. An _____ art collector

   bought all my paintings.

   _____

5. If a product is popular, you can

   _____ that its price will

   go up. _____

K BODY SYSTEMS

Fill in each blank.

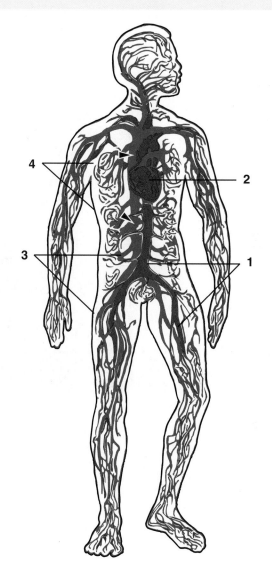

1. _____
2. _____
3. _____
4. _____

L **WRITING STORIES**

Write a story about this picture of Tyrone and Thelma. Your story should tell what happened **before** the picture, what happened **in** the picture, and what happened **after** the picture.

| conversation | braids | clasped hands | couch | consider |

_____

_____

_____

_____

_____

_____

_____

_____

_____

_____

A SENTENCE COMBINATIONS

Combine the sentences with **especially.**

1. Cats walk quietly.
Cats walk the most quietly when they are hunting.

_____

_____

_____

2. Her cheeks are red.
Her cheeks are reddest after she's been outside.

_____

_____

_____

3. Their house is dirty.
Their house is dirtiest after a party.

_____

_____

_____

4. Basketball games are fast.
Basketball games are fastest when the score is tied.

_____

_____

_____

B ECONOMICS RULES

Answer the questions.

1. What's the rule about when you buy products in large quantities?

_____

_____

_____

_____

> A woman buys five pounds of beef. A supermarket buys 5,000 pounds of beef.

2. Who buys large quantities of beef?

_____

3. So who pays less for each pound of beef?

_____

4. How do you know?

_____

_____

Mr. Erving pays $50 for each pair of Rocket tennis shoes he buys. The shoe store pays $25 for each pair of Rocket tennis shoes it buys.

5. Who pays less for each pair of tennis shoes?

_____

6. So who buys tennis shoes in large quantities?

_____

7. How do you know?

_____

_____

Store A buys 50,000 cans of King beans.
Store B buys 500 cans of King beans.

8. Which store pays less for each can of beans?

_____

9. How do you know?

_____

_____

10. Which store could charge less for beans?

_____

C EDITING

Underline the redundant sentences.
Circle and correct the punctuation errors.
Cross out and correct the wording errors.

Blue River flooded because there was a bad rainstorm last night. Water was all over the land. People was riding around their houses in boats. The people got together today and decided to construct a big levee along the river. They will make a big wall next to the river. The levee will cost a lot of money, but they will be worth it

D PARTS OF SPEECH

Underline the nouns. Draw **one** line **over** the adjectives. Draw **two** lines **over** the articles. Circle the verbs.

1. That man has many useless acquisitions.

2. His older brother is acquiring a new car.

3. Acquisitive shoppers circulated in the mall.

4. The long film had a happy ending.

E INFERENCE

Put the statements below the story in the right order.

Rosa and Sue took their vacation in May. They packed their car with clothes and cameras, and then started to drive to Mexico. On the way, they stopped off in Arizona. The sun was very hot, so they went swimming. They bought some silver rings. They ate tacos and hot chili. Then they crossed the Mexican border, and they drove toward the sea. When they found a cozy little hotel beside a sandy beach, they stopped. They stayed at the hotel for a week. They ate good Mexican food and swam in the clear warm water every day.

They ate tacos and hot chili.   _____

They packed their car.   _____

They found a cozy little hotel.   _____

They drove toward the sea.   _____

They crossed the Mexican border.   _____

They stopped off in Arizona.   _____

F SENTENCE ANALYSIS

Rewrite the passage in six sentences.

The largest private residence in the United States is Biltmore House, which is owned by the Vanderbilt family. Although it is an American house, it looks like a French castle. Biltmore House requires a huge staff because it has 250 rooms.

_____

_____

_____

_____

_____

_____

_____

_____

_____

_____

_____

G ECONOMICS RULES

Answer the questions.

1. What's the rule about when the demand is less than the supply?

_____

_____

_____

> Rose's Toy Shop has 10 baseballs. More than 20 people want to buy baseballs.

2. Which is greater, the supply or the demand?

_____

3. What will happen to the price of baseballs?

_____

4. How do you know?

_____

_____

_____

> In May, baseballs cost $6 each. In November, baseballs cost $4 each.

5. What happened to the price of baseballs?

_____

6. Which was greater, the supply or the demand?

_____

7. What will the baseball manufacturers try to do?

_____

_____

_____

> Name two ways that the manufacturers can do that.

8. _____

_____

9. _____

_____

> Last winter, baseballs cost $3 each. This spring, baseballs cost $5 each.

10. What happened to the price of baseballs?

_____

11. Which was greater, the supply or the demand?

_____

H INFERENCE

Use the facts to fill out the form.

> Facts: Your name is Julia Rosen. You are applying for a loan. You rent a house at 288 Alder Street, Dallas, Texas, for $950 a month. You work as a clerk for the Dallas Chemical Company, where you make $2,400 a month. You pay about $150 a month for utilities, $400 a month for car payments, and $50 a month for TV payments.

1. Name _____

2. Full address _____
   _____

3. Check one:
   own house ☐   rent house ☐

4. Employer _____
   _____

5. Position _____

6. Salary _____

7. Total monthly payments _____

8. Subtract line 7 from line 6 _____

I SIMILES

Complete the items about the words in the boxes.

dancer   rubber

1. Tell how the objects could be the same.
   _____
   _____

2. Write a simile about the objects.
   _____
   _____

hair   sunshine

3. Tell how the objects could be the same.
   _____
   _____

4. Write a simile about the objects.
   _____
   _____

Lesson 58

J **WRITING DIRECTIONS**

Write the instructions.

$$\overset{\textbf{2}}{\underset{\textbf{3}}{\text{acquisition}}} \;\Big|\; \textbf{1}$$

1. _____

   _____

   _____

2. _____

   _____

   _____

3. _____

   _____

   _____

A ECONOMICS RULES

Answer the questions.

1. What's the rule about products that are readier to use?

   _____

   _____

   _____

2. What's the rule about when you buy products in large quantities?

   _____

   _____

   _____

> Liquid milk costs more than powdered milk.

3. Which is readier to use when you obtain it?

   _____

4. How do you know?

   _____

   _____

> A grocery store buys larger quantities of canned soup than a person does.

5. Who pays less for canned soup?

   _____

6. How do you know?

   _____

   _____

> Lincoln School pays $3 per case of soup. John's Mart pays $2.50 per case of soup.

7. Who pays less per case of soup?

   _____

8. Who buys larger quantities of soup?

   _____

9. How do you know?

   _____

   _____

Lesson 59

B SENTENCE COMBINATIONS

Combine the sentences with **especially**.

1. Roses smell good.
   Roses smell best after it rains.

   _____

   _____

   _____

2. Mike eats a lot.
   Mike eats the most when he's tired.

   _____

   _____

   _____

3. Her respiration is slow.
   Her respiration is slowest when she sleeps.

   _____

   _____

   _____

4. The air is dry.
   The air is driest in the winter.

   _____

   _____

   _____

C DEFINITIONS

Fill in each blank with the word that has the same meaning as the word or words under the blank.

1. The man was _____ with
   (lucky)
   money.

2. She made many _____
   (smart)
   predictions.

3. The test was full of _____
   (not smart)
   questions.

4. That _____ man hurt his
   (not lucky)
   spinal cord.

5. Jim's father has been

   _____ for two weeks.
   (not employed)

D BODY RULES

Circle each bone that will move. Draw an arrow to show which way it will move.

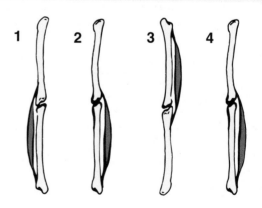

E ECONOMICS RULES

Answer the questions.

1. What's the rule about what manufacturers try to do?

   _____

   _____

   _____

   | The Fast Eat Shop didn't sell any doughnuts last week. |

2. Which was greater, the supply or the demand?

   _____

3. What will happen to the price of doughnuts?

   _____

4. What will the Fast Eat Shop try to do?

   _____

   _____

   _____

   | Name two ways it can do that. |

5. _____

   _____

6. _____

   | The demand for eggs at the Fast Eat Shop is less than the supply of eggs. |

7. What will happen to the price of eggs at the Fast Eat Shop?

   _____

8. How do you know?

   _____

   _____

   _____

   | Today, the price of doughnuts went up at the Fast Eat Shop. |

9. Which is greater, the supply or the demand?

   _____

10. How do you know?

    _____

    _____

F EDITING

Underline the redundant sentences.
Circle and correct the punctuation errors.
Cross out and correct the wording errors.

Cats purr when they are eating. Cats purr when they is sleeping. Cats also purr when people pet them. Cats purr for many reasons. We don't know how cats purr however we do know which cats can purr, and which cats can't. Small cats, such as house cats and bobcats can purr. Big cats, such as lions and leopards, can't purr. Tigers can't purr.

G   SENTENCE ANALYSIS

Rewrite the passage in six sentences.

> Egypt and Mexico have many pyramids. Southern Mexico has beautiful pyramids, particularly near Mexico City. Some of these Mexican pyramids are more than 1,000 years old, but they are much newer than the Egyptian pyramids.

H   CONTRADICTIONS

Underline the contradiction and circle the statement it contradicts. Then tell **why** the underlined statement contradicts the circled statement. Make the underlined statement true.

Clair had just finished high school, and she wanted to make a lot of money. Because so many people rode bikes, she decided to start making bicycle seats. She made 1,000 seats, but nobody wanted them. Clair tried to think up ways to get rid of the seats. * She put ads on television that told how comfortable the seats were. She offered a free pen with every seat. Pretty soon, she had to raise her prices. She started to think that making seats wasn't such a good idea after all.

I FOLLOWING DIRECTIONS

Follow the directions about the sentence in the box.

The _____ is a tube that

goes from the mouth to the stomach.

---

1. Fill in the blank.

2. Circle the word that tells where the tube goes to.

3. Cross out the nouns.

4. Above the first verb, write the name of the body system the sentence tells about.

J INFERENCE

Put the statements below the passage in the right order.

David tried to be a smart shopper. On Saturday, David went shopping. Before he went shopping, David read a consumer report about buying food. When he went shopping, David looked for good deals. He bought grade B eggs because they were cheaper than grade A eggs, but just as good. He acquired a big bag of flour because the big bag cost less per pound. He also bought a big bag of dog food. He obtained raw potatoes because they were cheaper than frozen potatoes. Instead of buying a hot chicken dinner, David bought a chicken he could cook himself. David paid a lot of money for the food he acquired, but he would have paid a lot more if he hadn't been such a smart shopper.

He read a consumer report
   about food.   _____

He looked for good deals.   _____

He obtained grade B eggs.   _____

He bought a chicken to cook.   _____

He paid a lot of money.   _____

K FOLLOWING DIRECTIONS

Follow the directions.

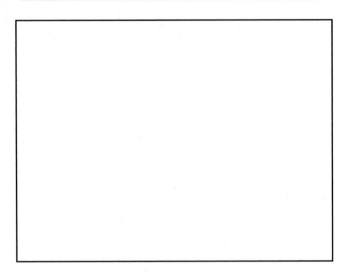

1. Draw a vertical line in the box.

2. Draw another vertical line to the left of the first line.

3. Draw a slanted line from the bottom of the first line to the top of the second line.

4. Above the shape, write the noun that comes from the verb **respire.**

<table>
<tr><td colspan="1" align="center">WORD LIST</td></tr>
</table>

WORD LIST

acquire (v) to get

acquisition (n) something you acquire

acquisitive (a) that something likes to acquire things

conclusion (n) the end or something that is concluded

criticism (n) a statement that criticizes

demand (n) how well something sells

digest (v) to change food into fuel for the body

erode (v) to wear things down

explanatory (a) that something explains

manufactured (a) that something has been made in a factory

motor nerve (n) a nerve that lets you move

production (n) something that is produced

sensory nerve (n) a nerve that lets you feel

supply (n) how much there is of something

L WRITING STORIES

Write a story about this picture of Kyle the writer. Your story should tell what happened **before** the picture, what happened **in** the picture, and what happened **after** the picture.

writer	computer	novel	characters	plot	setting

_____

_____

_____

_____

_____

_____

_____

_____

_____

_____

_____

_____

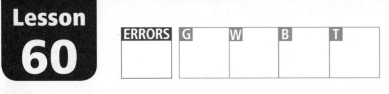

A ECONOMICS RULES

Answer the questions.

1. What's the rule about buying products in large quantities?

   _____

   _____

   _____

2. What's the rule about products that are readier to use?

   _____

   _____

   _____

> St. Mary's Hospital pays less per head of lettuce than Dr. Green does.

3. Who buys larger quantities of lettuce?

   _____

   _____

4. How do you know?

   _____

   _____

> Goode Muffins are ready to eat immediately. Great Muffins are ready to eat in half an hour.

5. Which muffins are readier to use?

   _____

6. Which muffins cost more?

   _____

7. If you want to save money, which muffins are better to buy?

   _____

8. If you want to save time, which muffins are better to buy?

   _____

> Fran's Cafe buys 50 pounds of chicken each week. Mick's Diner buys 500 pounds of chicken each week.

9. Who buys larger quantities of chicken?

   _____

10. Who pays less for each pound of chicken?

   _____

B DEFINITIONS

Fill in each blank with the word that has the same meaning as the word or words under the blank.

1. Susan was _____ for the
   (not prepared)
   pop quiz.

2. Jim concluded that Bob's story was

   _____.
           (not believable)

3. She is too

   _____ to eat.
      (not happy)

4. We were

   _____ to acquire this
          (lucky)
   car.

5. Dick made an _____
                    (not smart)
   selection.

C REWRITING PARAGRAPHS

Rewrite the paragraph in four sentences. If one of the sentences tells **why,** combine the sentences with **because.** If two sentences seem contradictory, combine them with **but.** Move part of the predicate in sentences that you don't combine.

Louis Armstrong came to Chicago in the 1920s. He started his own band. He began to make recordings. Louis Armstrong's recordings were probably the most important jazz recordings ever made. Louis Armstrong's recordings inspired jazz musicians all over the country. Pretty soon, jazz bands were formed everywhere. Most jazz bands were formed in Chicago and New York.

_____

_____

_____

_____

_____

_____

_____

_____

_____

_____

_____

_____

_____

_____

D EDITING

Underline the redundant sentences.
Circle and correct the punctuation errors.
Cross out and correct the wording errors.

Most people likes to play sports. Some people don't. Men that lived thousands of years ago had footraces. They had games, to see who could throw a spear the farthest. They had games to see who could run the fastest. Today, we play basketball football and many other games. People played sports thousands of years ago. People will still be playing and watching sports years from now. There will be sports fans in the future.

E SENTENCE COMBINATIONS

Circle the word that combines the sentences correctly. Combine the sentences with that word.

1. Hector acquired a car.
    Hector still rides his bike.
    which   because   but

    _____

    _____

    _____

2. That book was predictable.
    That book was most predictable near the end.
    especially   however   because

    _____

    _____

    _____

3. Tom was going to the party.
    His friend Pam was going to the party.
    especially   and   which

    _____

    _____

    _____

4. The doctor examined Berta's leg.
    The doctor did not look at her femur.
    which   although   particularly

    _____

    _____

    _____

    _____

5. That young girl participates in many sports.
    Her brother participates in many sports.
    who   and   although

    _____

    _____

    _____

F ANALOGIES

Complete the analogies.

1. **Tell a part each object has.**

   A car is to

   _____

   as a television is to

   _____ .

2. **Tell what each object runs on.**

   A car is to _____ as

   a television is to

   _____ .

3. **Tell what class each object is in.**

   A car is to _____ as

   a television is to

   _____ .

G FOLLOWING DIRECTIONS

Follow the directions.

1. Draw a vertical line in the box.

2. Draw a line that slants down to the right from the bottom of the vertical line.

3. Draw a muscle that covers the right side of the vertical line and attaches to the right side of the slanted line.

4. Draw an arrow that shows which way the muscle will move the slanted line.

H INFERENCE

Put the statements below the story in the right order.

> Marta was studying to be a doctor. In her first year of medical school, she learned all about the skeletal system. At the end of the year, Marta was tested on what she had learned. She had to name every bone in the skeleton. Marta named every bone except the upper leg bone, which she couldn't remember. She passed the test anyway, and she began studying the muscular system.
>
> In a few months, Marta could name every muscle and tell which bone each muscle was attached to. Marta studied all the time, and she only went to the movies once a month. Marta knew that she would have to study hard six days a week for the next three years.

She did not fail the test. _____

She could name every part of the muscular system. _____

She couldn't remember what the femur was called. _____

She was tested on the skeletal system. _____

She learned all about the system of bones. _____

She began studying the system of muscles. _____

I CONTRADICTIONS

Tell which fact each statement relates to. Make each contradiction true.

> A. Canned carrots are readier to use than raw carrots.
> B. When you buy carrots in large quantities, you pay less for each unit.

1. She bought raw carrots to save time. _____

2. She bought cases of carrots to save money. _____

3. She bought a can of carrots to save time. _____

A EVIDENCE

Write **R** for each fact that is **relevant** to what happened. Write **I** for each fact that is **irrelevant** to what happened.

Sam bought a big jar of peanut butter.

1. Big jars of peanut butter cost less per pound than little jars of peanut butter. _____

2. Sam has black hair. _____

3. Sam eats a lot of peanut butter. _____

4. There was a sale on peanut butter at the store. _____

5. Sam likes to make meatballs. _____

B ECONOMIC RULES

Answer the questions.

1. What's the rule about products that are readier to use?

_____
_____
_____

2. What's the rule about buying products in large quantities?

_____
_____
_____
_____

The Sport House buys larger quantities of Zip skis than the Winter Shop.

3. Who pays less for Zip skis?

_____

4. Who probably sells Zip skis at a lower price?

_____

John's Sporting Goods pays $50 for each pair of Zip skis. The Sport House pays $40 for each pair of Zip skis.

5. Who pays less for each pair of Zip skis?

_____

6. Who buys Zip skis in larger quantities?

_____

7. How do you know?

_____

Sue and John shop at the same store. Last night, they both had roasted chicken for dinner. Sue's dinner cost $7. John's dinner cost $3.

8. Whose dinner cost more?

_____

9. Whose dinner was readier to eat when it was obtained?

_____

10. Who spent more time fixing dinner?

_____

Lesson 61

C DEDUCTIONS

Write the conclusion of each deduction.

1. Some rock is made of sand.
   Marble is a rock.

   _____

   _____

2. Plants use carbon dioxide.
   Poison oak is a plant.

   _____

   _____

3. Some bones protect body parts.
   The patella is a bone.

   _____

   _____

D BODY RULES

Label each nerve.
Then write a message for each nerve.

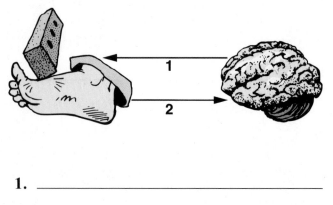

1. _____

2. _____

E FOLLOWING DIRECTIONS

Follow the directions.

1. Draw a box inside the box.

2. Draw a vertical line from the middle of the bottom horizontal line to the middle of the top horizontal line.

3. To the right of the middle line, print the name of the muscle that covers the back of the humerus.

4. To the left of the middle line, print the name of the muscle that covers the front of the humerus.

F INFERENCE

Read the passage and answer the questions.
- Circle the **W** if the question is answered by words in the passage. Then underline those words.
- Circle the **D** if the question is answered by a deduction.

Ms. Jackson runs the only flour mill in Zork City. In October, her mill produces only 1,000 pounds, which is half as much flour as Zork City needs each month. Because the demand is so much greater than the supply, Ms. Jackson charges $1 a pound for her flour.

Mr. Ross thinks he can make money if he starts another flour mill in Zork City that will compete with Ms. Jackson's mill. In November, he puts 1,500 pounds of flour up for sale at 75 cents a pound. Everybody starts buying Mr. Ross's flour. Then Ms. Jackson, who needs to sell her flour, lowers her price to 50 cents a pound. Everybody starts buying Ms. Jackson's flour again.

Each mill keeps lowering the price of flour until the price is as low as it can be. This is called a **price war,** and it always makes consumers very happy.

1. Why can Ms. Jackson charge so much for flour in October?

_____

_____

_____

_____ **W D**

2. Which was greater in November, the supply or the demand?

_____ **W D**

3. Why did Mr. Ross sell his flour for less than Ms. Jackson's flour?

_____

_____ **W D**

4. What did Mr. Ross do after Ms. Jackson lowered her price to 50 cents a pound?

_____

_____

5. Flour prices went down in November because of the price war. Give another reason why they went down.

_____

_____

_____ **W D**

6. If both mills end up charging 40 cents a pound for flour, how can one mill attract more customers?

_____

_____

7. Why might price wars make consumers happy?

_____

_____ **W D**

G EDITING

Underline the redundant sentences.
Circle and correct the punctuation errors.
Cross out and correct the wording errors.

Last summer, everybody in Mudville want a pair of sandals. Mr. Jones ran the only shoe store in town. There was a big demand for sandals. Mr. Jones got, lots of sandals from a manufacturer. No other place in town sold sandals. Mr. Jones made one dollar on each pair of sandals that he selling. One day, Mr. Jones selled ninety pairs of sandals. He made ninety dollars from sandal sales that day.

H REWRITING PARAGRAPHS

Rewrite the paragraph in four sentences. If one of the sentences tells **why,** combine the sentences with **because.** If two sentences seem contradictory, combine them with **however.** Move part of the predicate in sentences that you don't combine.

Thousands of jazz musicians were making recordings and playing concerts by 1930. Most jazz musicians played in big bands. Most jazz musicians also formed small groups. The greatest big-band leader was Duke Ellington. Duke Ellington played the piano. Fletcher Henderson was also good. Count Basie was also good.

_____

_____

_____

_____

_____

_____

_____

_____

_____

_____

_____

_____

_____

_____

I SIMILES

Complete the items about the words in the box.

| eyes | steel |

1. Tell how the objects could be the same.

_____

_____

2. Write a simile about the objects.

_____

_____

J **SENTENCE COMBINATIONS**

Circle the word that combines the sentences correctly. Combine the sentences with that word.

1. Water is erosive.
Wind is erosive.

which   **particularly**   **and**

_____

_____

2. Motor nerves carry messages from the brain.
Motor nerves let you move.

particularly   **which**   **however**

_____

_____

_____

_____

3. The teacher has to write reports.
His principal has to write reports.

especially   **and**   **because**

_____

_____

_____

4. She likes to explain her work.
She likes best to explain her painting.

who   **especially**   **because**

_____

_____

_____

5. Stars look small.
Stars are big.

who   **although**   **because**

_____

_____

K WRITING STORIES

Write a story about this picture of Armando. Your story should tell what happened **before** the picture, what happened **in** the picture, and what happened **after** the picture.

saxophone	practice	sheet music	school band	concert

_____

_____

_____

_____

_____

_____

_____

_____

A EDITING

Underline the redundant sentences.
Circle and correct the punctuation errors.
Cross out and correct the wording errors.

Some peoples read magazines. Some people don't. The store had, many different kinds of magazines John wanted to acquire a magazine, so he go to the store. The store had a wide selection of magazines. John looked, for a magazine about cars. The store had ten different car magazines. John try to decide which one to buy. The store had more than one car magazine. John didn't know which one she wanted.

B DEFINITIONS

Fill in each blank with the word that has the same meaning as the word or words under the blank.

1. Turnips upset his _____.
   (act of digesting)

2. That big old house needs to be

   _____.
   (changed)

3. It is _____ to run on ice.
   (not smart)

4. Susan was _____ for
   (not prepared)
   her camping trip.

5. Bob drew an _____ set
   (not lucky)
   of cards.

C SENTENCE ANALYSIS

Rewrite the passage in six sentences.

The Great Pyramid, which is one of the Seven Wonders of the World, took years to build. Many people died building the pyramid, especially slaves. Gold and jewels were hidden inside the pyramid for many years.

_____

_____

_____

_____

_____

_____

_____

_____

_____

_____

_____

_____

D EVIDENCE

For each sentence followed by a blank, write the number of the rule that relates to that sentence.

> 1. When you buy products in large quantities, you pay less for each unit.
> 2. Products that are readier to use cost more.

Don spends a lot on food. He always gets cooked chicken instead of raw chicken. He only buys a quart of milk at a time. _____ He thinks that if he had more space to store food, he might save money. _____ He thinks that if he had more time to fix dinner, he might save money. _____ Don thinks about saving money a lot, and someday he might do something about it. But until then, he will keep buying TV dinners. _____

E ECONOMICS RULES

Answer the questions.

1. What's the rule about buying products in large quantities?

_____

_____

> Rosa buys 10 loaves of bread a day. Josie buys 100 loaves of bread a day.

2. Who buys larger quantities of bread?

_____

3. Who pays less for each loaf of bread?

_____

4. How do you know?

_____

_____

> Store X charges less for Health Bread than Store Y.

5. Which store probably pays less for Health Bread?

_____

6. Which store probably buys Health Bread in larger quantities?

_____

> Cooked potatoes are readier to use than raw potatoes.

7. Which potatoes cost more?

_____

8. How do you know?

_____

_____

9. If you want to save time, is it better to buy cooked potatoes or raw potatoes?

_____

10. If you want to save money, is it better to buy cooked potatoes or raw potatoes?

_____

F INFERENCE

Read the passage and answer the questions.
- Circle the **W** if the question is answered by words in the passage. Then underline those words.
- Circle the **D** if the question is answered by a deduction.

> Mr. Bock runs the only pen factory in Zork City. Mr. Bock makes his pens cheaply, and they are not very good. But he can still sell them because the demand is so high. However, Ms. Flap starts another pen factory in Zork City. Her pens are better made, and they cost the same as Mr. Bock's. Pretty soon, everybody is buying Ms. Flap's pens.
>
> Mr. Bock begins to make his pens even better than Ms. Flap's. People start buying his pens again. Each factory keeps improving its pens until the pens are of top quality. The people of Zork City are very happy, except for Mr. Bock, who liked the early days better.

1. Why weren't Mr. Bock's pens very good?

_____

_____

2. Why did people in Zork City buy his pens?

_____

_____

3. Why did Ms. Flap make her pens better than Mr. Bock's pens?

_____

_____ W D

4. What might have happened to Mr. Bock if he had kept on making the same old pens?

_____

_____

_____ W D

5. Car manufacturers always compete with each other. Here are some ways that cars have improved because of competition: better gas mileage, more legroom, disk brakes. Name three more.

_____

_____

_____

6. Name another manufactured product that has improved because of competition.

_____

7. How has that product improved?

_____

_____

Lesson 62

G ANALOGIES

Write what each analogy tells.

> - what each object is made of.
> - where you find each object.
> - what makes each object run.
> - what class each object is in.

1. An engine is to gas as a lightbulb is to electricity.

   _____

   _____

2. An engine is to a car as a lightbulb is to a lamp.

   _____

   _____

3. An engine is to metal as a lightbulb is to glass.

   _____

   _____

H SENTENCE COMBINATIONS

Circle the word that combines the sentences correctly. Combine the sentences with that word.

1. Robin resides in a fancy home.
   Robin acquires many expensive things.

   who   but   although

   _____

   _____

   _____

2. People complain about the price of coffee.
   The price of coffee has gone up.

   however   who   because

   _____

   _____

3. Her heart beats fast.
   Her heart beats faster when she runs.

   particularly   although   and

   _____

   _____

4. The heart works all the time.
   The lungs work all the time.

   especially   and   although

   _____

   _____

5. Some regulations protect consumers.
   Consumers still get cheated.

   which   but   particularly

   _____

   _____

I PARTS OF SPEECH

Underline the nouns. Draw **one** line **over** the adjectives. Draw **two** lines **over** the articles. Circle the verbs.

1. That smart shopper is buying grain in large quantities.

2. Her older friend participates in many different activities.

3. Those manufacturers are hiring forty new workers.

4. The river has eroded a cave under this cliff.

J WRITING DIRECTIONS

Write the instructions.

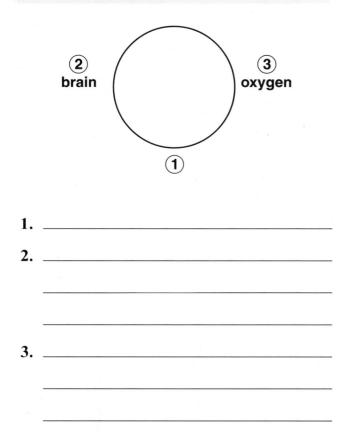

1. _____

2. _____

   _____

   _____

3. _____

   _____

   _____

K CONTRADICTIONS

Make each statement mean the same thing as the statement in the box.

> The faster the water moves, the more erosive it is.

1. The faster the water moves, the faster it wears things down.

2. The faster-moving the water, the less it erodes.

3. Things are eroded faster by fast-moving water.

4. The faster the water moves, the slower it wears things down.

Lesson 63

ERRORS	G	W	B	T

A EDITING

Underline the redundant sentences.
Circle and correct the punctuation errors.
Cross out and correct the wording errors.

Ms Sullivan was a pencil manufacturer. She made pencils in a factory. Ms. Sullivan got up at 7 a.m. every day of the week and went to his factory. She even went to work on Sundays. Ms. Sullivan's factory was clean, and modern Her workers was happy because she paid them a lot of money. Ms. Sullivan were well-liked, which is rare for a boss. The workers in the factory got good paychecks. They thought Ms. Sullivan was okay.

B PARTS OF SPEECH

Underline the nouns. Draw **one** line **over** the adjectives. Draw **two** lines **over** the articles. Circle the verbs.

1. A fussy man rearranged his living room three times.

2. The baseball pitcher considered her next pitch.

3. That shop has rearranged its shelves.

4. Your body digests food and circulates blood.

C WRITING DIRECTIONS

Write the instructions.

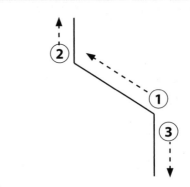

1. _____

   _____

   _____

2. _____

   _____

   _____

3. _____

   _____

   _____

D SENTENCE COMBINATIONS

Circle the word that combines the sentences correctly. Combine the sentences with that word.

1. The man acquired a lawnmower.
   His son acquired a lawnmower.
   however   because   and

   _____

   _____

   _____

2. We went backpacking this weekend.
   We didn't walk much.
   however   particularly   because

   _____

   _____

   _____

3. Some arteries are big.
   Arteries are biggest near the heart.
   however   especially   which

   _____

   _____

   _____

4. Ms. Thomas is very rich.
   Ms. Thomas manufactures hospital beds.
   although   who   especially

   _____

   _____

   _____

   _____

5. Bob was marching in the parade.
   Ron was marching in the parade.
   and   but   especially

   _____

   _____

   _____

E CONTRADICTIONS

Make each item mean the same thing as the statement in the box.

Exercise improves your circulation.

1. Running can make your blood circulate better.

2. The respiration of your blood can be improved by doing sit-ups.

3. If you exercise every day, you will have a better circulatory system.

4. You will improve your digestion if you get a lot of exercise.

F INFERENCE

Put the statements below the story in the right order.

John worked in a big manufacturing plant in Maryland. Every day was the same. He got up at six o'clock. He got to work at seven o'clock. He punched his time card and had a cup of coffee. Then he stood next to a long belt for eight hours, examining animal crackers. If an animal cracker didn't look like a bear or a lion or a kangaroo, John took the cracker off the belt and threw it away.

At five o'clock, when John went home, his wife met him at the door. "I made you a birthday cake," she said. John was surprised. He had forgotten it was his birthday. When his wife put the cake on the table, John fell over laughing. The cake was in the shape of a lion. It looked like a big animal cracker. His wife said, "It didn't come out the way it should have. But why don't you taste it?"

He did. It was really good. He started to eat it.

His wife said, "Don't eat it all now. I fixed your favorite dinner."

John said, "Thank you," and gave her a big hug.

He was surprised. _____

He took crackers off a belt. _____

He ate some cake. _____

He drank some coffee. _____

He hugged his wife. _____

He got to work at seven o'clock. _____

G SIMILES

Make up a simile for each item.

1. The lawn was soft and flat.

   _____

   _____

2. The car was big and slow.

   _____

   _____

H DEFINITIONS

Write a word that comes from **acquire** or **participate** in each blank. Then write **verb, noun,** or **adjective** after each item.

1. Soccer is a _____

   sport. _____

2. Mary was selected to

   _____ in the school

   play. _____

3. Some people choose to limit their

   _____ in sports.

   _____

4. Jim can't afford to

   _____ any more

   shoes. _____

5. A car is an expensive

   _____.

   _____

I BODY SYSTEMS

Fill in each blank.

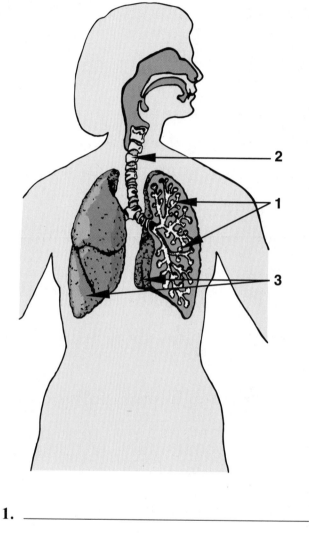

1. _____
2. _____
3. _____

J EVIDENCE

For each sentence followed by a blank, write the number of the rule that relates to that sentence.

> 1. Hot air holds more water than cold air.
> 2. When hot air rises, it cools off.

Hot air often blows across the Pacific Ocean toward the West Coast of the United States. When it reaches the West Coast, this air is carrying a great deal of water. _____ The air is then forced up by mountains along the coast. By the time it reaches the mountaintops, the air is quite cool. _____ The air can no longer hold all its water. _____ As a result, the west side of the mountains gets a lot of rain.

K SENTENCE ANALYSIS

Rewrite the passage in six sentences.

> German shepherd dogs were first used to protect herds of sheep, especially large herds. Then they were used by the police, who trained them to sniff out criminals. Today, they are used as watchdogs and as guide dogs for the blind.

_____

_____

_____

_____

_____

_____

_____

_____

_____

_____

_____

_____

L WRITING STORIES

Write a story about this picture of Carmen. Your story should tell what happened **before** the picture, what happened **in** the picture, and what happened **after** the picture.

bakery	pie crust	rolling pin	oven	flour

_____

_____

_____

_____

_____

_____

_____

_____

_____

_____

_____

_____

_____

_____

_____

_____

_____

_____

ERRORS | G | W | B | T

A DEFINITIONS

Fill in each blank with the word that has the same meaning as the word or words under the blank.

1. The woman liked to

_____ flowers.
(put in order)

2. Joe _____ his plan.
(thought about again)

3. That man _____ his
(put in order again)
checkerboard.

4. John decided to

_____ his story.
(write again)

5. Ron is _____ getting
(thinking about)
a new job.

B SIMILES

Complete the items about the words in the box.

hands   ice

1. Tell how the objects could be the same.

_____

_____

2. Write a simile about the objects.

_____

_____

C BODY RULES

Draw in the arrows. Write **vein** or **artery** in each blank. Also write **oxygen** or **carbon dioxide** in each blank.

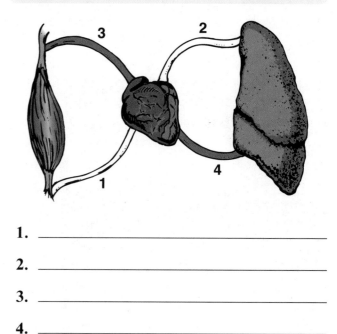

1. _____

2. _____

3. _____

4. _____

D ECONOMICS RULES

Answer the questions.

1. What's the rule about when the demand is greater than the supply?

_____

_____

_____

Last year, Johnson's lowered the price of its product.

2. Which was greater, the supply or the demand?

_____

3. How do you know?

_____

_____

4. What will Johnson's try to do?

_____

_____

_____

Name two ways that Johnson's can do that.

5. _____

_____

6. _____

_____

Johnson's keeps running out of its product now.

7. What will happen to the price of the product?

_____

8. How do you know?

_____

_____

_____

Johnson's manufactures 1,000 products a week. It has orders for 2,000 products a week.

9. Which is greater, the supply or the demand?

_____

10. What will happen to the price of the product?

_____

E INFERENCE

Put the statements below the story in the right order.

> Because Henry had worked in construction for many years, he decided to build his own residence. He bought some land in the mountains near a fast-flowing river. He got his friend Burt to help him build. Burt offered much constructive criticism, but he couldn't hammer nails. He kept hitting his fingers.
>
> Finally, the house was built and Henry moved in. At night, he could hear the river gurgling and the wind blowing through the pine trees. In the morning, he sat on his porch in the warm sunshine and could see only pine trees, the river, and green meadows. Henry was very happy.

The house was finished at last. _____

He had worked at building
things for a long time. _____

He felt good. _____

He acquired some property. _____

He heard water making noises. _____

He got a pal of his to aid him. _____

He made up his mind to
construct his own home. _____

F CONTRADICTIONS

Underline the contradiction and circle the statement it contradicts. Then **tell** why the underlined statement contradicts the circled statement. Make the underlined statement true.

The kids in the Kendall family loved potatoes, and they ate them every night. Because the family didn't have much money, Mrs. Kendall always got the cheapest potatoes. Her husband did not participate in the shopping because he was looking for a job. * One night, the family was sitting around eating potatoes Mrs. Kendall bought at a restaurant. Mr. Kendall said, "I have a big surprise. I got a job today." Everybody was very happy, and Mrs. Kendall went to the store to get more potatoes.

_____

_____

_____

G EDITING

Underline the redundant sentences.
Circle and correct the punctuation errors.
Cross out and correct the wording errors.

The man went from house to house, trying to get peoples to buy cups. People did not need cups, so the man wasn't selling very many. The man was a salesperson, but there was no demand for his product. He tried to make people want the cups by telling them that the cups was fun to drink out of. Not many people fell for this line. The man modified, his sales pitch. When he tried to sell the cups, he gave people a different line.

H REWRITING PARAGRAPHS

Rewrite the paragraph in four sentences. If one of the sentences tells **why,** combine the sentences with **because.** If two sentences seem contradictory, combine them with **although.** Move part of the predicate in sentences that you don't combine.

Many things happened to jazz in the 1930s. The 1930s are also known as the Swing Era. The saxophone became more important than the trumpet. The saxophone could make many new sounds. Many saxophone players became famous. Coleman Hawkins, Lester Young, and Johnny Hodges became the most famous. Many young musicians started playing the saxophone because it was so popular.

Lesson 64

I BODY SYSTEMS

Fill in each blank.

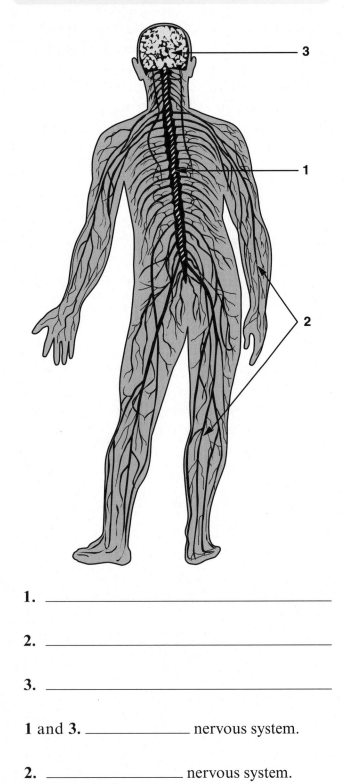

1. _____

2. _____

3. _____

1 and 3. _____ nervous system.

2. _____ nervous system.

J FOLLOWING DIRECTIONS

Follow the directions.

1. In the box, print the noun that means **something you acquire.**
2. Draw a horizontal line under that word.
3. Draw a vertical line under the horizontal line.
4. Under the vertical line, print the noun that means **a place where someone lives.**

WORD LIST

acquire (v) to get
acquisition (n) something you acquire
circulation (n) the act of circulating
fortunate (a) lucky
intelligent (a) smart
protective (a) that something protects
redundant (a) that something repeats
    what has already been said
regulate (v) to control
regulatory (a) that something regulates
reside (v) to live somewhere
respiration (n) the act of respiring
selective (a) that something is careful
    about selecting things
unfortunate (a) not lucky
unintelligent (a) not smart

328   *Lesson 64*

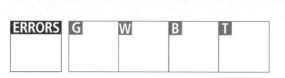

ERRORS	G	W	B	T

A CONTRADICTIONS

Underline the contradiction and circle the statement it contradicts. Then tell **why** the underlined statement contradicts the circled statement. Make the underlined statement true.

Fred was a cement producer. He made cement for sidewalks, for new houses, and for driveways. To make cement, he needed lots of sand and gravel. When he ran out of sand and gravel, Fred went to the sand and gravel store. Fred always tried to save money at the store. * The store sold both 50- and 100-pound bags of sand. One day, Fred obtained quite a bit of sand and gravel from the store. He loaded the 50-pound bags into his truck and drove away. The truck was so heavy that it got a flat tire.

_____

_____

_____

_____

B REWRITING PARAGRAPHS

Rewrite the paragraph in four sentences. If one of the sentences tells **why,** combine the sentences with **because.** If two sentences seem contradictory, combine them with **but.** Move part of the predicate in sentences that you don't combine.

Billie Holiday was the greatest singer of the Swing Era. Billie Holiday had an amazing voice. Her voice was not very loud. Her voice had great power. Her most famous recordings were made with Lester Young. Lester Young played the tenor saxophone. You should buy some Billie Holiday CDs if you get the chance.

_____

_____

_____

_____

_____

_____

_____

_____

_____

_____

_____

_____

_____

C FOLLOWING DIRECTIONS

Follow the directions.

1. Draw a vertical line in the box.

2. Draw a line that slants down to the left from the bottom of the vertical line.

3. Draw a muscle that covers the left side of the vertical line and attaches to the left side of the slanted line.

4. Draw an arrow that shows which way the muscle will move the slanted line.

D DEFINITIONS

Fill in each blank with the word that has the same meaning as the word or words under the blank.

1. The woman _____
   her dress.   (adjusted again)

2. The city is full of

   _____ buildings.
   (constructed again)

3. Mary will _____ the
                (put in order)
   basement for her party.

4. Joe _____ his
          (thought about again)
   selection.

5. The boss _____ his
   desk.   (put in order again)

6. Wanda has to _____
   her homework.   (do again)

E SIMILES

Tell **two** ways the things compared are **not** the same. Tell **one** way the things compared **are** the same.

Her fingernails are like knives.

1. _____

   _____

2. _____

   _____

3. _____

   _____

F INFERENCE

Read the passage and answer the questions.
- Circle the **W** if the question is answered by words in the passage. Then underline those words.
- Circle the **D** if the question is answered by a deduction.

> You know that products that are readier to use cost more. Manufacturers know that people will pay more for something that saves time and effort. Linda gets off work at five o'clock. She wants to go to a film at six o'clock, and she also wants to eat dinner. If she fixes dinner at home, she might not make it to the film on time. Besides, she is very tired from working all day and does not feel like working any more. So she goes to a restaurant. The dinner she gets in the restaurant probably costs three times as much as the dinner she could have fixed at home, but Linda doesn't care. She feels happy that someone other than herself is doing all the work.

1. Why will people pay more for products that are readier to use?

_____

_____

2. Give two reasons why Linda does not want to fix dinner at home.

_____

_____

_____

_____

_____ **W D**

3. Why does the restaurant dinner cost so much more?

_____

_____ **W D**

4. The next day, Linda fixes dinner at home. Give at least two possible reasons why she does that.

_____

_____

_____

5. Who probably spends more on food, a person who works part-time or a person who works full-time?

_____

_____ **W D**

6. Why?

_____

_____

_____

G ECONOMICS RULES

Answer the questions.

1. What's the rule about what manufacturers try to do?

   _____

   _____

   _____

| The Acme Motor Company manufactures 5,000 trucks a week. People buy 4,000 trucks a week. |

2. Which is greater, the supply or the demand?

   _____

3. What will happen to the price of trucks?

   _____

4. What will the Acme Motor Company try to do?

   _____

   _____

   _____

Name two ways that Acme can do that.

5. _____

   _____

6. _____

   _____

| Last year, trucks cost $25,000. This year, trucks cost $24,000. |

7. What happened to the price of trucks?

   _____

8. Which is greater, the supply or the demand?

   _____

9. How do you know?

   _____

   _____

H EDITING

Underline the redundant sentences.
Circle and correct the punctuation errors.
Cross out and correct the wording errors.

   Duke Ellington was the greatest jazz band leader what ever lived. He formed his first band in the 1920s which was when jazz first became popular. Although many of the players changed the band stayed together for almost fifty year. No band leader was better than Ellington. Everybody wanted to play with Ellington, so he had no trouble finding the best players. The Ellington band could really swing All kinds of players wanted to belong to it.

I WRITING STORIES

Write a story about this picture of Mr. Rodriguez and his grandson Diego. Your story should tell what happened **before** the picture, what happened **in** the picture, and what happened **after** the picture.

fishing pole	wharf	reel	bait	splash

_____

_____

_____

_____

_____

_____

_____

_____

_____

_____

_____

_____

_____

_____

_____

_____

_____

_____

Glossary

A

abdominal muscle	(n) the muscle that goes from the ribs to the pelvis
acquire	(v) to get
acquisition	(n) something you acquire
acquisitive	(a) that something likes to acquire things
adjective	(n) a word that comes before a noun and tells about the noun
arrange	(v) to put in order
arteries	(n) the tubes that carry blood away from the heart

B

biceps	(n) the muscle that covers the front of the humerus
brain	(n) the organ that lets you think and feel
bronchial tubes	(n) the tubes inside the lungs

C

capillaries	(n) the very small tubes that connect the arteries and veins
carbon dioxide	(n) a gas that burning things produce
central nervous system	(n) the body system made up of the brain and spinal cord
circulate	(v) to move around
circulation	(n) the act of circulating
circulatory	(a) that something involves circulation
circulatory system	(n) the body system that moves blood around the body
conclude	(v) to end or figure out
conclusion	(n) the end or something that is concluded
conclusive	(a) that something is true without any doubt

consider	(v) to think about
construct	(v) to build
construction	(n) something that is constructed
constructive	(a) that something is helpful
consumable	(a) that something can be consumed
consume	(v) to use up or eat
consumer	(n) something that consumes
critical	(a) that something criticizes
criticism	(n) a statement that criticizes
criticize	(v) to find fault with

D

demand	(n) how well something sells
digest	(v) to change food into fuel for the body
digestion	(n) the act of digesting
digestive	(a) that something involves digestion
digestive system	(n) the body system that changes food into fuel

E

erode	(v) to wear things down
erosion	(n) what happens when something is eroded
erosive	(a) that something erodes
esophagus	(n) the tube that goes from the mouth to the stomach
examine	(v) to look at
explain	(v) to make something easier to understand
explanation	(n) something that explains
explanatory	(a) that something explains

F

femur	(n) the upper leg bone
fortunate	(a) lucky

G

gastrocnemius (n) the muscle that covers the back of the lower leg

H

heart (n) the pump that moves the blood

humerus (n) the upper arm bone

I

intelligent (a) smart

irrelevant (a) that something does not help to explain what happened

L

large intestine (n) the organ that stores food the body cannot use

liver (n) the organ that makes chemicals that break food down

lung (n) a large organ that brings air into contact with blood

M

manufacture (v) to make in a factory

manufactured (a) that something has been made in a factory

manufacturer (n) something that manufactures

modification (n) a change

modified (a) that something is changed

modify (v) to change

motor nerve (n) a nerve that lets you move

mouth (n) the part that takes solid and liquid food in

muscular system (n) the body system of muscles

N

nerve (n) a wire in the body that carries messages

nervous system (n) the body system of nerves

noun (n) a word that names a person, place, or thing

O

obtain (v) to get

oxygen (n) a gas that burning things need

P

participate (v) to take part in something

participation (n) the act of participating

participatory (a) that something involves participation

pelvis (n) the hip bone

peripheral nervous system (n) the body system made up of the nerves that lead to and from the spinal cord and the brain

predicate (n) the part of a sentence that tells more

predict (v) to say that something will happen

predictable (a) that something is easy to predict

prediction (n) a statement that predicts

produce (v) to make

production (n) something that is produced

productive (a) that something produces a lot of things

protect (v) to guard

protection (n) something that protects

protective (a) that something protects

Q

quadriceps (n) the muscle that covers the front of the femur

Glossary

R

rearrange (v) to put in order again

reconsider (v) to think about again

redundant (a) that something repeats what has already been said

regulate (v) to control

regulation (n) a rule

regulatory (a) that something regulates

relevant (a) that something helps to explain what happened

reside (v) to live somewhere

residence (n) a place where someone resides

residential (a) that a place has many residences

respire (v) to breathe

respiration (n) the act of respiring

respiratory (a) that something involves respiration

respiratory system (n) the body system that brings oxygen to the blood

ribs (n) the bones that cover the organs in the chest

S

select (v) to choose

selection (n) something that is selected

selective (a) that something is careful about selecting things

sensory nerve (n) a nerve that lets you feel

simile (n) a statement that tells how things are the same

skeletal system (n) the body system of bones

skull (n) the bone that covers the brain

small intestine (n) the organ that gives food to the blood

spinal cord (n) the body part that connects the brain to all parts of the body

spine (n) the backbone

stomach (n) the organ that mixes food with chemicals

subject (n) the part of a sentence that names

supply (n) how much there is of something

T

trachea (n) the tube that brings outside air to the lungs

trapezius (n) the muscle that covers the back of the neck

triceps (n) the muscle that covers the back of the humerus

U

unfortunate (a) not lucky

unintelligent (a) not smart

V

veins (n) the tubes that carry blood back to the heart

verb (n) a word that tells the action that things do

A Tell **two** ways that the things compared are **not** the same. Tell **one** way that the things compared **are** the same.

The cat's claws were like knives.

---

1. _____

_____

2. _____

_____

3. _____

_____

B Underline the contradiction.
Circle the statement it contradicts.

Mabel was always kind to animals. She never ate meat, and she didn't wear leather shoes. She owned a dog, a cat, and several fish. * One night, Mabel ate dinner in a restaurant. She ordered salad, beans, and steak. Then she left a big tip for the waiter.

C Write **brain, nerves,** or **spinal cord** in each blank.

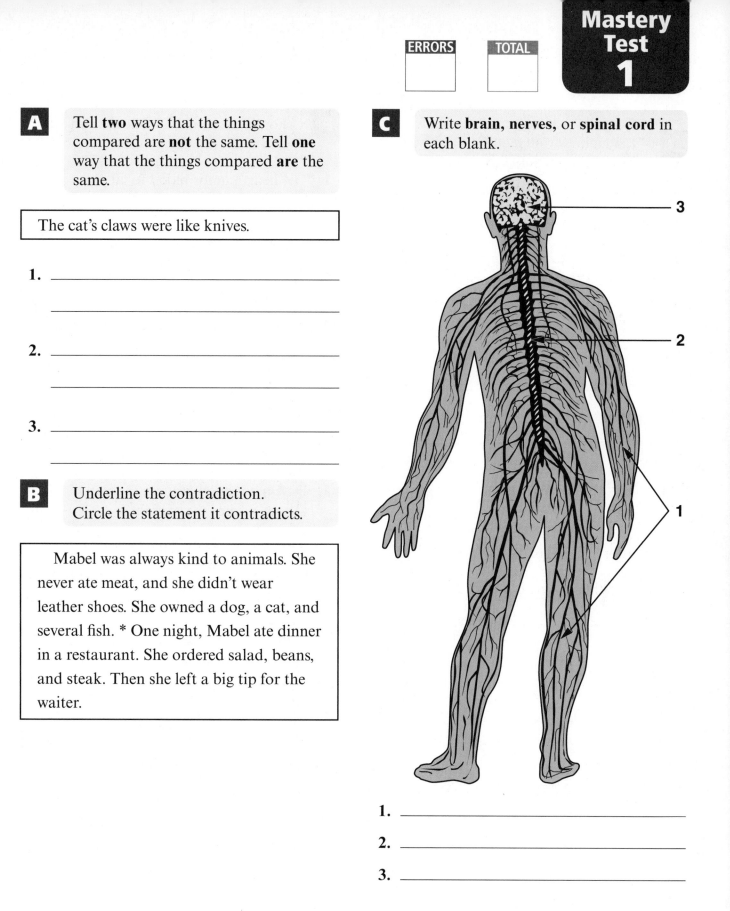

1. _____

2. _____

3. _____

D Complete each sentence with a word that comes from **modify.** Then write **verb, noun,** or **adjective** after each item.

1. Tailors often have to

    _____ the length of

    pants. _____

2. The painter made several

    _____ to her

    painting. _____

3. Sibyl is _____ her

    hair style. _____

E Complete each sentence with a word that comes from **digest** or **conclude.** Then write **verb, noun,** or **adjective** after each item.

1. The small intestine is part of the

    _____ system.

    _____

2. A deduction includes both a rule and a

    _____.

    _____

3. After hearing the case, the jury

    _____ that the suspect

    was not guilty. _____

F For each sentence, circle the subject and underline the predicate.

1. The heart pumps blood to all parts of the body.

2. Running up the hill is hard work.

3. The waxing moon glowed brightly in the night sky.

G For each item, underline the common part.
   • If one of the sentences tells **why,** combine the sentences with **because.**
   • If neither sentence tells why, combine them with **who, which,** or **and.**

1. Devon got good grades at school. Devon studied every night.

    _____

    _____

    _____

2. Leah was the tallest girl in class. Gabriel sat next to Leah.

    _____

    _____

    _____

H For each item, underline the common part. Then combine the sentences with **who** or **which**.

1. The hills have many oak trees.
   The hills are green in the spring.

   _____

   _____

   _____

2. The nurse relaxed on the weekend.
   The nurse worked five days a week.

   _____

   _____

   _____

I Read the passage and answer the questions.
   • Circle the **W** if the question is answered by words in the passage. Then underline those words.
   • Circle the **D** if the question is answered by a deduction.

Your respiratory system brings oxygen, which is a gas in the air, into contact with your blood. When you breathe in, air goes down your trachea and into the bronchial tubes in each lung. The bronchial tubes branch off into smaller and smaller tubes. When the air reaches the ends of the bronchial tubes, capillaries in the lungs take in some of the oxygen. That oxygen is now in contact with your blood.

---

1. Which system brings oxygen into contact with your blood?

   _____ **W   D**

2. Which is probably wider, your trachea or one of your bronchial tubes?

   _____ **W   D**

3. After the air reaches the ends of your bronchial tubes, which system does it come into contact with?

   _____ **W   D**

J Complete the instructions.

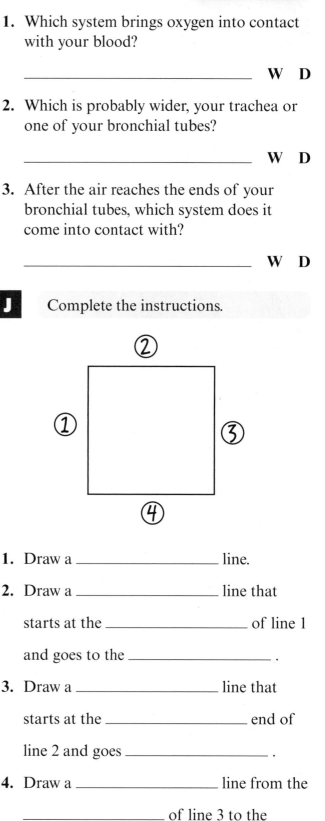

1. Draw a _____ line.

2. Draw a _____ line that

   starts at the _____ of line 1

   and goes to the _____ .

3. Draw a _____ line that

   starts at the _____ end of

   line 2 and goes _____ .

4. Draw a _____ line from the

   _____ of line 3 to the

   _____ of line 1.

A Complete the items.

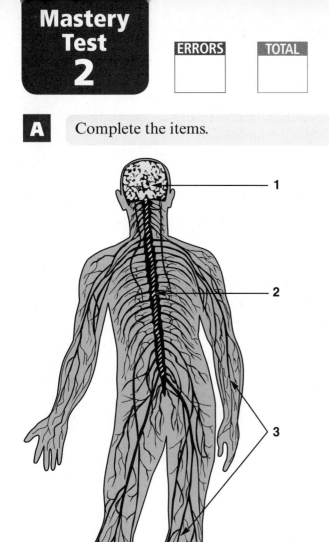

1. What is the name of part 1? _____

2. What is the name of part 2? _____

3. What is the name of part 3? _____

4. Parts 1 and 2 are the _____ nervous system.

5. Part 3 is the _____ nervous system.

B Draw in the arrows. Write **vein** or **artery** in each blank.

1. _____

2. _____

3. _____

4. _____

C Complete each sentence with a word that comes from **consume.** Then write **verb, noun,** or **adjective** after each item.

1. That rich _____ buys

   fancy clothes. _____

2. Rocks are not a _____

   product. _____

3. Those _____ are careful

   with their money. _____

D For each sentence, circle the subject and underline the predicate. Then rewrite the sentence by moving part of the predicate.

1. The wind blows hardest at the crest of the hill.

_____

_____

2. The players were tired and sore after the game.

_____

_____

3. The dog and cat were sleeping under the bed.

_____

_____

_____

E Follow the instructions about the sentences in the box.

> The bird sat on the branch. The bird had caught a worm. The branch was covered with moss.

1. Underline the common part that is at the end of one sentence and the beginning of another. Then combine those sentences with **who** or **which.**

_____

_____

_____

2. Circle the common part that is at the beginning of two sentences. Then combine those sentences with **who** or **which.**

_____

_____

_____

F Use the facts to fill out the form.

> **Facts:** Your name is Oscar Feliz. You are a bus driver who is applying for a job as a truck driver. You are now making $840 a week. Your address is 146 Heather Circle, Wheeling, West Virginia. Your wife's name is Lucinda Feliz.

A. Write your last name on line 1.

B. On line 3, write the state in which you live.

C. Write your wife's first name on line 4.

D. On line 2, write your weekly salary.

1. _____

2. _____

3. _____

4. _____

G Read the passage and answer the questions.
- Circle the **W** if the question is answered by words in the passage. Then underline those words.
- Circle the **D** if the question is answered by a deduction.

> When you stub your toe, the message "toe hurts" goes from your toe to your brain. Your nerves don't really carry the words "toe hurts." What they do carry is a little bit of electricity. The electricity comes in very short bursts called **impulses.** If the toe doesn't hurt too much, the message may have just a few impulses per second. If the toe hurts a lot, the message may have many impulses per second. The greater the pain, the more impulses per second.

1. Which gives fewer impulses per second: clapping your hands as hard as you can or rubbing them together lightly?

   _____

   _____ **W** **D**

2. What are very short bursts of electricity called?

   _____ **W** **D**

3. Pain message A has 140 impulses per second. Pain message B has 50 impulses per second. Which message describes the most pain?

   _____

H Write the instructions.

conclusion ③

1. (what) _____

   _____

2. (what and where) _____

   _____

   _____

3. (what and where) _____

   _____

I For each sentence, write another word that means the same thing as the underlined part.

1. It is hard to change a mountain.

   _____

2. The police looked for true without any doubt evidence. _____

3. He upset his act of digesting by eating pickles. _____

A Make up a simile for each item.

1. A cat purred loudly.

_____

_____

_____

2. A woman was strong.

_____

_____

_____

B Underline the contradiction and circle the statement it contradicts. Then tell why the underlined statement contradicts the circled statement.

Hiroshi was the best hitter on his team, which was playing a baseball game. In the first inning, Hiroshi hit a home run. In the fourth inning, he hit a double. * In the seventh inning, Hiroshi came up to bat again. His team was losing three to nothing. Hiroshi hit a triple.

_____

_____

_____

C Label each nerve.
Write a message for each nerve.

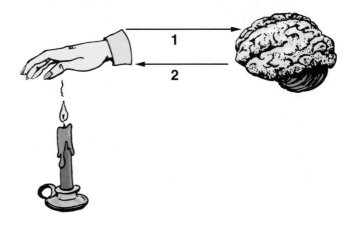

1. _____

_____

2. _____

_____

Mastery Test 3

D Complete each sentence with a word that comes from **explain** or **manufacture.** Then write **verb, noun,** or **adjective** after each item.

1. The student had to

   _____ why she was

   late for class. _____

2. That _____ makes

   pencils in a factory.

   _____

3. The guide gave an

   _____ talk on the

   history of the castle.

   _____

E For each sentence, write another word that means the same thing as the underlined part.

1. The short story had a thrilling <u>end</u>.

   _____

2. We need to build cars that <u>use up</u> less gas.

   _____

3. He rode a <u>changed</u> bike to work.

   _____

F For each sentence, circle the subject and underline the predicate. Then rewrite the sentence by moving part of the predicate.

1. You have to study more to improve your grades.

   _____

   _____

   _____

2. The woman got a good job because she was smart.

   _____

   _____

   _____

Mastery Test 3

G For each pair of sentences, underline the common part.
- Combine the contradictory sentences with **but.**
- Combine the other sentences with **who** or **which.**

1. The computer cost a lot of money.
The computer didn't work.

_____

_____

2. Her computer cost a lot of money.
She had thousands of songs on her computer.

_____

_____

_____

3. The computer had lots of memory.
The computer was white and blue.

_____

_____

_____

H Combine the sentences with **particularly.**

1. Felicia runs hard.
Felicia runs the hardest when she's in a race.

_____

_____

_____

2. That cat sleeps a lot.
That cat sleeps the most during the winter.

_____

_____

_____

I Use the facts to fill out the form.

Facts: You are applying for a passport. Your name is Brad Overstreet. Your social security number is 978-64-2367. You live at 1465 H Street, Salt Lake City, Utah. You were born on May 5, 1990. You need a passport because you want to visit China and Japan.

1. Social security number

_____

2. Countries you plan to visit

_____

3. How old are you?

_____

4. In what month were you born?

_____

J Read the passage and answer the questions.
- Circle the **W** if the question is answered by words in the passage. Then underline those words.
- Circle the **D** if the question is answered by a deduction.

Cars as we know them were first made around 1900. They cost a lot, and only rich people could buy them. A man named Henry Ford thought he could make a lot of money if he produced cheap cars that anybody could buy. He started the Ford Motor Company in 1903 and sold his first cars for $850, which was a lot cheaper than any other car. But Ford wanted to make his cars even cheaper. He followed one rule: **The lower the price, the bigger the sales.** Each year more people bought Fords. By 1914, a Ford cost only $500, and half of all cars made in the United States were Fords.

1. Why could only rich people buy cars around 1900?

   _____

   _____ **W   D**

2. Why did Ford keep lowering the price of his cars?

   _____

   _____

   _____

3. If 200,000 cars were made in the United States in 1914, how many of those were Fords?

   _____ **W   D**

K Write the instructions.

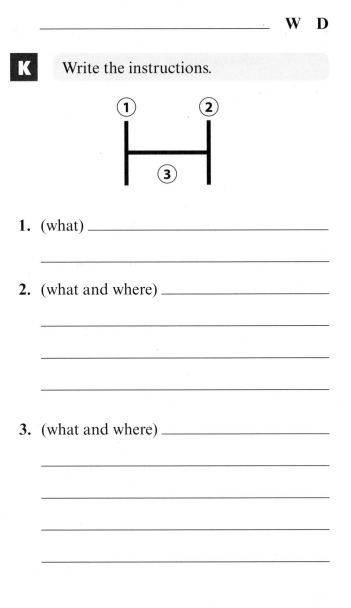

1. (what) _____

   _____

2. (what and where) _____

   _____

   _____

   _____

3. (what and where) _____

   _____

   _____

   _____

A Make up a simile for each item.

1. The car radio was very loud.

_____

_____

2. His clothes were old and worn.

_____

_____

_____

_____

_____

_____

_____

_____

_____

B Underline the contradiction and circle the statement it contradicts. Then tell why the underlined statement contradicts the circled statement. Make the underlined statement true.

Jacob knew that **demand** tells how well something sells. He also knew that **supply** tells how much there is of something. One day, Jacob decided to find out about the demand for wool coats at a clothing store. * Jacob walked into the store. Then he found a salesperson. He asked the salesperson how many wool coats the store had. The salesperson said, "I don't know."

C Tell if each event changed the **demand** or the **supply.**

The factory made 100 computers a day.
The factory sold 100 computers a day.

1. The factory ran out of computer screens, so it stopped making computers for a few days.

_____

2. Because of the problem with the screens, people started buying computers from another factory.

_____

3. The factory found new screens and started making computers again.

_____

D Complete each sentence with a word that comes from **circulate** or **respire**. Then write **verb, noun,** or **adjective** after each item.

1. It feels good to

_____ fresh air in

the morning. _____

2. The heart is part of the

_____ system.

_____

3. The doctor checked the man's

_____ by listening

to his lungs. _____

E For each sentence, write another word that means the same thing as the underlined part.

1. The shy student refused to take part in

class.

_____

2. Her house was filled with made in a

factory products.

_____

3. The vendors moved around through the

crowd.

_____

F Underline the common part of the sentence in the box. Write two sentences with that common part.

> Birds sing loudly, particularly in the morning.

1. _____

_____

2. _____

_____

G Read the passage and answer the questions.
- Circle the **W** if the question is answered by words in the passage. Then underline those words.
- Circle the **D** if the question is answered by a deduction.

Here's a rule about demand and supply: **When the demand is greater than the supply,** prices go up.

Ms. Lopez runs the only chicken farm near Mudville. In March, her chickens produce just as many eggs as Mudville needs, which is 1,000 dozen a month. Ms. Lopez sells the eggs for $1 a dozen, so she makes $1,000 that month.

In April, a big group of people moves into Mudville, and Mudville's demand for eggs goes up to 1,500 dozen a month. But Ms. Lopez's chickens are still producing only 1,000 dozen a month, and it becomes very hard for the people of Mudville to get all the eggs they need. People start to offer Ms. Lopez more for her eggs, just so they can be sure of getting some. Ms. Lopez, who likes the idea of making extra money, decides to raise the price to $1.25 a dozen. Because the demand is so high, she has no trouble selling all the eggs at the new price.

---

1. When do prices go up?

_____

_____

_____ **W** **D**

2. In which month was the demand higher, March or April?

_____

3. How much money did Mr. Lopez make from egg sales in April?

_____ **W** **D**

4. How could Ms. Lopez increase the supply of eggs in May?

_____

_____

_____

_____

H Write the instructions.

② **demand** _____ ①

③ △

1. _____

_____

2. _____

_____

_____

3. _____

_____

I Underline the redundant sentences.

Emily was afraid of heights. She lived in a one-story house. Her house did not have a second floor. One day, she had to go to an office in a tall building. She did not look out the office windows. Being in a high place filled her with fear. She was happy when she took the elevator back to the ground floor. There were many floors above the ground floor.

J Rewrite the passage in four sentences.
- If one of the sentences tells **why,** combine the sentences with **because.**
- If two sentences seem contradictory, combine them with **but.**

> Baseball pitchers throw many kinds of pitches. Baseball pitchers want to strike out batters. One particularly good pitch is the curveball. The curveball curves down and away from batters. Many batters swing at curveballs. Many batters often miss. Learning to hit a curveball takes time. Learning to hit a curveball takes practice.

1. _____

_____

_____

_____

_____

2. _____

_____

_____

_____

_____

3. _____

_____

_____

4. _____

_____

_____

A   Complete the items about the words in the box.

voice   thunder

1. Tell how the objects could be the same.

_____

_____

2. Write a simile about the objects.

_____

_____

B   For each sentence followed by a blank, write the letter of the rule which relates to that sentence.

A. Light moves faster than sound. B. Sound travels one mile in about five seconds.

   Lightning produces both lightning bolts and thunder. When you're in a thunderstorm, you can see lightning before you hear it. _____ You can figure out how far away lightning is by starting to count as soon as you see a lightning bolt. If you count to ten before you hear the thunder, you know that the lightning bolt is two miles away. _____ And if you only count to three, you know that the lightning bolt is less than a mile away. _____

C   Answer the questions.

1. What's the rule about when the demand is greater than the supply?

_____

_____

_____

In December, the demand for firewood is greater than the supply of firewood.

2. What will happen to the price of firewood?

_____

3. How do you know?

_____

_____

_____

D   Answer the questions.

1. What's the rule about when the demand is less than the supply?

_____

_____

_____

> In March, the demand for calendars is less than the supply of calendars.

2. What will happen to the price of calendars?

_____

3. How do you know?

_____

_____

_____

E   Answer the questions.

1. What's the rule about what manufacturers try to do to the demand and the supply?

_____

_____

_____

> A manufacturer makes 50 robots a month and sells 50 robots a month.

2. What will the manufacturer try to do to the demand?

_____

_____

3. Name one way the manufacturer could do that.

_____

_____

_____

F   Complete each sentence with a word that comes from **erode.** Then write **verb, noun,** or **adjective** after each item.

1. The constant rain is _____

our hill. _____

2. Wind and rain are both

_____ forces.

_____

3. You can prevent soil _____

by planting grass. _____

G For each sentence, write another word that means the same thing as the underlined part.

1. The teacher expected <u>the act of participating</u> from everyone.

   _____

2. After running hard, the man <u>breathed</u> deeply.

   _____

3. She made money by <u>making in a factory</u> rubber ducks.

   _____

H Rewrite the passage in four sentences.

> The fog near the ocean is thick, particularly in summer. Our house, which is a mile from the ocean, is often blanketed in fog during June.

1. _____

   _____

2. _____

   _____

3. _____

   _____

4. _____

   _____

I Read the passage and answer the questions.
- Circle the **W** if the question is answered by words in the passage. Then underline those words.
- Circle the **D** if the question is answered by a deduction.

Ms. Thomas runs the only dairy farm near Newton. In July, her cows produce just as much milk as Newton needs, which is 1,000 gallons a month. In August, a big group of people moves out of Newton, and Newton's demand for milk drops to 600 gallons a month. But Ms. Thomas's cows are still producing 1,000 gallons a month.

Ms. Thomas sells 600 gallons at the old price, and then she is stuck with 400 gallons that will soon go bad. She thinks she can get people to buy the 400 gallons if she lowers the price. Her idea works, and she sells all 400 gallons at the lower price.

---

1. In which month did Ms. Thomas make more money, July or August?

   _____ **W** **D**

2. How could Ms. Thomas increase the demand for milk without lowering the price?

   _____ **W** **D**

3. What will happen to the demand for milk if a big group of people moves to Newton in September?

   _____

J Underline the redundant sentences.

Carmen played on her school's soccer team. She was the goalie. She hadn't allowed any goals all year long. She was one of the best players on the team. Her job was to guard the goal. No one had scored against her this year. She had black hair and green eyes. She was better than most of the players on her team.

 A   Answer the questions.

1. What's the rule about products that are readier to use?

_____

_____

_____

Fresh orange juice costs more than frozen orange juice.

2. Which type of orange juice is readier to use when you obtain it?

_____

3. How do you know?

_____

B   Answer the questions.

1. What's the rule about when you buy products in large quantities?

_____

_____

_____

Mega Warehouse Store pays $2 per case of bottled water. Sam's Corner Market pays $3 per case of bottled water.

2. Who pays more per case of water?

_____

3. Who probably buys larger quantities of water?

_____

4. How do you know?

_____

_____

C   Complete each sentence with a word that comes from **acquire**. Then write **verb, noun,** or **adjective** after each item.

1. He used a credit card to

_____ groceries.

_____

2. She was so _____ that

her house was filled with objects.

_____

3. They are _____ camping

supplies for their trip.

_____

D   For each sentence, write another word that means the same thing as the underlined part.

1. Reading books can make you <u>smart</u>.

_____

2. Everybody felt sorry for the <u>not lucky</u> puppy.

_____

3. You should never be <u>not prepared</u> for a test.

_____

E Combine the sentences with **however.**

1. Hector talked for a long time.
   Hector had nothing to say.

   _____

   _____

   _____

2. Harriet petted her cat.
   Her cat did not purr.

   _____

   _____

   _____

F Combine the sentences with **especially.**

1. Justin talks in a loud voice.
   Justin talks loudest when he's excited.

   _____

   _____

   _____

2. Donna loves to play tennis.
   Donna loves to play tennis most in the
   morning.

   _____

   _____

   _____

G Put the statements below the passage
in the right order by numbering them
from 1 to 5.

> Laura practiced her violin for 30
> minutes every afternoon. First she took
> the violin out of its case and tightened the
> bow. Then she tuned the strings. When
> her strings were in tune, she played scales
> for five minutes. Then she did some finger
> exercises for a few more minutes. After
> that, she played the pieces her teacher had
> given her. She usually spent several
> minutes on each piece. After half an hour,
> she loosened the bow and put the violin
> away.

She spent several minutes playing
each piece.   _____

She tightened the bow.   _____

She played scales for five minutes. _____

She tuned the strings.   _____

She did finger exercises.   _____

H   Write the instructions.

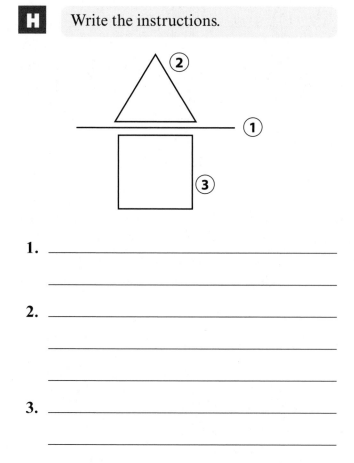

1. _____

_____

2. _____

_____

_____

3. _____

_____

_____

I   Edit the following passage.
- Underline the redundant sentences.
- Circle and correct the punctuation errors.
- Cross out and correct the wording errors.

A big dog jump in our pond yesterday. He got all wet, however, he dried quickly. It didn't take him long to stop being wet. Then he running around our yard. Our cats hissed at him from inside the house The dog just look at them. The cats were not outside. At last, the dog run away and did not come back

J Rewrite the paragraph in four sentences on the lines below.

- If one of the sentences tells why, combine the sentences with **because.**
- If two sentences seem contradictory, combine them with **however.**
- Move part of the predicate in sentences you don't combine.

> Hannah was studying medicine. Hannah wanted to be a doctor. She was interested in body systems. She was most interested in the skeletal system. She knew the names of most bones. She did not know the names of a few small bones. She studied the names of bones every night.

1. _____

_____

_____

2. _____

_____

_____

3. _____

_____

_____

_____

4. _____

_____

_____

A Make up a simile for each item.

1. A woman had large eyes.

_____

_____

2. A man had a clear voice.

_____

_____

B Complete the items about the words in the box.

jungle   oven

1. Tell how the objects could be the same.

_____

_____

2. Write a simile about the objects.

_____

_____

C Read the passage and do the items.

The Woody Forest has many different kinds of trees. It has pine trees that stay green all year long. It has maple trees that lose their leaves in the fall and grow new ones in the spring. * The Woody Forest is particularly beautiful in the winter. The pine trees are still green. The leaves on the maple trees are covered with snow. The air is cold, and the forest is quiet.

1. Underline the contradiction and circle the statement it contradicts.

2. Tell why the underlined statement contradicts the circled statement.

_____

_____

_____

_____

3. Make the underlined statement true.

D For each sentence followed by a blank, write the letter of the rule that relates to that sentence.

> A. Products that are readier to use cost more.
> B. When you buy products in large quantities, you pay less for each unit.

Carlos was a good shopper who liked to save money. When he went to the store, he always bought a large box of cereal instead of a small box._____ He also bought cold, raw chicken instead of hot, cooked chicken._____ He never bought frozen dinners that can be heated up in a few minutes._____ Instead, he made all his dinners himself. They were delicious.

E Answer the questions.

1. What's the rule about when the demand is greater than the supply?

   _____

   _____

2. What's the rule about when the demand is less than the supply?

   _____

   _____

> In July, the demand for airplane tickets is greater than the supply of airplane tickets.

3. What will happen to the price of airplane tickets?

   _____

4. How do you know?

   _____

   _____

   _____

F Answer the questions.

1. What's the rule about what manufacturers try to do to the demand and the supply?

   _____

   _____

   _____

   _____

> A manufacturer makes 1,000 chess sets a month and sells 950 chess sets a month.

2. What will the manufacturer try to do to the demand?

   _____

3. Name one way the manufacturer could do that.

   _____

   _____

   _____

G Complete the items.

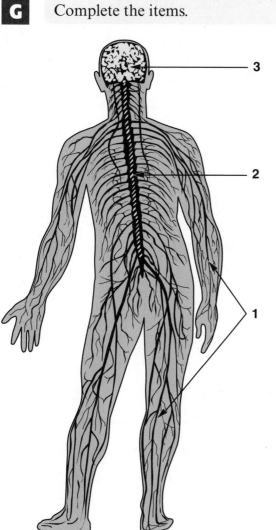

1. What is the name of part 1?

   _____

2. What is the name of part 2?

   _____

3. What is the name of part 3?

   _____

4. Parts 2 and 3 are the _____
   nervous system.

5. Part 1 is the _____
   nervous system.

H Draw in the arrows. Shade in each tube that carries dark blood. Tell what gas each tube carries.

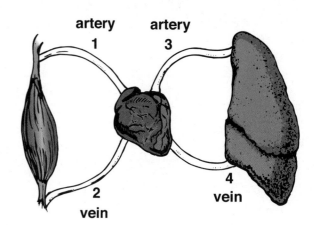

1. _____

2. _____

3. _____

4. _____

I For each sentence, write another word that means the same thing as the underlined part.

1. The students had to <u>put in order again</u> their desks.

_____

2. Good speakers <u>think about</u> their words carefully.

_____

3. An <u>smart</u> dog can learn several commands.

_____

4. The <u>not lucky</u> boy lost his wallet yesterday.

_____

5. A diamond ring is an expensive <u>something you acquire</u>.

_____

6. Your <u>involves digestion</u> system changes food into fuel.

_____

J Complete each sentence with a word that comes from **erode** or **participate**. Then write **verb, noun,** or **adjective** after each item.

1. We could see the _____

on the hills after the big storm.

_____

2. Everybody joins in during this

_____ game.

_____

3. The mountain stream kept

_____ its banks.

_____

4. Everyone wanted to

_____ in the school

play. _____

K For each sentence, write another word that means the same thing as the underlined part.

1. The guide <u>made easier to understand</u> the history of the town.

_____

2. You need to <u>breathe</u> deeply before diving into water.

_____

3. Geraldo made a small <u>change</u> to his skateboard.

_____

4. A falling apple gives <u>true without any doubt</u> proof of gravity.

_____

5. Good <u>people who consume</u> know how to save money.

_____

6. Blood is always <u>moving around</u> in your body.

_____

L For each item, circle the word that combines the sentences correctly. Then combine the sentences with that word.

1. The man worked hard.
   The man worked hardest on Mondays.
   because   especially   and

   _____
   _____

2. Greta put on her coat.
   Greta still felt cold.
   however   which   particularly

   _____
   _____
   _____

3. The bronchial tubes bring oxygen to the blood.
   The bronchial tubes are inside the lungs.
   although   especially   which

   _____
   _____
   _____
   _____

M For each item, circle the word that combines the sentences correctly. Then combine the sentences with that word.

1. Rachel loved to read.
   Rachel did not like novels.
   because   especially   although

   _____
   _____
   _____

2. Getting a job is hard.
   Getting a job is hardest during the winter.
   particularly   which   because

   _____
   _____
   _____

3. The glass of water got hot.
   The glass of water was sitting in the sun.
   who   because   however

   _____
   _____
   _____

N Rewrite the passage in four sentences.

> Although music is fun to hear, it is hard to play. You have to practice for many hours, especially if you want to play for other people.

1. _____
   _____

2. _____
   _____

3. _____
   _____

4. _____
   _____
   _____

O Put the statements below the passage in the right order by numbering them from 1 to 5.

Lee was hungry, so he decided to make a sandwich. First he put two pieces of bread in the toaster. Then he found some ham and cheese in his refrigerator. When the bread finished toasting, he put mustard on both pieces. Then he put the ham on one piece and the cheese on the other. He sat down at his table and ate the sandwich. After eating, he drank a glass of milk.

Lee sat down at his table. _____

Lee put mustard on both pieces of toast. _____

Lee drank a glass of milk. _____

Lee decided to make a sandwich. _____

Lee found some ham and cheese. _____

P Use the facts fill out the form.

Facts: Your name is Ricardo Mendez. You are applying to be a student at Tuliop College. You are now a student at John Jay High School in Columbus, Idaho. You have a 3.5 grade point average. Your favorite subject is math. You are on your school's soccer team. You collect baseball cards.

1. Last name _____

2. Grade point average _____

3. Sports played _____

4. City and state

   _____

5. Hobbies

   _____

   _____

Q Write the instructions.

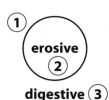

1. _____

2. _____

   _____

   _____

3. _____

   _____

   _____

R Label each nerve.
Write a message for each nerve.

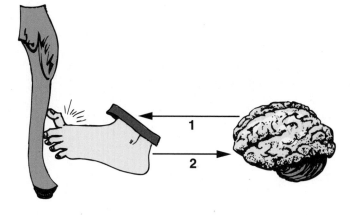

1. _____

2. _____

S Edit the following passage.
• Underline the redundant sentences.
• Circle and correct the punctuation errors.
• Cross out and correct the wording errors.

The sky is always changing. It was blue this morning however, now it was gray. This evening, it will probably be pink The sky is different all the time. I like the sky in the evening especially during sunset. When the sun goes down the sky change color. I think it will be pink tonight.

T For each sentence, circle the subject and underline the predicate. Then rewrite the sentence by moving part of the predicate.

1. The cows felt safe on the other side of the fence.

   _____

   _____

   _____

   _____

2. Tree branches sag after a heavy rain.

   _____

   _____

U Read the passage and answer the questions.
- Circle the **W** if the question is answered by words in the passage. Then underline those words.
- Circle the **D** if the question is answered by a deduction.

You can save money when you shop if you figure out how much something costs **per unit.** Pretend that a two-pound bag of King Rice costs 70 cents and a three-pound bag of Queen Rice costs 90 cents. If you do the math, you can figure out that King Rice costs 35 cents **per pound** and Queen Rice costs 30 cents **per pound.** You can save money by buying Queen Rice.

Many grocery stores help you figure out how much something costs per unit. The stores put little labels next to the products they sell. The labels show how much each product costs per pound, per gallon, or per some other unit. Look for these labels the next time you're in a grocery store.

1. How much do you save per pound if you buy Queen Rice?

   _____ **W** **D**

2. What unit would the label next to a bottle of milk use: pounds, gallons, or inches?

   _____ **W** **D**

3. A ten-pound bag of Felix Cat Food costs seven dollars. A five-pound bag of Oscar Cat Food costs five dollars. Which cat food costs less per unit?

   _____

4. How do grocery stores help you figure out the cost per unit?

   _____

   _____

Answer Key for Fact Game 1

2. Lynn was wearing a cast because her femur was broken.

3. a. magazine, circulation
   b. The, a
   c. glossy, large
   d. has

4. a. To breathe cold air
   b. can hurt

5. He went running because he needed some exercise.

6. a. verb
   b. adjective
   c. noun

7. a. Swimming in that lake
   b. is a bad idea

8. a. respiratory system
   b. trachea
   c. bronchial tubes
   d. lungs

9. a. red
   b. almost black

10. a. He made many modifications to his speech.
    b. She modified the plans for her new house.

11. a. oxygen
    b. carbon dioxide

12. a. That office needs many modifications.
    b. The racer modified her sports car.

Answer Key for Fact Game 2

2. Pam, who lives in Fulton, is a baseball player.

3. a. adjective
   b. noun

4. a. nervous system
   b. respiratory system

5. a. The brain and the spinal cord make up the central nervous system.
   b. The nerves that lead to and from the spinal cord and the brain make up the peripheral nervous system.

6. Pam lives in Fulton, which is in New York State.

7. a. artery
   b. oxygen
   c. carbon dioxide

8. a. The class concluded when the bell rang.
   b. He completed the deduction by drawing a conclusion.

9. a. adjective
   b. verb

10. a. brain
    b. spinal cord
    c. nerves

11. a. It takes a long time to digest your dinner.
    b. Too much candy can upset your digestion.

12. a. Ideas: Fingers are not made of chopped meat; Sausages aren't part of a body.
    b. Ideas: They're both fat; They're both round.

Answer Key for Fact Game 3

2. Jill was very hungry, but she didn't eat dinner.

3. a. The teacher's <u>explanatory</u> comments helped us solve the problem.
   b. The student's <u>explanation</u> was hard to understand.

4. a. The nerves that let you feel are called sensory nerves.
   b. The nerves that let you move are called motor nerves.

5. These chairs cost a lot of money, but they are falling apart.

6. a. The nerves that carry messages *to* the brain are called <u>sensory</u> nerves.
   b. The nerves that carry messages *from* the brain are called <u>motor</u> nerves.

7. a. To make money, his older brother writes books.
   b. Because it was raining, she put on her hat.

8. a. sensory
   b. motor
   c. sensory

9. a. noun
   b. noun

10. a. If you buy products in a store, you are a <u>consumer</u>.
    b. If something can be consumed, it is <u>consumable</u>.

11. a. On the moon, nothing can grow.
    b. To finish the project, my sister stayed up all night.

12. a. verb
    b. adjective

Answer Key for Fact Game 4

2. a. She wanted to <u>participate</u> in the play.
   b. That school has no <u>participatory</u> sports.

3. a. noun
   b. noun

4. Your circulatory system works hard, particularly when you exercise.

5. a. verb
   b. adjective

6. a. supply
   b. demand

7. Tom had to cut the grass, but he didn't have a lawn mower.

8. a. demand
   b. demand

9. a. almost black
   b. red

10. Pete watches TV, particularly on weekends.

11. a. sensory
    b. motor

12. a. That new factory will <u>manufacture</u> laptop computers.
    b. Cars are a good example of a <u>manufactured</u> product.

Answer Key for Fact Game 5

2. a. When you exercise, your <u>circulation</u> increases.
   b. The cows <u>circulated</u> around the pasture yesterday.

3. Jessie is going to the party. Len is going to the party.

4. Although he doesn't exercise, he is in good shape.

5. a. noun
   b. verb

6. When the demand is greater than the supply, prices go up.

7. Idea: It will go up.

8. a. Asthma is a <u>respiratory</u> disease.
   b. Your body is <u>respiring</u> all the time.

9. Manufacturers try to make the <u>demand</u> greater than the supply.

10. Although she modified her explanation, it was still unclear.

11. Doris runs every day. Doris is in training.

12. Idea: It will go down.

Answer Key for Fact Game 6

2. a. The ocean is <u>eroding</u> this beach.
   b. Some parts of that mountain have had lots of <u>erosion</u>.

3. a. instant oatmeal
   b. instant oatmeal

4. a. noun
   b. adjective

5. Whales are not fish; however, they live in the sea.

6. She loves to read. She doesn't own any books.

7. When you buy products in large quantities, you pay <u>less</u> for each unit.

8. She plays basketball, especially in the winter.

9. Products that are readier to use cost <u>more</u>.

10. a. Our team <u>acquired</u> new hats for the game.
    b. He spends lots of money on <u>acquisitions</u>.

11. Anna made the trip with Yoko. Yoko is her best friend.

12. a. Giant Mart
    b. Giant Mart